HBJ Reading Program

Margaret Early

Bernice E. Cullinan
Roger C. Farr
W. Dorsey Hammond
Nancy Santeusanio
Dorothy S. Strickland

LEVEL 10

Archways

HBJ **HARCOURT BRACE JOVANOVICH, PUBLISHERS**
Orlando   San Diego   Chicago   Dallas

Acknowledgments

For permission to reprint copyrighted material, grateful acknowledgment is made to the following sources:

Atheneum Publishers, Inc.: "Telling Time" from *Think of Shadows* by Lilian Moore. Copyright © 1975, 1980 by Lilian Moore.

Bradbury Press, an affiliate of Macmillan, Inc.: From *The Year of the Comet* by Roberta Wiegand. Copyright © 1984 by Roberta Wiegand.

Curtis Brown, Ltd.: Chapter 11 from *How Juan Got Home* by Peggy Mann. © 1972 by Peggy Mann. Published by Coward, McCann & Geoghegan, Inc.

Carolrhoda Books, Inc., 241 First Avenue North, Minneapolis, MN 55401: From *Space Challenger: The Story of Guion Bluford* (Titled: "Space Challenger") by Jim Haskins and Kathleen Benson. Copyright © 1984 by Jim Haskins and Kathleen Benson.

Childrens Press: From *Leontyne Price: Opera Superstar* by Sylvia B. Williams. Copyright © 1984 by Regensteiner Publishing Enterprises, Inc. From *The Mystery of the Rolltop Desk* by Evelyn Witter. Copyright © 1977 by Regensteiner Publishing Enterprises, Inc.

Coward, McCann & Geoghegan: Adapted from *And Then What Happened, Paul Revere?* by Jean Fritz. Copyright © 1973 by Jean Fritz.

Dial Books for Young Readers: Adapted from *The Patchwork Quilt* by Valerie Flournoy, pictures by Jerry Pinkney. Text copyright © 1985 by Valerie Flournoy; pictures copyright © 1985 by Jerry Pinkney.

Aileen Fisher: "Until We Built a Cabin" from *That's Why* by Aileen Fisher.

Garrard Publishing Company, Champaign, IL: From *Putting the Sun to Work* by Jeanne Bendick. Copyright 1979 by Jeanne Bendick.

Harcourt Brace Jovanovich, Inc.: "Reading Circle Graphs" and from "The Mountain States Long Ago" in *HBJ Social Studies: States and Regions*. Copyright © 1985 by Harcourt Brace Jovanovich, Inc. From "Is Air Matter?" in *HBJ Science*, Level Orange, Grade 4. Copyright © 1985 by Harcourt Brace Jovanovich, Inc. From "What a Tooth Is Like" in *HBJ Health*, Level Orange, Grade 4. Copyright © 1983 by Harcourt Brace Jovanovich, Inc. Pronunciation key from p. 33 and the short key from p. 35 in *HBJ School Dictionary*. Copyright © 1985 by Harcourt Brace Jovanovich, Inc.

Harper & Row, Publishers, Inc.: Complete text, abridged and adapted, from *High Sounds, Low Sounds* by Franklyn Branley. Copyright © 1967 by Franklyn M. Branley. Published by Thomas Y. Crowell. "Wind Circles" from *Out in the Dark and Daylight* by Aileen Fisher. Copyright © 1980 by Aileen Fisher. Adapted and abridged from pp. 15–47 in *Childtimes* by Eloise Greenfield and Lessie Jones Little. Copyright © 1979 by Eloise Greenfield and Lessie Jones Little; copyright © 1971 by Pattie Ridley Jones. Published by Thomas Y. Crowell. Complete text, abridged and adapted, and illustrations from *SELF-PORTRAIT: Trina Schart Hyman*, written and illustrated by Trina Schart Hyman. Copyright © 1981 by Trina Schart Hyman. "Lewis Has a Trumpet" from *Dogs & Dragons, Trees & Dreams* by Karla Kuskin. Copyright © 1958 by Karla Kuskin. Chapters 3–10, abridged and adapted from the story *From Anna* (Titled: "Anna's New Beginning") by Jean Little. Copyright © 1972 by Jean Little. Abridged and adapted from pp. 14–33 in *Me and My Family Tree* by Paul Showers. Copyright © 1978 by Paul Showers. Published by Thomas Y. Crowell. Slightly adapted from *My Robot Buddy* by Alfred Slote. Text copyright © 1975 by Alfred Slote.

D.C. Heath and Company: "Learning from Other Countries" in *Heath Social Studies* by Gloria P. Hagans. Copyright © 1985 by D. C. Heath and Company.

Highlights for Children, Inc., Columbus, OH: "Ballet Is for Everyone" by Susanne Banta Harper from *Highlights for Children*, March 1985. Copyright © 1985 by Highlights for Children. "Just Because I'm Left-Handed" by Linda McCollum Brown from *Highlights for Children*, April 1984. Copyright © 1984 by Highlights for Children, Inc.

Houghton Mifflin Company: Abridged from *Help! I'm a Prisoner in the Library* by Eth Clifford. Copyright © 1979 by Ethel Clifford Rosenberg.

James Houston: From *Songs of the Dream People* (Titled: "A Central Eskimo Chant"), selected and edited by James Houston. Copyright © 1972 by James Houston.

Barbara A. Huff: "The Library" by Barbara A. Huff. Copyright © 1972 by Barbara A. Huff.

International Reading Association and George Coon: from "Homophones" by George Coon in *The Reading Teacher*, April 1976.

Alfred A. Knopf, Inc.: From *The Queen Who Couldn't Bake Gingerbread: An Adaptation of a German Folk Tale* (Titled: "The Queen Who Couldn't Bake Gingerbread") by Dorothy Van Woerkem. Copyright © 1975 by Dorothy Van Woerkom.

Laidlaw Brothers, a division of Doubleday & Company, Inc.: From pp. 234–235 in *Living in World Regions* by Beverly Jeanne Armento et al. Copyright © 1985 by Laidlaw Brothers, Publishers.

Little, Brown and Company, in association with The Atlantic Monthly Press: From pp. 15–48 in *McBroom Tells the Truth* by Sid Fleischman. Text copyright © 1966 by Sid Fleischman.

Macmillan Publishing Company: "Roads" from *Poems* by Rachel Field. Published by Macmillan, New York, 1957. From pp. 59–60 in *The Earth and Its People* (Macmillan Social Studies), Grade 4 by John Jarolimek, Senior Author, and Mae Knight Clark. Copyright 1985 by Macmillan Publishing Company, a division of Macmillan, Inc. Circle graph from p. 242 in *Series M: Macmillan Mathematics*, Grade 4 by Tina Thoburn and Jack E. Forbes, Senior Authors, and Robert D. Bechtel. Copyright © 1985 by Macmillan Publishing Company, a division of Macmillan, Inc.

McIntosh & Otis, Inc.: From *Dvora's Journey* by Marge Blaine. Text copyright © 1979 by Marge Blaine. Published by Holt, Rinehart and Winston.

Eve Merriam: "Which Washington?" from *There Is No Rhyme for Silver* by Eve Merriam. Copyright © 1962 by Eve Merriam. All rights reserved. Published by Atheneum Publishers, Inc.

Charles E. Merrill Publishing Company: "How Muscles Help You Move" and "Muscle Injuries" from *Health: Focus on You*. Copyright 1982, 1984 by Bell & Howell Company. Published by Charles E. Merrill Publishing Company.

(continued on page 614)

Contents

Unit 2   # Skylights   **158**

Unit 3 Symphonies

296

Unit 4 Memories

Archways

DETOUR

STOP

DO NOT ENTER

ROAD CLOSED

END FREEWAY

NO LEFT TURN

WRONG WAY

KEEP RIGHT

Unit 1

Detours

What do we do when we want to go somewhere but the way is blocked? We probably take a detour, a different way around. Most often, we think of detours when we think of traveling and roads. During our travels, we may suddenly see a "detour" sign with an arrow that points us in a new direction. Despite the trouble, we may find that the detour is really an interesting road to take!

Some detours have nothing to do with real travel. Suppose we want to do something very badly, but a problem comes up that blocks our way. We may have to take a detour to get around that problem. The new path may be hard, but it may also lead to adventure.

In this unit you will read about detours that result in many different kinds of adventures. As you read the selections, look for the different kinds of detours the characters take, and see where these detours lead them.

Realistic Fiction

Some stories we read seem to tell about real characters and events. Yet the stories are not true. We call these stories **realistic fiction.**

Realistic fiction is not the same as fantasy. In realistic fiction there are no characters with magical powers, and there are no talking animals. The story takes place in the real world.

The characters in realistic fiction do the same kinds of things real people do. They laugh and cry about the same kinds of things real people laugh and cry about. The reader can easily imagine that he or she is one of the characters in the story. When a story reminds us of things real people do or ways they feel, we say that the story is "believable." Realistic stories are believable.

Read the following fictional paragraph. Think about why it is realistic fiction.

Janie threw the stick far out into the pond. In a flash Rex leaped into the pond and swam toward the stick. As he was swimming back with the stick, Rex noticed another dog racing toward the water. Rex began to bark. The stick floated silently away.

Janie could be a real person, and Rex could be a real dog. Their actions are believable. You might imagine yourself by that pond, throwing the stick and waiting for the dog.

Read the following sentences. Which ones could describe something from realistic fiction?

1. An elephant drives to school in a new green truck.
2. A girl takes care of a bird with a broken wing.
3. A man in a wheelchair learns to drive a car.
4. A fox says, "Oh, these grapes taste good!"

The second and third sentences are from realistic fiction. They describe things that could really happen in our world. The first and last sentences are not realistic. They describe something from fantasy. Animals do not talk or act like humans in realistic fiction.

Read and think about the following characteristics of realistic fiction:

- The characters and events seem real, but the story is not true.
- The story is believable.
- The story seems to take place in the real world.
- The story reminds us of things real people do or ways real people feel.

Think about these characteristics as you read each story in the unit. Is the story realistic fiction, or is it fantasy? How do you know?

In this selection, a detour into a library leads to adventure. Read to find out how two sisters try to get out of the library.

Look for details that show that this selection is realistic fiction. Are there any details that do not seem believable?

Help! I'm a Prisoner in the Library

by Eth Clifford

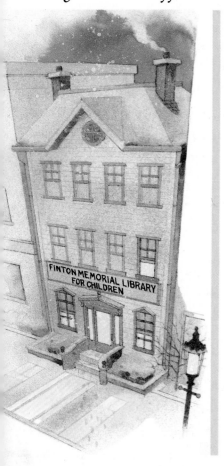

Mary Rose and her sister Jo-Beth came to Indianapolis from Fort Wayne with their father. In the middle of the city, during a snowstorm, the car ran out of gas. Their father walked to a nearby gas station for help while Mary Rose and Jo-Beth waited in the car. Then Jo-Beth decided she needed to find a rest room—right away!

The two sisters walked quickly to a nearby library, which looked like a big old house. They meant to stay there for only a few minutes, but they saw a large display in a back room and went to look at it.

While they were standing behind the display, the librarian prepared to close up the library. She checked all the rooms but did not see the two girls. After she locked the doors, she turned off the main lights and turned on the blue night lights. Then she went upstairs.

When the lights went out so suddenly, the two girls were so shocked they couldn't speak. Jo-Beth gave a small gasp. Mary Rose realized almost at once that they had forgotten about the time.

"The librarian's gone home. I'll bet she locked us in!" Mary Rose nodded her head. "And Daddy doesn't even know where we are."

Jo-Beth shivered. "I don't like these spooky blue lights. They make everything so weird." Mary Rose agreed.

Jo-Beth came out from behind the display and crept along to the front door, with Mary Rose right behind her. At the door, she pulled and tugged at the knob.

"What good is that? The doors are locked."

"I know they're locked," Jo-Beth snapped. She was so angry she kicked the door. "Whoever heard of locking a door *inside* with a key?"

Jo-Beth turned and stood with her back up against the door. The blue lights were even worse in here because the room was so big. Shadows crouched down from the walls and moved closer and closer. Jo-Beth swallowed hard, but the hollow sensation in her stomach refused to go away.

"Oh, Mary Rose," she sobbed. "We're never going to get out of here. The librarian's gone, and nobody knows where we are."

Mary Rose started to walk away from the door.

Jo-Beth promptly followed. "I don't want to stay here by myself. Where are you going?"

"I'm going to find the phone. You said at least one sensible thing. Nobody knows we're here. So I guess it would be a good idea to call somebody on the phone and tell them where we are."

"Who are you going to call?" Jo-Beth asked when Mary Rose found the phone. It was hidden on a shelf below the sign that read "Check Books Out Here."

Mary Rose didn't pay any attention. She dialed the operator, and a voice spoke to her at the other end. Mary Rose said, "I want to call Fort Wayne collect." She gave the operator her home number and her mother's name.

She listened to the voice on the phone, and then she hung up.

"The operator says the phones are down in Fort Wayne. On account of the blizzard."

"What's a blizzard?" Jo-Beth asked.

"It's a terrible snowstorm. *Mountains* of snow. And gusty winds." That's what they always said on TV in the weather reports. "Gusty winds."

"The operator said the blizzard was everywhere. Come on over to the window so we can look out and see it," Mary Rose said.

At one of the front windows facing out on the porch, the two girls rubbed the wet panes and tried to peer out. It was night — darkness came early in the winter. Still, the falling snow brightened the world outside, especially when the street lights gleamed on the twirling flakes.

"I know," Jo-Beth cried. "I'll make a sign and put it up on the window."

"You can if you want to. I'm going to call the police."

Jo-Beth ran back to the librarian's desk. She pulled drawers open until she found what she was looking for — a big sheet of paper, a thick black marking pen, and some tape. Meanwhile, Mary Rose picked up the phone.

"Operator," she said, "I want the police."

"H-e-l-p-!" Jo-Beth started to print.

"Are you in trouble?" the operator asked. She sounded suspicious.

"Yes, we are. Please. I want the police."

"How do you spell *prisoner*?" Jo-Beth asked.

A voice in Mary Rose's ear came on at the same time. The man spoke just as Mary Rose was saying to her sister, "Put down p-r-i-s-o-n . . ."

"Who is this?" the voice asked.

". . . e-r," Mary Rose finished quickly. "Is this the police?"

Jo-Beth shouted into the phone. "We're prisoners! We're prisoners in the library!"

"You kids stop playing with your phone," the officer scolded. "We have to keep all these lines open for emergencies." He slammed the receiver down so hard it made Mary Rose's ear tingle.

"Are they coming to get us?"

"He hung up on me. He didn't even want to *listen*."

Mary Rose wasn't a girl to give up easily. She lifted the receiver again.

"Hello, operator? I want the fire department."

Jo-Beth, meanwhile, was finishing her sign. It looked fine to her. In big letters, she had printed "Help! I'm a Prisoner in the Liberry."

"Now to hang it up in the window," Jo-Beth thought. A sign was better than a phone call. People believed in signs.

Mary Rose was having a problem.

"Aren't you the same little girl who just asked for the police?"

"Yes, but they hung up on me."

"Is your mother or father there?" the operator asked. When Mary Rose said no, the operator wanted to know, "Is there any grownup in the house at all?"

"That's what I'm trying to tell you." Why didn't people *listen*? "Nobody's here except me and my little sister. We're locked up in the . . ."

Without warning, the phone went dead. No sound came from it at all, not even a hum or a dial tone. At the same time, the lights went out and the room was swallowed up in darkness.

Jo-Beth called from the window in panic, "The lights just went off in the street." She started to run toward her sister. Mary Rose could hear her banging into things as she tried to find her way back to the librarian's desk and Mary Rose.

"I wish the blue lights would come back on," Jo-Beth whispered. "They were spooky, but they were better than nothing."

"The power line must be down." Mary Rose didn't feel nearly as brave as she sounded. "Stop shaking, Jo-Beth. Just think of it this way. We can't get out. But nobody can get in, either. So we're perfectly safe."

Jo-Beth relaxed a little. "I wouldn't mind it so much if it wasn't so dark."

"Maybe I can find a flashlight in one of these drawers." Mary Rose ran her fingers across the desk and down one side. In the very last drawer, she found a key ring with a tiny flashlight attached to it.

At that exact moment, there was a heavy thud over their heads, as if someone had fallen down.

The moaning started almost at once.

Jo-Beth grabbed her sister so hard that Mary Rose dropped the flashlight.

"Don't do that!" Mary Rose exclaimed. She dropped to her knees and started to fumble about on the floor for the flashlight.

"You said we were safe because the door was locked. You said nobody could get in. Well, *something* got in."

"There is no use arguing," Mary Rose thought. She had a big decision to make, and her sister was no help at all. The question was—should they hide downstairs, or should they go upstairs and see who, or what, was there?

Jo-Beth whispered, "I hate this place. I'm never going to come back. If we ever get out."

Mary Rose told her sister to be quiet. She listened hard, turning her head from side to side. The moaning had stopped, but that didn't mean that whatever was up there was gone.

She took a deep breath. "Jo-Beth, you can stay here if you want to, but I'm going upstairs and see what's up there."

Jo-Beth put out her hand as if to stop Mary Rose. She wanted to plead with Mary Rose not to leave her. But she knew what Mary Rose was like once she made up her mind about something.

"I'm going to sit right here on the floor," Jo-Beth said. Mary Rose shrugged. She began to walk away, toward the steps. "Wait," Jo-Beth cried. "You've got the light."

Mary Rose shrugged again. She beamed the light up at the stairway. She took another deep breath, closing her eyes for a moment. Then she put one hand on the banister and held on to the flashlight with the other. She didn't say a word when Jo-Beth raced after her, breathing hard.

"Let me walk in front of you. Please, Mary Rose. I'd rather have you right in back of me than . . ."

Her voice trailed off, but Mary Rose knew exactly what her sister meant because she could feel the awful quiet dark emptiness pressing in behind her.

Halfway up the stairs there was a broad landing. Jo-Beth stopped abruptly, so abruptly that Mary Rose ran into her and cracked her jaw on Jo-Beth's head.

"Don't ever do that again," Mary Rose said angrily. "I think you broke my jaw."

"I'll tell you one thing, Mary Rose. I'm not going up any more steps. If we do, it will be to our certain death." Jo-Beth liked the sound of that. She repeated it with joyful gloom. "Certain death."

"Great. Just great. That's what I love about you, Jo-Beth. You really know how to cheer a person up. Come on!"

Jo-Beth would have settled for staying on the landing, but Mary Rose was determined to complete the journey to the second floor.

Before long, the girls reached the head of the stairway and another wide landing, which turned around on both sides into two spacious hallways. In each hallway were a number of doors. At the farthest end on the left, a door was open. A light flickered from somewhere inside the room.

"Come on," Mary Rose said.

Jo-Beth held back. "You go first. You're older than I am. And bigger. And you have the flashlight. You can use it as a weapon if you have to."

Mary Rose looked down at the key ring and the tiny flashlight attached. She didn't bother answering. She just sighed and began to walk along the hallway.

Mary Rose peered in through the open doorway. She saw a large room, comfortably furnished, with a fire glowing in a large fireplace. That was the flickering light they had seen.

The two girls walked into the room, looking about curiously.

"Somebody lives here," Jo-Beth said finally. "I didn't know anybody ever lived in a library."

"That's what we must have heard, Jo-Beth. We must have heard the librarian. She must have knocked something over." Mary Rose's eyes began to shine with excitement. "Do you realize what this means?"

"We can get something to eat!" Jo-Beth felt relaxed enough now to remember that she was starved.

"No," Mary Rose said. "It means we can get out!"

You can find out what happens next to Mary Rose and Jo-Beth if you read the rest of the book Help! I'm a Prisoner in the Library *by Eth Clifford.*

1. How did Mary Rose and Jo-Beth get locked in the library?

2. What important things did Mary Rose and Jo-Beth do when they found out they were locked in the library?

3. Was Mary Rose's decision to go upstairs a good one? Explain.

4. What clue on page 6 tells you that the librarian might live in the building?

5. How do you think the girls will get out of the library?

Tell why each of the following details from the story seems to be from a realistic fiction selection.

1. Jo-Beth was so angry she kicked the door.

2. Mary Rose had to spell *prisoner* for Jo-Beth.

3. Jo-Beth wanted to walk up the stairs in front of Mary Rose, where it was lighter.

4. When the girls found the room upstairs, the first thing Jo-Beth thought about was food.

Prewrite

Study the situations below. Imagine what you would do if you found yourself in one of them.

---

1. You are at a library, and like Mary Rose and Jo-Beth, you have been locked in. Who is with you? What do you do to pass the time? What do you do to try to get out?

---

2. You are Mary Rose or Jo-Beth. Suppose there is no apartment above the library. List some possible ways to get out of the library. What would you do all night if no one came to rescue you until morning? How would you pass the time?

Compose

Choose one of the situations above, and write a paragraph that will answer the questions in that box.

Revise

Read your paragraph. Does it answer all the questions? Does it make sense? If not, add the information needed and revise your work.

The Library
by Barbara A. Huff

It looks like any building
When you pass it on the street,
Made of stone and glass and marble,
Made of iron and concrete.

But once inside you can ride
A camel or a train,
Visit Rome, Siam, or Nome,
Feel a hurricane,
Meet a king, learn to sing,
How to bake a pie,
Go to sea, plant a tree,
Find how airplanes fly,
Train a horse, and of course
Have all the dogs you'd like,
See the moon, a sandy dune,
Or catch a whopping pike.
Everything that books can bring
You'll find inside those walls.
A world is there for you to share
When adventure calls.

You cannot tell its magic
By the way the building looks,
But there's wonderment within it,
The wonderment of books.

A detour is "a new path." In this selection Juan has taken a detour. How do you think Juan will finally get "home"?

As you read, notice how the author uses informal language in dialogue to develop the characters.

How Juan Got Home

by Peggy Mann

Juan came from Puerto Rico to live with his uncle in New York City. When he arrived, he tried to make new friends. However, he spoke very little English, and the families in his uncle's neighborhood did not speak Spanish. Soon Juan wished that he could go back home.

One day Juan went to a Spanish neighborhood to buy food for a special meal. There Juan met Carlos, a boy about his age. Carlos invited Juan to play stickball, a street game that is a lot like baseball. Carlos was amazed when Juan hit the ball so far that it went past the third sewer cover, way up the street. A three-sewer hit was a very long hit. Juan's new friend asked him to play for the neighborhood team in the big game on Saturday.

When he got home, Juan burst into his uncle's apartment and announced the news. He was going to play on the team against the Young Princes!

Uncle Esteban seemed mightily pleased. He gave Juan a resounding thwack on the back and raised the boy's arm in the manner of a winning boxer. Then he asked, "Where are the *plátanos*[1] and the *gandules*[2] and the *ajíes*[3]?"

Juan gasped and clapped his hand over his mouth. He had left the groceries somewhere. But where?

"I'll go back," he told his uncle. "I'll find them!"

Uncle Esteban laughed. "Never mind," he said. "You've already found something a lot better."

The next afternoon, which was Saturday, Uncle Esteban made plans to go and watch his nephew in the big game. "Also," said Uncle Esteban, "I may find a few friends myself. Who knows?"

They arrived early. Carlos was sitting on the stoop of his house, waiting. But as soon as he caught sight of Juan he raced down the street to welcome him.

---

[1] plátanos [plä′tä•nōs]: Bananalike fruits.
[2] gandules [gän•doo′läs]: Pigeon peas.
[3] ajíes [ä•hē′äs]: Chili peppers.

"Man!" he said to Juan, breathless. "Am I glad to see you! I've been telling the team all about you. How a little kid—what are you, seven, eight years old?—can hit three sewers!"

Juan understood some of the sentences. He drew himself up with dignity. "I am ten years old."

"Oh," Carlos said. "So you're little for your age, that's all. But no matter how old you are—or how little—you're the first kid on this street that's hit three sewers all summer long." Then he looked at Juan and frowned. "What I'm wondering now is, was it just a lucky accident? Do you think you could ever do such a thing again?"

Since Juan did not understand, he merely grinned and nodded.

The game was scheduled for four o'clock. By three-thirty the entire neighborhood, it seemed, was out on the street. The steps of the brownstone stoops were as crowded as bleachers. The box seats set out by the areaways and the alleyways were all taken. Some people had even brought camp chairs and stools to sit out on the sidewalk. And the windows facing the street were filled with spectators gathered to watch the big game. Voices rose like a wall of sound.

Juan had never in his life felt so nervous. It was one thing to hit a stone with a stick across the Piñonas River with only his friends, Ricardo and Eduardo and Julio and Ramon, watching. It was quite something else to try to get a three-sewer hit under the eyes of all these staring strangers. Fervently he wished he had never ventured forth from his uncle's apartment to buy the things they needed for the special Spanish supper.

Uncle Esteban was chatting with some men who were setting out a card table on the sidewalk. He seemed to have forgotten all about Juan.

"C'mon," Carlos said. "I gotta be sure you know the rules of the game." He took Juan by the arm and brought him over to a very tall boy called Pee-Wee. This boy spoke good Spanish, and carefully explained to Juan about the pitcher, the catcher, the first, second, and third bases, and how to run from one to the next. "*¿Alguna pregunta?*"[1] said Pee-Wee then. "Any questions?"

The only question Juan had was how had he gotten into this mess. And how could he get himself out of it, and go back home to his uncle's house. But he managed to grin as though everything was fine and calm inside and he said, "I onnerstan'."

When it came his turn to stand up and bat, he felt faint with fear. All the eyes on the street seemed to be boring into him. As he stood at home plate holding the sawed-off mop handle, silence spread down the block. It was an exploding silence. Pee-Wee had told him that the word had gone around. This little kid had hit three sewers. Could he do it again? They all were watching; all were waiting.

---

[1] ¿Alguna pregunta? [äl•gōō'nä prä•gōōn'tä]: Any questions?

The pitcher was a tall black boy. "Batter up, champ," he called. "You the midget miracle man they been crowing about?"

Laughter rose from the Young Princes and from the people watching the game. Hooting, derisive laughter.

Anger clenched inside Juan's chest like a hard fist. Why were they making fun of him? Because he was a stranger? Because he was little for his age?

When the ball came flying toward him he slammed at it with all his strength, and watched then with stunned satisfaction as the ball sped down the street.

Everyone was screaming at him. "Run. . . . Run!" But he did not know what the word meant. Some kind of English *Bravo!*[1] maybe. He smiled at the standing, screaming sidewalk crowd and raised one hand over his head in a victory sign, as his uncle had done at home.

Pee-Wee ran up, and he began shaking him. "*¡Corre! ¡Corre!*"[2]

Suddenly Juan remembered the rules and started racing toward first base: the fender of a parked car. The screams of the crowd grew louder. He made it to second base, a chalked circle in the middle of the street. Pee-Wee was racing along beside him. "Keep going!" Pee-Wee shouted in Spanish. "The ball went under a truck. Keep running!"

He reached third base: the fire hydrant. And then came the sprint back. He slid onto home plate, his breath coming in hard gasps.

Carlos and Pee-Wee and the rest of his teammates were all around him, slapping him on the back and shouting, "Man, you got home! You made a home run! You got home!"

Pride swelling inside him, he sat on the curb, Carlos on one side of him, Pee-Wee on the other. Carlos instructed Pee-Wee to ask whether Juan would come over again and

---

[1]Bravo! [brä′vō]: Well done!

[2]¡Corre! ¡Corre! [côr′rā côr′rā]: Run! Run!

play on their team. And Juan instructed Pee-Wee to say sure, he would come! He'd come over here every day to play. Even when school started in September, he'd keep coming.

Pee-Wee translated this, and Carlos clapped Juan on the knee. "Man," he said. "You're in!"

Juan was up at bat four more times that afternoon. He hit no more home runs, but that didn't seem to matter. He had done it once, so there was always the hope he might do it again. Each time he stood up at bat an expected hush of anticipation spread down the street. They were with him, he knew. Even those on the other team. He was in! He belonged.

Between his times at bat he sat on the curbstone, Carlos on one side, Pee-Wee on the other. At first he spoke only to Pee-Wee, spoke only in Spanish. But by the end of the afternoon he was shouting and cheering like all the others as one of his teammates hit the ball and raced down the street.

"Come on, man! Move it!" Loud and proud he yelled the words—words of the English language.

1. How did Juan get "home"?

2. List three important things that happened in the story that helped Juan to get "home."

3. What parts of the story did you think were funny? Why?

4. Did you think that Juan would make a three-sewer hit in the big game? Why or why not?

5. Do you think Juan still wishes to return to Puerto Rico? Explain.

Apply the Skills

Tell which statements below are examples of formal language and which are informal language. How could you change each informal statement to make it formal?

1. "The ball went under a truck. Keep running!"

2. "C'mon," Carlos said, "I gotta be sure you know the rules of the game."

3. "I may find a few friends myself."

4. "You the midget miracle man they been crowing about?"

Prewrite

The chart below compares and contrasts baseball and stickball. Copy the chart and complete it by listing at least one more likeness and two more differences.

Likenesses	Differences
Players run around bases.	Baseball is played on a special field.
Players take turns hitting a ball.	

Compose

Choose one of the activities below.

1. Write a paragraph comparing and contrasting baseball and stickball.

2. Make a chart comparing and contrasting Juan and you, showing at least three ways you are alike and different. Use the chart to write a paragraph.

Revise

Read your paragraph. Have you included all the information listed in your chart? If not, revise your paragraph.

Schedules

A **schedule** is a plan of things to be done or a list of times telling when things will happen. There are many times when using a schedule can help you.

A doctor has a schedule. All the people who come to a doctor's office cannot see the doctor at the same time. Therefore, every doctor has a schedule that sets aside time for each person the doctor sees.

When the doctor says, "I want to see Bob Drake next Thursday afternoon," someone checks the doctor's schedule. From the schedule, the person can tell whether or not the doctor has time to see Bob that day. Perhaps the doctor's schedule looks like this one:

THURSDAY		October 21
A.M.	10:00	Lois Blake
	10:30	Tom Gomez
	11:00	Mary Trout
	11:30	Carol Beach
P.M.	1:00	David Cox
	1:30	Paul Mixon
	2:00	
	2:30	Pat Day
	3:00	
	3:30	Rose Green

Bob is told that he can come either at 2:00 P.M. or at 3:00 P.M. He chooses the time that fits into his plans for Thursday. If he chooses 3:00 P.M., his name is written on the line next to that time on Thursday's schedule. The doctor will not plan to see anyone else at that time on Thursday.

Train, Plane, and Bus Schedules

There are many other kinds of schedules. Trains, planes, and buses follow schedules, too. People who want to travel must know where the train, plane, or bus goes and when it leaves one place and arrives at the next. They find this information on a schedule. People use the schedules to plan their trips. By looking at the schedule, they know when the train, plane, or bus will leave and when it will arrive. They can then plan to get to the train station or airport or bus stop in plenty of time.

Bob may use a bus schedule to help him get to the doctor's office at the right time on Thursday afternoon. The bus schedule shown on the next page may help him.

Bob can see that this is the bus schedule he needs. A look at the top left corner tells him this is a schedule for Monday through Friday. It also tells him that these times are P.M., or afternoon, times.

The first column of the schedule lists the stops the bus makes. The next columns list the time that each bus arrives at each stop. Bob can use the schedule to plan which bus he will take.

RED LINE BUS COMPANY

Monday - Friday
P.M. Schedule

	Bus A	Bus B	Bus C	Bus D
Fifth Avenue	12:30	1:00	1:30	2:00
Cook Street	12:45	1:15	1:45	2:15
Lake Street	1:00	1:30	2:00	2:30
Flower Lane	1:15	1:45	2:15	2:45
Main Street	1:30	2:00	2:30	3:00
Palm Drive	——	2:15	2:45	3:15

Bob lives on Cook Street, near the bus stop. The doctor's office is on Palm Drive, across the street from the bus stop. So Bob knows he must go from the Cook Street stop to the Palm Drive stop.

When Bob uses this schedule, he starts at the bottom of the schedule. There he sees that the Palm Drive stop is the last on the bus route. Bob can also see that bus A does not go to Palm Drive.

The schedule shows Bob that bus B gets to Palm Drive at 2:15. If Bob uses bus B, he will have to wait forty-five minutes to see the doctor at 3:00. Next, Bob checks bus C. If he takes bus C, Bob will get to Palm Drive at 2:45, which would be fifteen minutes early. This seems like a good bus to take. Bob sees that bus D arrives at Palm Drive at 3:15, which is too late. Bob chooses bus C.

Now Bob works from the bottom up. He uses his finger to follow the column for bus C up to the time it arrives at the Cook Street stop. The bus he wants to take arrives at Cook Street at 1:45. Bob plans to leave his home no later than 1:35 to be sure he is at the stop when the bus arrives.

Juan and Uncle Esteban use a bus schedule, too. On Saturday they plan to make a special trip. They are going to a stickball game near Jackson Road. The trip is an easy one, because the game will be played close to the Jackson Road stop.

Juan and Uncle Esteban will get on the bus at Clove Street. The stickball game is at 9:30 A.M., and they don't want to be late. Their trip can be planned using the following bus schedule. Which bus should they take? Why?

WEEKENDS AND HOLIDAYS				
A.M.	BUS 1	BUS 2	BUS 3	BUS 4
Clove Street	—	8:35	8:51	9:10
Jewell Avenue	8:25	8:42	8:58	9:17
King Street	8:44	9:01	9:17	9:36
Queen Street	8:58	9:15	9:31	—
Jackson Road	9:06	9:23	9:39	9:48

Remember that a schedule is a plan of things to be done or a list of times telling when things will happen. Using a schedule can help you plan your time wisely and make your travels more enjoyable.

Uncle Joe must leave his special school to go live with his sister's family for a while. Read to see how this detour changes the family.

As you read, look for details that show that this selection is realistic fiction.

Making Room for Uncle Joe

by Ada B. Litchfield

Mom looked really serious as she read us the letter from Uncle Joe's social worker.

Uncle Joe is Mom's younger brother. He has Down's syndrome. People with Down's syndrome are mentally retarded and need help taking care of themselves. After Uncle Joe was born, his mother died, and no one else in the family could give him the care he needed. That's why he had been in a state hospital school for such a long time.

Uncle Joe had been happy at his school. But now it was closing, the letter said, and the people who lived there had to find other homes. Uncle Joe would have to live with us for a while. We were his only family.

"The social worker says she's looking for an apartment for Uncle Joe, but they are hard to find," Mom explained. "So your dad and I think Joe should stay with us until—"

"He'd better find an apartment fast," my older sister, Beth, shouted. "We can't have a retarded person living here forever!"

"He won't be here forever, Beth," I said. "It's just until he finds another place."

"Good grief," Beth said. "Doesn't anyone see how embarrassing this will be for all of us?" She burst into tears and ran out of the room.

"Let her go," Dad said when Mom tried to call Beth back. "She needs to think things over."

I had to think things over, too. Suppose Uncle Joe was a nuisance? Suppose he hung around me all the time? Suppose he messed with my baseball cards?

"Dan, helping Uncle Joe is something our family has to do together," Dad said, as if he were reading my thoughts. "Your mother and I will appreciate any help you and Beth and Amy can give us."

"I'll help Uncle Joe," Amy said.

Amy is only five and a half. What kind of help could she be?

"I'll help, too," I said, trying to sound cheerful. To tell the truth, I didn't feel cheerful at all.

I felt worse when I talked to my friend Ben the next day.

"Down's syndrome, eh?" Ben said with a know-it-all look on his face. "You should be upset. I saw a TV program about people with Down's syndrome. Their eyes slant and their noses look squashed in." He showed me with his fingers what he meant. "Does your uncle look like that?"

"I don't remember," I said. "I only saw him once when I was little."

I didn't know if what Ben said was true or not, but I didn't think it was a very helpful thing for a friend to say.

When I got home, I found Mom and Dad moving furniture around. They had moved the TV from the family room into the living room and the record player into Beth's room.

"We're making room for Uncle Joe," Mom said when she saw me. "You're just in time to help."

Dad and I brought an extra bed up from the basement into the family room. Uncle Joe would sleep there.

Early the next day, Mom and Dad drove to the state school to bring Uncle Joe home. All morning, Amy and Beth and I waited at the front window, watching for them to return. Finally, about noon, we saw our car turn into the driveway. In a few minutes, Mom and Dad came up the walk. Behind them came a short man carrying a suitcase and a small blue bag.

As soon as Beth saw them, she left the window and went into her bedroom.

Uncle Joe came into the house very slowly. His cap was on crooked. He was wearing a jacket with sleeves too short for his arms. His pants were too long for his legs. His eyes did slant a little, and his nose did look a little squashed in.

He looked around at everything in the room and at Amy and me. Then he smiled.

"Hi," he said. "My name's Joe. What's . . . uh . . . yours?"

"This is Dan," my father said. "And here's Amy."

Amy made a little bow, and I bobbed my head.

"And, oh, yes," Dad said, "there's one more." He left the room and came back holding Beth by the arm.

"This is Beth," Dad said.

"Hello, Beth," Uncle Joe said. "You're pretty."

"Thank you," said Beth. She looked surprised.

Dad took Uncle Joe's suitcase into the family room. Uncle Joe wouldn't let him take the blue bag. Instead, he brought it over to me.

"This is my bowling ball," he said, holding the bag up almost in my face. "My friend Ace gave it to me."

Soon after that we all sat down for lunch. All except Uncle Joe, that is. He sat in a chair by the china cabinet, holding his bowling ball on his lap.

"Come sit here, Joe," Mom said, pointing to the empty chair beside Amy. "Put that bowling ball down somewhere and come eat."

"No," Uncle Joe said, shaking his head. "I miss Ace. I need a friend with me . . . uh . . . when I eat lunch."

He hung his head and looked sad. Nobody seemed to know what to do, except Amy. She slid out of her chair, went over to Uncle Joe, and put her hand in his.

"I'll be your friend, Uncle Joe," she said. "You can eat with me." She pulled him to the table.

That was the beginning of Amy's friendship with Uncle Joe. As soon as we finished lunch, she showed him her library book. Every day after that, Uncle Joe and Amy spent a lot of time together with their heads bent over Amy's books. I don't think he always knew if she read the right words or not, but he listened carefully anyway, nodding his head. Showing off for someone made Amy very happy.

Yes, Amy and Uncle Joe got along fine right away, but for the rest of us, having Uncle Joe around wasn't easy.

He had to be reminded to wear his glasses, comb his hair, take a shower, and things like that. Somebody had to see that he put on matching socks.

Uncle Joe offered to help around the house, but he often seemed to get directions mixed up. Usually he was more trouble than help.

We didn't know what to do. Finally Mom got the idea that I should take him bowling. I didn't want to go, but before I knew what was happening, Uncle Joe had come out of his room wearing his bowling jacket and carrying his blue bag.

All the way to Bowl-a-rama, I hoped none of my friends would see us. I hadn't seen any of them—even Ben—for a few weeks. But we didn't see anyone I knew, and as soon as we started bowling, I forgot about everything else.

Uncle Joe was a good bowler. Sometimes he got a spare. Sometimes he got a strike.

Me? I was lucky if I knocked down any pins at all.

"It's okay, Danny," Uncle Joe kept saying in his slow way. "I . . . uh . . . know you can do it. You'll get a strike. Just . . . uh . . . keep trying."

And I did. I got a strike. On the very last frame, all the pins went down—whack, whack, whack—just like that!

We both shouted and jumped up and down.

Everyone around us looked, but I didn't care. I didn't even care when I saw Ben and two other guys from my school watching us.

At first, they just stared and nudged each other. I could tell they were looking for something to laugh at. When they finally came over to us, I introduced them to Uncle Joe.

"I'm glad to meet you . . . Ben . . . and John . . . and Eli," Uncle Joe said. He shook each of their hands and smiled at them. They looked down at the floor and shuffled their feet, but Uncle Joe didn't seem to notice.

"Would you like to bowl with us?" he asked.

They all nodded yes. Ben and Eli had bowled before, but John hadn't. Uncle Joe showed him how to hold the ball and encouraged him the way he had encouraged me.

In no time at all, everybody seemed to forget that Uncle Joe had Down's syndrome. We were all just trying to knock down bowling pins. We were all just having fun.

After that, Ben and my other friends started coming over to the house again. They were always kind to Uncle Joe, and he loved to talk with them.

After a while, things seemed to go better at home. Mom and Dad took more time showing Uncle Joe how to do simple jobs. Uncle Joe began to be a real help around the house. He could carry in groceries and help put them away. He liked to peel carrots and potatoes for dinner. He helped wash and polish the car. He helped Amy put the new bell on her tricycle, and he helped me paint a display rack for my baseball cards.

But what about Beth?

For a long time, Beth acted almost as if Uncle Joe didn't exist. He never bothered her, but sometimes he would sit quietly in the living room and listen while she practiced her piano lesson. Once he clapped, but that startled her so much he never did it again.

Then one day, when he thought no one was around, Uncle Joe sat down at the piano and played "Chopsticks."

Everyone in the family came running, and we clapped so loudly for him that he played it again.

"My friend Ace showed me how to do that," Uncle Joe said, grinning.

Beth went over to the piano. "I know how to play another part of that piece," she said. She sat down next to Uncle Joe and taught him how to play "Chopsticks" as a duet.

Later, Beth showed Uncle Joe how to play other tunes. Sometimes he played them over and over so many times we all got tired of listening, but we felt good because Beth was being kind to Uncle Joe.

By the time spring came, things had settled down into what Mom called a "comfortable routine."

Then another letter came from Uncle Joe's social worker.

Mom read the letter to us. It said that Uncle Joe would be leaving. Everything had finally been arranged. Uncle Joe would share an apartment with two other men in the city. He would work at a sheltered workshop close to where he lived.

A sheltered workshop is a place where some handicapped people are taught to do special jobs. They sort nuts and bolts, put together small motors, package things to send through the mail, or do other simple tasks. The work is easy, and they are paid for doing it.

At first, Uncle Joe seemed pleased. He had Mom read the letter again and again.

I was sure he felt good about having a place of his own and a job of his own. He wanted to take care of himself.

I was sure my parents felt good about not having to be responsible for Uncle Joe anymore.

We would all be glad to have the family room back again so we could entertain our friends there.

We'd always known that Uncle Joe would be leaving sometime. So why did everyone look so sad that night at dinner?

"I'm going to miss you, Uncle Joe," Amy said. She burst into tears.

"I'll miss you, too," said Uncle Joe. He began to look very unhappy.

"Who will listen to me practice for my recital now?" Beth said. Tears were running down her cheeks, too.

"Hey, I'm not going to cry about this," I said to myself, taking a drink of water. But there was a lump in my throat, and I choked so badly I had to leave the table.

I knew I was going to miss Uncle Joe something awful.

When I came back, even my father looked as if he'd been crying. He cleared his throat and blew his nose.

"Listen," he said at last, "your mother and I have been talking this over for quite a while. We thought you all might be pretty upset if Joe leaves. We don't see why Uncle Joe has to live somewhere else if he doesn't want to. We are his family. I can drive him to that workshop every day on my way to the office, and he can take the bus back. What do you say, Joe? Would you like to stay with us?"

Uncle Joe looked thoughtful for a long time. He pulled at his hair. Then he started to grin. "I want to stay here. Yes, I do . . . I can work hard and . . . uh . . . pay for my food. I want to stay here all the time forever with my family."

"Then it's settled," Mom said. "I'll call the social worker right away and tell her we'd all like Uncle Joe to stay with us."

"Yippee!" shouted Amy. She climbed into Uncle Joe's lap and gave him a big hug.

And Uncle Joe? He looked so happy, nobody cared that he had forgotten to comb his hair. Or that there was a mess of crumbs around his plate and more on the floor. We all knew that in many ways Uncle Joe is a neat guy.

We were glad he had come to stay with us . . . all the time, forever.

1. How did knowing Uncle Joe change Dan's family?
2. What were three things that Uncle Joe did that made him important to the family?
3. Was Mom's idea that Dan take Uncle Joe bowling a good one? Explain.
4. How do you know that Dan's friends learned to accept Uncle Joe?
5. Why did the family decide that Uncle Joe should stay with them instead of going to the new apartment?

1. Name three things Dan did in the story that show us he could be a real person.
2. Uncle Joe and Dan wanted to take a bus from the Oak Street stop to the Fourth Avenue stop. Which bus would get them there by 2:00 P.M.?

	Leave Oak Street	Arrive Fourth Avenue
Bus 6	1:24 P.M.	1:51 P.M.
Bus 7	1:41 P.M.	2:13 P.M.
Bus 8	1:52 P.M.	2:21 P.M.

Prewrite

Think about the ways life changed when Uncle Joe came to live with Dan's family. Copy and complete the chart below. List each change as an advantage or a disadvantage.

Advantages
1. Uncle Joe was with the family now.
2.
3.

Disadvantages
1. The family had to be responsible for Uncle Joe.
2.
3.

Compose

Using the reasons you have listed, write a paragraph that tells why it was or was not a good idea for Uncle Joe to live with the family.

Revise

Read your paragraph. Make sure you have included all the facts from the list you chose. Correct your work if necessary.

Comparisons and Contrasts

When you think of ways that things are alike, you are making a **comparison.** How are carrots and oranges alike? Both are parts of plants. Both are about the same color. Both are foods. Both are good for the body. There are other ways carrots and oranges are alike. Can you think of any?

When you think of ways that things are different, you are making a **contrast.** How are carrots and oranges different? A carrot is a vegetable, but an orange is a fruit. Carrots grow in the ground, but oranges grow on trees. There are other ways carrots and oranges are different. Can you think of any?

Now read the following paragraph. Note the ways eagles and penguins are being compared and contrasted.

Eagles are birds that fly high in the sky. They build their nests near the tops of cliffs or in tall trees. They have claws for feet. Penguins are birds, too, but they cannot fly. They build their nests on the ground. Penguins live near the cold waters of the sea, and they have webbed feet that make them good swimmers. Both birds have wings and feathers and beaks. Penguins eat mostly fish, but eagles will eat almost any small animal.

One way to sort out the characteristics of things is by using a chart. Look at the following chart. The top half of the chart lists the ways eagles and penguins are alike. The bottom half lists the ways eagles and penguins are different.

Comparisons	
<u>Eagles</u>	<u>Penguins</u>
They are birds.	They are birds.
They have feathers.	They have feathers.
Contrasts	
<u>Eagles</u>	<u>Penguins</u>
They fly.	They swim.
They have claws.	They have webbed feet.

Read the paragraph about eagles and penguins again. What other comparison can you add to the chart? Did you notice that both eagles and penguins have wings and beaks?

What contrasts can you add to the chart? Where do eagles and penguins live? What do they eat? Eagles nest in cliffs and in tall trees. Penguins nest on the ground. Eagles eat small animals, but penguins eat mostly fish.

Read the paragraph on the following page. Look for the ways in which the planets Mars and Venus are alike and the ways in which they are different. Then make your own chart. List the ways Mars and Venus are compared and the ways they are contrasted.

Venus and Mars are the two planets closest to Earth. Mars is named after the Roman god of war. Venus is named after the Roman goddess of beauty. The surface of Mars can be seen from Earth. Venus, though, is clouded by thick gases. Both planets have active volcanoes. Mars has two moons. Venus has none. Venus is much hotter than Earth. Mars is much colder than Earth. Scientists have sent spaceships from Earth to both planets to try to find out more about them.

Textbook Application: Comparisons and Contrasts in Science

Writers often use comparisons and contrasts to explain ideas or to present new information. Sometimes writers present new information by comparing and contrasting it with information the reader may already have. Read these two examples from science books. The sidenotes will help you recognize the comparisons and contrasts that the writer has used.

In this sentence the writer compares the size of a virus with the size of a period. The writer helps you understand how small a virus is.

A virus is very small. You need a very strong microscope to see it. A microscope can show the virus enlarged 1,000 times. Four thousand viruses could fit on the period at the end of this sentence.

Look at these pictures of frogs. Each frog is from a different population. Their colors are different. They are also different sizes.

In this paragraph the writer asks you to contrast the two types of frogs.

Read the following article from another science book. Look for the ways the author uses comparison and contrast. Read the sidenotes and answer the questions.

LIVING THINGS NEED ENERGY

Where do plants and animals get their energy?

Have you ever tried to work or play when you have not had enough to eat? You get tired easily when you have not eaten enough food. You need food to give you energy.

All living things need energy. Living things need energy to move and grow. Living things die if they do not get enough energy.

Where do green plants get their energy? Like other living things, green plants get energy from food. But green plants are different from other living

This sentence compares green plants with other living things. How are all living things alike?

These two sentences contrast green plants with other living things. How are the plants different from other living things?

things. Green plants can produce, or make, their own food. Green plants use sunlight, water, and air to produce food in their leaves. Plants store some of this food in their roots, stems, and leaves. Because plants produce their own food, they are often called producers (prə•dü′ sərz).

 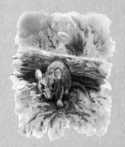

In this paragraph, notice how the writer compares and contrasts the ways animals get energy.

These sentences contrast how animals such as a mouse and a hawk get energy.

This sentence uses comparison to explain how all animals get energy.

Where do animals get their energy? All animals must consume, or eat, food to get energy. Since animals consume food, they are often called consumers (kən•sü′mərz). Some animals, like this mouse, eat green plants. These animals get energy right from the green plants. Some animals, like this hawk, eat other animals. They get energy from the animals they eat. But what if a hawk eats a mouse? The mouse got its energy from green plants. By eating a mouse, a hawk gets energy that once came from green plants. In fact, all animals depend on energy that comes from green plants.

—*Silver Burdett Science,* Silver Burdett

50

Compare green plants with other living things. How are they alike? Both need energy to move and grow. Both get energy from food. Contrast green plants with other living things. How are they different? Green plants produce their own energy. Animals do not.

How are all animals alike? When you compare them, you will find that all energy that animals use comes from green plants. How are some animals different from other animals? When you contrast them, you will find that some animals eat plants, and some animals eat other animals.

When you read, you will often find comparisons and contrasts. Ask yourself whether the author is using comparisons and contrasts to explain ideas or to present new information. Knowing why the author is using comparisons and contrasts will help you understand better what you are reading.

In this selection, Tom goes to live on a farm for the summer. This detour leads him to an adventure with a black fox. Read to see how Tom helps the black fox.

As you read, compare Tom's feelings about the fox with those of his aunt and uncle.

The Midnight Fox

by Betsy Byars

Five summers ago, Tom discovered a beautiful black fox in the woods near his aunt and uncle's farm. The more Tom watched the fox, the more the fox became special to him.

The trouble began when the black fox killed a turkey and a hen that belonged to Aunt Millie. Uncle Fred wanted to stop the black fox from killing any more animals. So one day he caught the black fox's baby and put it in a cage. He planned to use the baby fox as bait to trap the mother.

In this story Tom thinks back to that day and to the night that followed, when he was forced to make an important decision,

Sometimes at night when the rain is beating against the windows of my room, I think about that summer on the farm. It has been five years, but when I close my eyes I am once again by the creek watching the black fox come leaping over the green, green grass. She is as light and free as the wind, exactly as she was the first time I saw her.

Or sometimes it is that last terrible night, and I am standing beneath the oak tree with the rain beating against me. The lightning flashes, the world is turned white for a moment, and I see everything as it was — the broken lock, the empty cage, the small tracks disappearing into the rain. Then it seems to me that I can hear, as plainly as I heard it that August night, above the rain, beyond the years, the high, clear bark of the midnight fox.

"Are you getting sick?" Aunt Millie asked at supper that night.

"I guess I'm a little tired."

"Well, I should think so! Helping with the pump out in the broiling sun all morning and then tracking that fox all afternoon. It's a wonder you don't have heat stroke. You eat something though, hear? You have to keep up your strength."

I finished my supper and went up to my room. I did not even look out the window, because I knew I could see the rabbit hutch by the garage and I never again wanted to see that baby fox cowering against the wall.

It seemed to get dark quickly that night. Uncle Fred was already out on the back porch. He had brought out a chair and was sitting with his gun beside him, pointing to the floor. I never saw anyone sit any quieter. You wouldn't have noticed him at all, he was so still.

I stood behind him inside the screen door. Through the screen I could see the tiny fox lift his black nose and cry again. Now, for the first time, there was an answer — the bark of his mother.

I looked toward the garden, because that's where the sound had come from, but Uncle Fred did not even turn his head. In a frenzy now that he had heard his mother, the baby fox moved about the cage, pulling at the wire and crying again and again.

Just then there was the sound of thunder from the west, a long rolling sound, and Aunt Millie came to the door beside me and said, "Bless me, is that thunder?" She looked out at the sky. "Was that thunder, Fred?"

"Could be," he said without moving.

We stood in the doorway, feeling the breeze, forgetting for a moment the baby fox.

Then I saw Uncle Fred's gun rise ever so slightly in the direction of the fence behind the garage. I could not see any sign of the fox, but I knew that she must be there. Uncle Fred would not be wrong.

The breeze quickened, and abruptly the dishpan which Aunt Millie had left on the porch railing clattered to the floor. For the first time Uncle Fred turned his head and looked in annoyance at the pan and then at Aunt Millie.

"Did it scare your fox off?" she asked.

He nodded, then shifted in the chair and said, "She'll be back."

In just this short time the sky to the west had gotten black as ink. Low on the horizon, forks of lightning streaked the sky.

"Now, Fred, don't you sit out here while it's thundering and lightning. I mean it. No fox is worth getting struck by lightning for."

He nodded, and she turned to me and said, "You come on and help me shut the windows."

I started up the stairs, and she said again, "Fred, come on in when it starts storming. That fox'll be back tomorrow night, too."

I went upstairs and started closing the windows. I had just gotten one window down when I heard the gunshot. I had never heard any worse sound in my life. It was a very final sound, like the most enormous period in the world. Bam. Period. The end.

I ran out of my room and down the steps. I went out the back door, opening it so fast I hit the back of Uncle Fred's chair. I looked toward the rabbit hutch, said "Where?" and then looked at the back fence. Then I looked down at Uncle Fred, who was doing something with his gun.

"Missed," he said.

Suddenly I felt weak. My legs were like two pieces of rope, like that trick that magicians do when they make rope come straight up out of a basket and then say a magic word and make the rope collapse. My legs felt like they were going to collapse at any second. I managed to force these two pieces of rope to carry me up the stairs and into the room.

I closed two windows, and the third one, in sympathy perhaps, just banged down all by itself. Then I sank to the bed.

I lay in bed for a long time, still in my clothes, and then I got up very carefully. I walked over to the window and looked out at the tree that Aunt Millie's sons used to just run up and down all the time like monkeys. I opened the window, pushed out the screen, reached out into the rain, and felt for the smooth spot Aunt Millie had told me was worn into the bark of the tree.

I took off my shoes and knelt on the window sill. There was an enormous flash of lightning that turned the whole world white for a moment. Then I climbed out onto the nearest branch and circled the trunk round with my arms.

I thought that I could never get one step farther. I thought that I could never move even one muscle or I would fall.

After a while, though, I began to sort of slip down the tree. I never let go of the main trunk for a second. I just moved my arms downward in very small movements.

If there were smooth spots on those branches, my feet never found them. They only touched one rough limb after another. Slowly, I kept inching down the tree, feeling my way, never looking down at the ground. Finally, my foot reached out for another limb and felt the cold wet grass. It shocked me for a moment. Then I jumped down, landing on my hands and knees.

I got up and ran to the rabbit hutch. The baby fox was huddled in one corner of the pen. The lightning flashed and I saw him watching me.

"I'm going to get you out," I said.

There were bricks stacked in a neat pile under the hutch and I took one and began to bang it against the lock. I was prepared to do this all night if necessary, but the lock was an old one and it opened right away.

I unhooked the broken lock, opened the cage, and stepped back against the tree.

The baby fox did not move for a moment. He cried sharply. From the bushes there was an answering bark.

The lightning flashed again, and in that second he jumped and ran in the direction of the bushes. He barked as he ran. There was an immediate answer, and then only the sound of the rain. I waited against the tree, thinking about them. Then I heard the black fox bark one more time as she ran through the orchard with her baby.

Suddenly the rain began to slacken, and I walked around the house. I had never been so wet in my life. Now that it was over I was cold, too, and tired. I looked up at the tree and there didn't seem to be any point in climbing back up. In just a few hours everyone would know what I had done anyway. I went up on the porch and rang the doorbell.

It was Aunt Millie in her cotton robe who turned on the porch light and peered out through the side windows at me.

I must have been an awful sight, for she flung open the door at once and drew me in.

"What are you doing out there? What are you doing?"

"Who is it?" Uncle Fred asked as he came into the hall.

"It's Tom," Aunt Millie said.

They both turned and looked at me, waiting for an explanation. I cleared my throat and said, "Uncle Fred and Aunt Millie, I am awfully sorry but I have let the baby fox out of the rabbit hutch." I sounded very stiff and formal, and I thought the voice was a terrible thing to have to depend on, because I really did want them to know that I was sorry, and I didn't sound it the least bit. I knew how much Uncle Fred had looked forward to the hunt and how important getting rid of the fox was to Aunt Millie, and I hated for them to be disappointed now.

There was a moment of silence. Then Aunt Millie said, "Why, that's perfectly all right, isn't it, Fred?

Don't you think another thing about that. You just come on to bed. You're going to get pneumonia standing there in that puddle. I'll get you some towels."

Uncle Fred and I were left in the hall alone, and I looked up at him.

"I'm sorry," I said again.

He looked at me. I knew he was seeing through all the very casual questions I had been asking all summer about foxes, and seeing through the long days I had spent in the woods. I think those pieces just snapped into place right then in Uncle Fred's mind. I knew that if there was one person in the world who understood me, it was this man.

He cleared his throat. "I never liked to see wild things in a pen myself," he said.

Aunt Millie came down the hall and threw a towel over my head and started rubbing. "Now get upstairs. I am not going to have you lying in bed with pneumonia when your mother arrives."

We went into my room. Then she turned down my bed, went out, and came back with a glass of milk.

"I'm sorry about your turkey and hen," I said.

"Oh, that! It was more the heat than anything else. Just don't think about it anymore. The fox and her baby are miles away from here now, and they'll never come back to bother my birds. That's one thing about a fox. It learns."

She turned out the light and said, "It is starting to rain again. I declare we are going to be flooded out." Then she went downstairs.

The rest of the summer went by quickly. Pretty soon my visit to the farm began to seem hazy.

But then sometimes at night, when the rain is beating against the windows of my room, I think about that summer and everything is crystal-clear. I am once again beside the creek. The air is clean and the grass is deep and very green. I look up and see the black fox leaping over the crest of the hill, and she is exactly as she was the first time I saw her.

Or I am beneath that tree again. The cold rain is beating down upon me, and my heart is in my throat. And I hear, just as plainly as I heard it that August night, above the rain, beyond the years, the high, clear bark of the midnight fox.

1. Why did Uncle Fred want to kill the black fox?

2. How did Tom save the fox?

3. Do you think that Tom acted bravely? Why or why not?

4. When Tom described the fox (on page 53), what words did he use to help you know that he wanted the fox to be free?

5. What did Uncle Fred say to Tom to show him that he understood why Tom set the baby fox free?

Compare and contrast Tom's feelings about the fox with those of his aunt and uncle. How were Tom's feelings about the fox like his aunt's? How were they different? How were Tom's feelings about the fox like his uncle's? How were they different?

Prewrite

Sometimes when Tom hears the sound of rain beating against the windows of his room, he is reminded of the summer he spent on his aunt and uncle's farm. Copy the chart below and complete it by listing what place or event each sound makes you remember.

What do you think about when you hear . . .
a baby cry?
a dog bark?
a siren sound?
a door slam?

Compose

Choose one of the sounds from the chart. Write a paragraph that describes the place or event that the sound makes you remember. Be sure to include enough details to make the place or event seem real to a reader.

Revise

Read your paragraph. Is it a good description of the place or event? If not, revise your work by adding more details.

In this selection, a boy and his grandma escape down a river on a raft. Read to find out why Trouble River is a good name for the river.

As you read, think about how the author has used informal language in dialogue to develop the characters.

Trouble River

by Betsy Byars

Dewey had just built the raft. He had planned to explore the quiet part of Trouble River near his home. Now his raft faced a real test.

When the outlaw Indians had come, Dewey and his grandma and his dog, Charlie, had escaped on the raft. They hoped to make it down the river to Hunter City. Dewey's mother and father were visiting there. They would know what to do. For now, however, Dewey and his grandma were on their own.

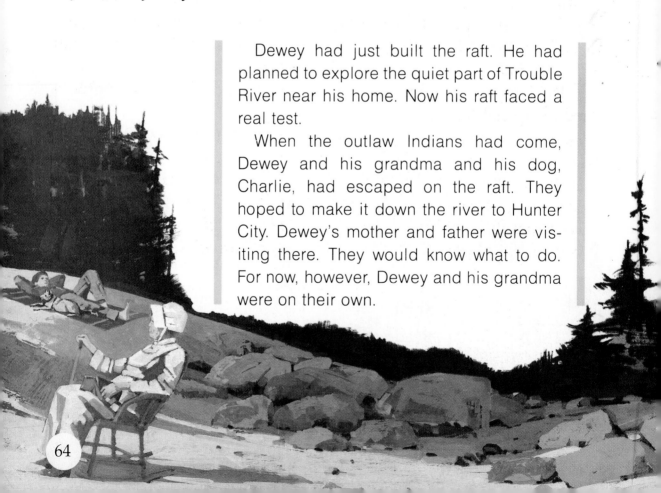

At dusk they stopped in the shelter of an old, dry creek bed. There was a widened sandy place where a pool had once formed. Dewey set his grandma's rocker on the sand. Then he spread his blanket on the rise above it.

They ate what was left of the cornmeal cakes. They also ate some fresh berries that Dewey had gathered.

"Try to get some sleep," Dewey's grandma said.

"Yes'm."

He had been sitting on the edge of the blanket, drawing a stick through the sand. Now he turned. Charlie was curled up in the center of the blanket, so Dewey lay beside him. He was so tired that his body ached, but he could not sleep. He lay with his hands locked behind his head.

"Push that dog off the blanket," his grandma said. "I swear that worthless thing'll be up in my chair next."

"He's all right, Grandma." Dewey hugged the dog to him. He had the lonely feeling that he and Grandma and Charlie were the only living creatures left in the world. He buried his face in the dog's fur and waited until the tears in his eyes had dried.

"Grandma," he said after a while.

"What is it now? I thought you were asleep."

"I was wondering, Grandma, what's going to happen to us." The thought had been troubling him all afternoon.

She paused and then she said, "There is something inside a person — I don't know how to give it a name exactly — but when something bad happens to you, well, a person thinks, This here's the end. I've thought it. I thought it when I had to come live out here on the prairie. I crawled up in that wagon and I said to myself, 'This here's the end.' I reckon you'll think it more than once in your life. Then a little time passes, a week or maybe a year. This something inside a person — whatever you'd call it — makes you come alive again."

"I wonder if I could be like that," Dewey said.

"You could if there was anything to you at all," she said. "Now get some sleep. You can't be steering us into Hunter City tomorrow if you don't get some sleep."

Dewey lay on his back for a long time, looking up at the sky. When sleep finally came, it was troubled.

He awoke, wet with sweat in the chilly air. Then he realized that it was not a dream that had awakened him. Charlie had risen on the blanket and was looking up into the darkness, a low growl deep in his throat. His teeth showed white beneath his raised upper lip.

This had seemed the ideal spot to camp when Dewey had first seen it. It was sheltered and protected. Now he realized that it would be easy for an enemy to slip up on them.

Dewey waited. He could see nothing. Then, from the bushes above, he heard a snarl and the rising howl of a wolf. He said in a low voice, "Grandma, wake up."

"What? What?" she said. She awakened so suddenly that her cane jabbed deep into the soft sand.

"Grandma, I think there are wolves up there."

"Wolves!" she said. She was fully awake now, for she feared them. "They'll eat us alive."

Her voice was helpless and old. Her hands clutched the arms of her rocker so tightly that the veins stood out.

In the shadows, a wolf, snarling and threatening, crossed to the edge of the creek bed.

Dewey said quickly, "Let's go."

He took his grandma by the arm, and with the other lifted the heavy rocker. "Charlie," he said firmly, "come."

Reluctantly, Charlie followed the boy as he stumbled toward the raft under his load.

"Help me, boy," his grandma gasped. "Help me!"

"I am, Grandma. I am."

He threw the chair on the raft. Before she was seated, he began to push the raft away from the shore with his oar.

"I'm not set yet," she said. Then, "But go on, boy, go on."

On the shore a wolf howled, a high, lonely sound. Then the other wolves took up the chorus. They ran in a pack to the bank and started for the raft, reaching out over the water with open jaws.

Charlie barked sharply. He stood on the edge of the raft, crouched as if he were about to jump into the water.

"Oh!" said Dewey's grandma with a sigh. She rose slightly and moved her chair to the center of the raft. "Oh! don't stop no more, boy," she said. "Whatever happens, don't stop no more. Those awful wolves."

"I can keep going if you can, Grandma."

Trouble River wound through the prairie like an animal on the scent of its prey. It hurried, then slowed. It twisted, then straightened. Then, at last, after its long and twisted journey, it began to gain speed before it rushed right into Big River. There, at the joining of the two rivers, would be Hunter City.

"Seems like we're picking up a little speed, doesn't it, boy?" she said, and her voice was lighter. "Maybe we'll get there by morning."

"Yes'm."

Dewey smiled. He dipped his paddle into the water and again began to feel the glow of confidence. He felt that the worst of the journey was over. Surely by morning they would be in Hunter City. He had no way of knowing about the stretch of treacherous water that lay ahead.

Dewey kept his eyes on the shores of the river. In the moonlight he occasionally saw the wolves slinking on the shore, but it did not trouble him. As long as he kept the raft in the center of the river, he and his grandma would be safe from them.

He poled the raft closer to the far bank.

"Keep it steady, boy," his grandma said. "This is no time to be upsetting now that we're almost there."

"No'm."

Charlie had given up growling at the wolves and now sat uneasily by Grandma's feet. The blanket had been lost in the rush for the raft. Now he had nothing to lie on. The water licking between the logs made him uneasy. He stuck his cold nose up into Grandma's hand.

"You worthless critter," she said. "You think I got nothing better to do than to hold your nose?" Still, she patted his head before she withdrew her hand. "I reckon we'll all be glad to see friendly faces, the dog, too."

Now they fell silent. Only the sound of Dewey's oar dipping into the water broke the silence. Dewey had no idea of the time. He knew daylight was still hours away.

He bent to reach under the raft, feeling the strips of hide. Some of them had begun to fray because of the constant rubbing of the logs, but he thought there was no danger. The raft would see them through.

He changed position and began to rub some of the stiffness out of his arms. His bare feet were cold against the wet logs. Suddenly he wanted to be in Hunter City so badly that his knees began to shake. He dipped his oar deep into the water to speed their progress.

By dawn they were gaining speed again. The river had straightened, and now the water rushed toward its goal, Big River.

"Maybe you better slow us down, boy," Grandma said. It was the first she had spoken in hours, though she had not been asleep. "It's not that I don't want to get there fast as you do."

"Yes'm, I will."

"It's just that I don't want to get upset."

"I'll slow her down."

He plunged his oar into the water, bracing himself, and waited for the raft to slow, but this seemed to have no effect.

"Slow her down." Grandma jabbed her cane into the air. "Now, boy."

"I am," he said. Again he swept the oar against the current, then added in a low voice, "Much as I can."

"Perhaps the raft will slow itself when we round that bend," Grandma said. She took her cane, set it across her lap, and held it along with the handle of her satchel in both hands.

"We're really moving," he said.

"What, boy?" she shouted over the noise of the water.

"I said we're really moving."

"Well, you don't need to tell me that." She looked uneasily at the wild river.

The river had narrowed. The shore was close on either side, but try as he would, Dewey could not move the raft from the rush of the current. All his paddling did nothing.

"Are we slowing any, boy?" she asked.

"No'm." He gasped as the raft tipped in the rough current. The water was now white with foam.

Grandma in her chair leaned forward tensely. Dewey gripped his oar. Charlie, on his feet now, whined and moved about unsteadily behind Grandma's chair. They listened closely, without moving.

So it was that they heard the rapids before they saw them. It was a wild noise that filled the air like the hum of a million insects.

"What *is* that, boy?" his grandma shouted.

He did not answer, for both of them knew. Dewey watched wide-eyed as the little raft swept around the bend in the river. Then Dewey gasped, and he heard his grandma scream.

There, stretching below them, were the rapids. Through a treacherous crack in the bluffs, the water ran, dashing against rocks, throwing spray high into the air.

"Get down, boy," Grandma cried.

He heard her when he was already on his knees, thrown by the force of the first waterfall. He slung one arm about Charlie and then crouched under his grandma's rocker. His other arm held the chair to the raft.

Water washed over Dewey, drenching him.

They plunged, turned twice, and fell as if they were dropping to the center of the earth. Dewey was in the air for a moment, and then they struck the water. The rocking chair hit Dewey on the shoulder.

"Grandma," he cried. Water was in his mouth, his eyes. He thought they had plunged under the water and were lost. He swallowed the icy water and sucked it into his nose as he gasped for breath.

Then, suddenly, it was over. It was like coming out of a nightmare, for they came through the dark shadows of the bluffs into the early morning sunlight. The sun turned the rippling water golden, and then the river widened to fill the broad valley beyond.

Dewey lifted his head. The dog, his fur flattened over his body, strained to be free. Dewey let him go. Charlie looked around, ready to leap for safety, then found to his surprise that he was safe. The water was smooth now, unhurried, with only the faint sound of the rapids behind to remind them of their recent danger.

"Grandma?" Dewey said.

There was no answer.

"Grandma!" He straightened and raised himself to one knee. "Grandma!"

"I'm still here, boy," she said in a voice that sounded small and far away.

"Are you all right?"

He looked at her. Her clothes were stuck against her thin body. Her hair, always so neatly bound behind her head, now hung in wet wisps. The bonnet she had guarded so carefully hung like a limp rag behind her. But her satchel, wet and flattened over the objects it contained, was still held safely in her lap.

Suddenly Dewey got to his feet. He put one hand up to his eyes to shield them from the sun.

"Grandma, Grandma!" He covered her thin shoulder with his hand. "Grandma, yonder's Hunter City!"

1. Why was Trouble River a good name for the river in this story?
2. What troubles did Dewey and his grandma have on their way to Hunter City?
3. What part of the story did you think was the scariest? Why?
4. What words did the author use on page 70 to help you hear the sound of the rapids?
5. How do you know that Dewey's raft survived the "real test" of Trouble River?

Read the following examples of informal language in dialogue. Tell how you might say each line using formal language.

1. "This here's the end."
2. "I reckon you'll think it more than once in your life."
3. "I'll slow her down."
4. "Grandma, yonder's Hunter City!"
5. "Are we slowin' down any?"

Prewrite

Think about the story "Trouble River." What were the problems that Dewey and his grandma faced? How were these problems solved? Copy the chart below and complete it by listing the solution for each problem.

Problem	Solution
outlaw Indians	
wolves	
rapids	

Compose

Choose one of the problems that Dewey and his grandma faced, and write a paragraph describing the problem and how it was solved. Include sentences that give details to make your paragraph interesting.

Revise

Read your paragraph. Have you stated the problem at the beginning of the paragraph? If not, revise the paragraph. Also, check your work to make sure you have used enough details and have included the solution to the problem.

As you read this biography, think about the two stories you just read by this author. Recall details from those stories that reflect the author's own experiences in life.

Look for the details that support the main ideas about Betsy Byars's life.

Betsy Byars

by Arlene Pillar

When Betsy Byars's four children were young, they read early drafts of their mother's books. They would draw small arrows pointing down next to parts they thought were boring. Next to parts they thought were interesting, they drew arrows pointing up. The children were Mrs. Byars's greatest critics. Today, many books later, we know that children reading Betsy Byars's books would draw arrows pointing up on nearly every page. Children enjoy reading what she writes.

Betsy Comer Byars was born on August 7, 1928, in Charlotte, North Carolina. She grew up there. Her family lived part of the time in the city and part of the time in the country. As a child, Betsy had rabbits, a goat, a rooster, and a dog. She loves animals, and this love is obvious in her book *The Midnight Fox* when she describes the black fox. Mrs. Byars writes that the fox's "black fur was tipped with white . . . as if the moon were shining on her fur, frosting it."

Betsy studied English at Queens College in North Carolina. When she graduated, Betsy was not thinking of becoming a writer. She says, "I thought writers spent their time in front of a typewriter, and that seemed boring." Writing became important only after she married Edward Byars and was at home raising three daughters and a son. She began by writing for magazines that adults read. Today, Mrs. Byars is one of the best-loved writers of books for young people.

"When I first started writing," Betsy Byars says, "I wrote daily, beginning when my kids left for school in the morning and ending at three o'clock when they got home." She is sure that she would never have written anything without putting in all those long days. Mrs. Byars adds, "Writing is something that has to be learned, like playing the piano, and a writer has to put in many, many hours."

Betsy Byars has been a writer for more than twenty years. One of the things she has learned from her job is that making up stories about young people is very interesting. She is never bored. This certainly shows how much her thinking has changed since her college days.

The ideas for Betsy Byars's stories tend to come from things that really happened. For example, she once really saw a fox in the woods, as Tom did in *The Midnight Fox*. The idea, however, is only the beginning. It may take Mrs. Byars a full year to write a book. Then she may spend another year "thinking about it, polishing it, and making improvements."

Mrs. Byars puts facts about herself, her friends, and her family in her stories. The dog in *Trouble River* is a lot like her own dog. Sara in *The Summer of the Swans* has big feet. Betsy did, too, at that age. The idea for *The Night Swimmers* came from friends, who told her a true story about some nighttime visitors to their swimming pool. *The 18th Emergency,* about a bully, shows the fear that Betsy had as a child. There was a bully in her own school.

Many things interest Betsy Byars. These interests lead to ideas. For example, the idea for *The Summer of the Swans* came from a story in her college magazine. At the university there were swans that kept leaving their beautiful lake for less pleasing ponds. In her mind, she moved the swans to West Virginia, and the story began.

Mrs. Byars's stories tell of the problems some boys and girls face. She is skilled at showing how young people feel, think, and act, so her characters make young readers feel a part of what is happening. Some of the subjects she writes about are fears, growing pains, and taking chances. Many young people have experienced these things for themselves, and they are pleased when Mrs. Byars explores them on the printed page.

Betsy Byars believes in showing life the way it is. Sometimes life is not very nice. Endings are not always happy. Problems are not always solved. Mrs. Byars believes that her readers can understand life's hard truths. As Roy says in *The Night Swimmers,* it is like swallowing spinach: the "experience makes you stronger."

Betsy Byars's books have been translated into many languages. Some have been made into movies for televi-

sion. Also, they bring in lots of fan mail. Mrs. Byars gets
about two hundred letters a week from young people.
However, adults also think she is a wonderful writer. In
1971, she won the Newbery Medal for *The Summer of
the Swans*. Many of her other books have won important
prizes, too.

Betsy Byars lives with her husband in South Carolina.
They have a cat named Tiger and a dog named Harvey.
She does most of her writing in the winter months. In
the summer, she and Mr. Byars spend a lot of time gliding in their sailplane. They put the plane together and
take it apart themselves. The Byarses enjoy flying, and
they enjoy traveling around the United States to do it.
Of course, as she travels, Betsy Byars is always looking
for ideas. She wants to be sure to keep those arrows
pointing up.

1. How does the story "The Midnight Fox" reflect Betsy Byars's childhood?

2. What three things that really happened to her did Betsy Byars use for story ideas?

3. How do you think that Betsy Byars's children helped their mother write better stories?

4. What words did Betsy Byars use to tell you that writers need to practice writing?

5. Why are Betsy Byars's stories popular with children?

Think about the following main ideas that were discussed in the biography of Betsy Byars. Choose one of the main ideas, and list three details from the selection that support that main idea.

1. Betsy Byars's interests lead to ideas for stories.

2. Betsy Byars's stories tell of the problems children face.

3. Betsy Byars's books are popular.

Prewrite

Betsy Byars gets ideas for stories from things that really happen. Copy and complete the chart below. Think of an idea for a story Betsy Byars might write after seeing each thing. Write a sentence that tells the main idea of such a story. The first one is done for you.

1. a wild horse in a field	A girl finds a wild horse and takes pictures of it.
2. an eagle with a broken wing	
3. a dog taking care of a kitten	

Compose

Choose one of the ideas from the chart to write a story with a beginning, a middle, and an ending. Use enough descriptive details to make the characters seem real.

Revise

Read your story. Have you described the characters well? Does your story have a beginning, a middle, and an ending? If not, revise your work.

Fact and Opinion

Some sentences state facts. Some sentences give opinions. Read the following sentence:

Tourists spend over a billion dollars a year in Thailand.

This sentence states a fact. The statement can be proved. Records are kept of the amount of money tourists spend in Thailand. You can find the information in an encyclopedia or another source. A **fact,** then, is something that can be proved.

Another kind of statement gives an opinion. An **opinion** tells what a person feels, thinks, or believes. An opinion may be based on facts, but it is a judgment. An opinion cannot be proved.

Sometimes a writer may signal an opinion by using certain words. Some of these signal words are *in my opinion, it seems to me,* and *I think.*

Read the following sentence:

I think tourists spend too much money in Thailand.

It cannot be proved that tourists spend too much money in Thailand. That is the writer's opinion. The words *I think* signal that an opinion follows.

Very often, opinions are given without signal words. Look at the picture and read each farmer's statement. Which statement presents a fact? Which statement presents an opinion?

The first statement presents a fact. The farmers can prove how long they have been growing corn. The second statement presents an opinion. The second farmer is telling what he thinks they should do. The first farmer may or may not agree with this opinion. You could add signal words to the second statement to make it read "I think next year we should grow wheat."

Writers often present both facts and opinions in the same article. You may agree that all the facts are true. However, you may not agree with the opinions. Before you can judge the opinions, you must be able to separate them from the facts.

Now read the following paragraph. In it the writer gives both facts and opinions. Which are the facts? Which are the opinions? How do you know?

Few rivers are as impressive as the Thames River in England. The Thames flows past Oxford

University, the oldest university in Britain. It also flows by a number of old royal palaces. On sunny summer days, hundreds of people picnic along the river's banks. The Thames River is Britain's most historic river and also the one the British people enjoy the most.

The first sentence ("Few rivers are as impressive as the Thames River in England") gives an opinion. The word *impressive* describes how the author feels about the Thames River. It would be impossible to prove this statement.

The next three sentences state facts. You could prove each of these statements. How? You could look in an encyclopedia and at a map of Britain to prove the second and third sentences. Someone could prove the fourth sentence by counting the people who picnic along the Thames on sunny summer days.

The last sentence ("The Thames River is Britain's most historic river and also the one the British people enjoy the most") gives an opinion. It is based on facts, but the facts are used to support the writer's opinion. Another person might not agree with this opinion. Notice the word *most* in the last sentence. Like the word *impressive* in the first sentence, *most* is a clue that the writer is giving an opinion.

As you read, look carefully for facts and opinions. Remember, facts can be proved. Opinions tell how someone feels or what someone thinks.

Read the following paragraph. Look for facts and opinions. Then answer the questions that follow.

Siberia covers over one half of the Soviet Union. It is rich in natural resources. However, its climate is harsh and unpleasant. Temperatures there can fall as low as −50°C. Many of the Siberian people still herd reindeer, as they have for centuries. As long as the climate does not change, the people will not change.

1. Which statements are opinions?
2. Which opinion does not have any clue words?
3. Which opinion is supported by a fact?

Textbook Application: Fact and Opinion in Social Studies

In textbooks, authors usually state facts. However, authors may sometimes state their own opinions. Most authors support their opinions with facts. Supporting opinions with facts leads to sound conclusions. Read the following selection, looking for facts and for opinions based on facts. The sidenotes will help you.

A crowded farming area The rich soil and the climate make the North China Plain a good place for farming. About 60 percent of China's wheat is grown here. Only the United States and the Soviet Union grow more wheat than China. The North China Plain produces about half of China's cotton. The Soviet Union is the only country that produces more cotton than China. Other important crops are soybeans, vegetables, and

The word *good* helps you know that this is an opinion.

These statements are facts that can be found in an almanac. They support the opinion.

What other facts and opinions can you find?

> tobacco. China leads the world in the production of rice, but most of this crop is grown in southern China.
>
> —*States and Regions*, Silver Burdett

There are no sidenotes for the next article. As you read, look for opinions and supporting facts.

> ### The Land of the Netherlands
>
> Some of the land in the Netherlands is covered with water, because it is below sea level. Hundreds of years ago, the Dutch began draining the water from this land. Land that has been drained by pumping the water from it is called a polder. Today the Dutch are still adding land to their country by making new polders.
>
> The Dutch make a polder by first building a dike, or a wall of soil and stone, around the land that is covered with water. Then they pump the water into canals. Canals are found in almost every part of the Netherlands. The canals carry the water to the North Sea. Windmills were once used to pump the water into the canals. Today most of the pumps are powered by electric motors.
>
> —*Living in World Regions*, Laidlaw Brothers

Did you find an opinion in this article? No, there are only statements of fact. What opinions do you think could have been included that would be supported by the facts in the article?

There are no sidenotes for the next article either. Read it and answer the questions at the end.

Learning from Other Countries

People never copy another country's ideas exactly. Instead, they change them to fit their own way of life. The idea that all children should attend school started in Germany. This idea spread to countries everywhere. Yet all schools are not alike.

Schools in Canada are different from schools in the United States. Children in Canada learn how to read and write in both French and English, because these two languages are equally important in Canada. In the United States, French is not a main language. Most schools in the United States do not teach French until the later grades.

—*Regions Near and Far,* D. C. Heath

In this article the author has an opinion about schools. What is it? What facts does the author give to support this opinion?

Remember, statements of fact can be proved. Opinions are judgments and cannot be proved. Sometimes articles have opinions that seem to be supported by the facts. As you read, look for the writer's opinions and how the writer supports those opinions. Then decide whether or not you agree with them.

In this selection, you will read the true story of a steamboat journey that had some detours. Read to find out where these detours led.

As you read, see how some people's opinions change when they are given new facts.

The Amazing Voyage of the *New Orleans*

by Judith St. George

In 1809 steamboats traveled only on the eastern rivers. That wasn't good enough for Nicholas Jacobus Roosevelt. He believed that steamboats had a future on western rivers, too.

What a difference in frontier life steamboats would make. They could travel easily down and up the Ohio and Mississippi rivers, carrying both goods and news.

Two other steamboat men,

Robert Fulton and Robert Livingston, dreamed the same dream as Nicholas Roosevelt. The three men became partners. Together they planned to build a steamboat and test it on the western rivers.

There was never any question as to who would be in charge. Nicholas Roosevelt would build the steamboat. Nicholas Roosevelt would also take it on its two-thousand-mile journey.

But first, the partners decided, Mr. Roosevelt must study and map the rivers. Good. Nicholas would take his new bride, Lydia, with him.

Along the way, Mr. Roosevelt got a lot of advice. When the Roosevelts' flatboat reached Louisville just above the Falls of the Ohio, riverboatmen hooted. "A paddlewheeled steamboat make it over the Falls? Never! Why, those rocks and rapids would break up a deep-hulled steamboat in no time."

Mr. Roosevelt paid them no mind. After he had studied and measured the Falls for three weeks, he was sure a steamboat could safely make it. Watch for me in a year or two, he promised when he left Louisville. I'll be back in my steamboat and show you.

When the Roosevelts reached the Mississippi River, the Mississippi riverboatmen hooted, too. "Maybe a steamboat can navigate on deep, calm, eastern rivers like the Hudson. However, a steamboat can never make it through the terrible currents and snags and floating islands of our great river. You'd be throwing away your time and money."

In December 1809, six months after starting out from Pittsburgh by flatboat, Nicholas and Lydia Roosevelt reached New Orleans. Mr. Roosevelt had listened and watched and studied and measured. Now his mind was made up. He was sure a steamboat could navigate the western rivers. He couldn't wait to start building it.

The following spring, in 1810, Nicholas and Lydia Roosevelt again traveled to Pittsburgh. There, in a shipyard at the Forks of the Ohio, Mr. Roosevelt began to build his steamboat. He took charge of every detail.

Nothing was too good, or too costly, for Mr. Roosevelt's steamboat. Finally, after eighteen months, and $38,000, the *New Orleans* was finished.

On October 20, 1811, the *New Orleans* was ready to start its long journey. Many of the Roosevelts' Pittsburgh friends came down to the shipyard to watch. Mr. Roosevelt was everywhere. He was running back and forth, making last-minute changes, and giving orders to his crew.

Why, there was Lydia Roosevelt boarding the *New Orleans* as well. She was leading her huge Newfoundland dog, Tiger. The Pittsburghers were surprised. What if the boat blew up or hit a snag and sank? Surely Mr. Roosevelt wasn't going to let his wife risk her life on such a foolish venture.

Mr. Roosevelt was puzzled. Risk? There was no risk. Hadn't he, Nicholas Roosevelt, seen to the planning and building of every inch of the *New Orleans*? Of course Mrs. Roosevelt was going.

And of course she did. It was impossible to be married to Nicholas Roosevelt and not have some determination of one's own. No, Mrs. Roosevelt was not one to sit home by the fire knitting. She would rather be on another two-thousand-mile adventure with her husband.

"Whooooot!" Smoke blew from the tall smokestack.

Hats flew in the air. Ladies waved their handkerchiefs. Though the Pittsburghers did wish the Roosevelts all good luck, they were certain the steamboat would never reach New Orleans. Nicholas and Lydia waved good-bye in return. They were just as certain of their success.

Together they watched the curve of unbroken forest pass by as they steamed down the majestic Ohio River.

After a week of pleasant traveling, the *New Orleans* dropped anchor in the stream across from Cincinnati. It seemed as if all twenty-six hundred inhabitants had gathered on the riverbank to watch. The Roosevelts had met the people of Cincinnati two years before when they had floated by flatboat down the Ohio River. Mr. Roosevelt had said he would return in a steamboat, but no one had believed him. Now here he was.

Two days after leaving Cincinnati, the *New Orleans* stopped near the waterfront town of Louisville, Kentucky. It was midnight, and the moon lit up the night as bright as day. The Great Comet of 1811 stretched halfway across the sky, its tail over a hundred million miles long. The engineer released the safety valve. A shriek of escaping steam pierced the quiet.

At the noise, the people of Louisville jumped from their beds and rushed to the banks of the Ohio River. They were sure that the comet had fallen from the sky, hissing and whistling as it sank in the Ohio River.

What they found was almost as amazing as a comet. A 116-foot-long bright blue steamboat sat at anchor. A ribbon of smoke was pouring from its smokestack. There to greet them were Mr. and Mrs. Roosevelt and their Newfoundland dog, Tiger.

When the people of Louisville got over their surprise, they gave a public dinner in honor of the Roosevelts. They had grown fond of Nicholas and Lydia two years before. That was the time when the Roosevelts had spent three weeks in Louisville studying the Falls. Besides, they respected Mr. Roosevelt as a man of his word. He had promised to come back to Louisville in a steamboat, hadn't he? Well, there it was, paddlewheels and all.

In return, the Roosevelts invited their Louisville friends to a dinner aboard the *New Orleans.*

When everyone was eating and talking and having a good time, machinery began to clank. Deep rumblings sounded below. The *New Orleans* was moving.

The guests jumped to their feet and ran from the dining cabin. They were certain that the anchor cable had broken and the *New Orleans* was drifting downstream toward the Falls of the Ohio, just below Louisville.

No such thing. The *New Orleans* wasn't drifting downstream toward the Falls at all. She was chugging along nicely upstream against the current.

The *New Orleans* didn't go far,

only a mile or two, but it was far enough. Showman that he was, Mr. Roosevelt had proved to the people of Louisville that his steamboat could go upstream against the current, just as well as down.

Mr. Roosevelt had never been very good at waiting. Like most determined people, when he had something to do, he wanted to do it . . . now. But he had a good long wait in Louisville, more than a month. It was all because the Ohio River was low. It was too low for the *New Orleans* to pass safely over the two miles of treacherous rocks and rapids of the Falls of the Ohio. Like it or not, Mr. Roosevelt had to wait until the rains fell and the river rose.

Every day Mr. Roosevelt measured how deep the river was. Day after day the river didn't rise. Mr. Roosevelt had to do something to keep busy. So he and his crew boarded the *New Orleans* and steamed back up the Ohio River 141 miles to Cincinnati.

After a few days in Cincinnati, Mr. Roosevelt steamed back to Louisville to wait some more.

Days passed. Now the crew was as impatient as Mr. Roosevelt, and the December weather didn't help. It was heavy and still, with no air moving. The sun was a red globe in a leaden, cloudless sky. Sometimes it seemed as if a huge wet sheet covered the countryside.

Then, when everyone was about to burst with impatience, the Ohio River began to rise. Day after day, Mr. Roosevelt measured the depth of the river. Finally, after ten days, the river stopped rising. Mr. Roosevelt was sure the river would rise no higher. It was now or never. Nicholas Roosevelt, being Nicholas Roosevelt, decided it was now.

Most of the Roosevelts' Louisville friends came to the banks of the Ohio River to say good-bye. Most of them were worried.

The *New Orleans* may have gone upstream, even all the way to Cincinnati. However, it would never, ever make it safely over the terrible rapids and limestone rock ledges of the Falls of the Ohio.

If the *New Orleans* were to pass over the Falls, it would have to travel faster than the current, which was very fast indeed. A special Louisville pilot who knew every rock and eddy of the Falls had come aboard. The engineer built up a powerful head of steam. Sparks and black smoke ribboned from the tall smokestack. The safety valve whistled. The paddlewheels turned faster than they ever had before. The *New Orleans* flew out of sight of the Roosevelts' friends.

The deafening thunder of the rushing water drowned out all sound. The special pilot had to signal to the helmsman with his hands. Black limestone ledges could be seen through the foam. Flying spray soaked everyone as all hands braced themselves. The *New Orleans* was going so fast it seemed as if it would fall right into the swirling waters.

After the *New Orleans* was out of sight, the people of Louisville waited for word. They waited so long, they finally decided the *New Orleans* had gone down with everyone on board. Sadly they started toward their homes.

"Ho, there!" It was a young man on horseback riding up the pike. "I just saw the most amazing sight," he called.

Everyone rushed around him.

"A floating sawmill with a deckful of passengers and a dog as big as a pony just flew over the Falls of the Ohio. They bounced and bucked and the whole sawmill shook, ready to break apart. It was going faster and louder than anything I ever saw."

"Were there any survivors?" the people asked.

"The whole sawmill survived. It's setting right below the Falls, a'steaming and a'puffing. Every-one on board is dancing and shouting for joy. Now doesn't that beat all?"

Author's note: *Nicholas Roosevelt was the great-granduncle of President Theodore Roosevelt. He reached New Orleans in his steamboat on January 12, 1812. Until it sank in 1814, the* New Orleans *carried freight and passengers between Natchez and New Orleans. It never did go all the way back up the rivers, but other steamboats soon made that long journey. By 1817 steamboats were regularly traveling both up and down the Ohio and Mississippi rivers.*

1. Where did Nicholas Roosevelt and his wife travel on the steamboat?

2. How did the voyage of the *New Orleans* change people's beliefs about steamboats?

3. What did you like best about Nicholas Roosevelt?

4. What did you read that made you think that people liked the Roosevelts?

5. How did Nicholas Roosevelt solve the problem of passing over the Falls of the Ohio?

Apply

the

Skills

Read the following sentences. Which ones present facts? Which present opinions? Tell how you know.

1. "Why, those rocks and rapids would break up a deep-hulled steamboat in no time."

2. Nicholas Roosevelt was the great-grand-uncle of President Theodore Roosevelt.

3. When everyone was eating and talking and having a good time, machinery began to clank.

4. "I just saw the most amazing sight."

Prewrite

Nicholas Roosevelt dreamed of building a steamboat to travel the western rivers of the United States. These are the steps he took to reach his goal.

1. decided what he wanted to do

2. talked and planned with others

3. studied and mapped the rivers

4. took charge of all building details

Compose

Choose one of the activities below.

1. Pretend you want to be a professional sports star. List the steps you would need to take to reach that goal. Write a paragraph that tells what you would need to do.

2. Use blocks to list the steps you must take to reach a goal that you have. Write a paragraph telling what the goal is and how you will try to achieve it.

Revise

Make sure you have identified your goal and included all the steps needed to achieve it.

In this selection, a girl and her family set out for America from their home in Russia. As you read, think about how this family feels as they travel toward their new life.

Watch for time clues. They will tell you how long this part of the journey takes.

Dvora's Journey

by Marge Blaine

In 1904, a feeling of unrest and dissatisfaction existed among many people in Russia. They were unhappy with the conditions under which they were forced to live. Life was especially hard for Russian Jews.

Dvora, a Jewish girl, and her family made plans to escape from Russia into Poland. From there they hoped to travel all the way to America to start a new life. They thought that they would have more opportunities and more freedom in America.

The family faced many dangers and hardships on their journey. Perhaps the most dangerous time came when they arrived at the river.

We drew closer and closer to the river. Papa stopped the cart near the edge. Tall grass grew along the bank. Behind the grass were bushes and a few trees. I could see the other side, far across the water.

"Everyone out!" Papa called. "All the bundles, too!"

"But where are we going?" I asked. "There's nothing here."

Papa pointed. "Look," he said. "In the grass. Can you see the little house? That's where we'll stay."

I followed Papa's finger. Almost hidden by the grass was a straw hut. Did Papa mean we'd stay there? I guess he did, because he carried our belongings inside. Then Papa climbed back on the wagon.

"Where are you going, Papa?" Saul asked.

"To the village. I have to find the man who's going to guide us across."

I thought being indoors after three days in the cart would be a relief, but the hut was terrible. It was dark and it smelled.

"Can we go outside?" Minnie asked as soon as Papa left. "We can play near the river."

"No, children," Mama told us. "You'll have to stay inside. We don't want anyone to find us here."

Papa didn't come back until late. Although he was tired, he was smiling.

"Is everything all right, Jacob?" Mama asked.

Papa nodded. "I found Peter, the man I wanted. He'll get us across the river and into Poland."

"What took you so long, Papa?" Yossel asked.

"Well, it was hard to find Peter. I just couldn't walk around the village asking, 'Where's the man who smuggles Jews into Poland?' could I?"

We laughed. "I guess not," Saul said. "How *did* you find him?"

"Don't ask! It was some job. And then I had to find someone to buy the cart and the horse, too. But we're all set now."

We stayed in the hut for five days and nights. It

was awful, cooped up in the darkness with nothing to do. We took turns peeking through the door, watching the birds that hid in the grass or the changing shape of the clouds.

One afternoon I heard Saul ask Papa, "What if Peter doesn't come?"

"He'll come. Don't worry," Papa said.

"But what if he took your money and doesn't take us across?" Saul sounded worried.

My father shook his head. "I'm not so foolish," he explained. "I gave him half. Half here and half when we're safe in Poland. My friend Sol told me that's the way to do it."

Finally Papa left for town. When he came back, he had good news. "Tonight's the night," he told us. "Tonight we're leaving Russia." He looked around the hut. "Make sure everything's ready. Peter will be here after dark."

We waited in the darkness in front of the hut. No one said a word. Other families stood in groups along the bank.

It was chilly and I pulled my shawl tight. I heard a rustling in the bushes behind us. "I hope it's Peter," I whispered to Rivkeh, "and not the border guards."

"Sshhh! No talking," Papa reminded us.

Overhead I saw the stars and the moon, the last time I'd see the stars of Russia. "Are the same stars in Poland? And do they have stars in America?" I wondered. Before I had a chance to ask Saul, a man stepped out of the woods.

He began walking toward the water, motioning for us to follow. We stopped at the edge of the river. "Not a sound now," Peter warned. "The guards have guns and we don't want anyone shot!"

Stealing the border suddenly seemed real, not a game we were playing. If we made it, we'd be free, free from soldiers who took what they wanted without paying, free from the army, free to go to America. And if we didn't make it? I tried not to think about that.

"How are we going to get across?" I heard Minnie ask. "There aren't any boats."

"Walk!" my father told her, settling the heavy bundle holding his tools more securely on his back. "We're going to walk."

All around were gasps and splashing sounds as people began making their way into the water. The group that had been nearest to us, three men, two women, and a girl about my age, was already quite far out. I could see their outline in the moonlight: the strangely shaped mass of their bundles, small circles for their heads, and the longer shapes of their bodies, cut in half by the water. It looked pretty deep to me.

"Come on. Let's go," Papa repeated. "And don't let anything drop. If it falls into the river, we won't get it back."

Rivkeh and I stepped forward. My foot touched the water. "Aaiii!" I almost screamed. It was icy. How would I be able to walk through it?

I had no choice. In went my other foot. With each step I took I felt the water climb higher. It seemed even colder than it had at first. I pulled my shawl tighter in an effort to keep at least some of me warm. The river got deeper as we went farther in.

"What about our dresses?" I hissed to Rivkeh. "If it gets any deeper, they'll be soaked!"

"Try to hold your skirt up with your free hand."

"Free hand! I don't have any. One's keeping my bundle from falling into the water, and the other's holding my shawl."

"Well, just do the best you can."

I felt the current at my legs, trying to pull me downstream. I kept going, one foot after another, trying to keep from falling, trying to stay straight ahead, hoping the guards were busy along another part of the river.

We were almost halfway across by now and no one had tried to stop us. I began to think we'd make it, but my feet were getting worse. They felt as though they were turning to ice. At least the river wasn't getting any deeper now. I kept my skirts up as well as I could, hoping they'd stay dry.

Just then I heard a smothered cry from up ahead.

The girl I'd noticed before grabbed wildly at her bundle. I saw her arm reach out, trying to save it. She leaned over as far as she could, but it was gone. The current had taken it.

Far off I heard another splash and a cry, only it was too far away to see what had happened.

We kept walking. The water was shallower by now and somehow less cold. I saw trees and bushes along the bank and hurried to reach it. At last we were on the other side.

I looked to make sure we were all safe. I saw Papa, Mama, and Minnie. Minnie's skirts must have fallen into the water, because they clung to her legs. Mine were just a little wet along the bottom, but my legs felt clammy anyway.

Saul and Yossel were the last ones out. "Oh, Yossel!" Mama cried. "What happened?"

Yossel was soaked. Water dripped from his hair, down his shoulders, and onto the ground. "I slipped," he said. "Saul grabbed my hand and pulled me out."

Saul had one wet arm across Yossel's back, but the rest of him was dry. "It's a good thing I was right there," Saul told us.

"Let me change you," Mama said. "There's dry clothing right here."

"We can't stop, Esther," Papa ordered. "We're not out of Russia yet."

Mama wrapped her shawl around Yossel and we started off, following the others along a small path in the woods. Soon we came out into a field. It stretched far out in the distance. Stubble from corn scraped my legs.

There must have been forty or fifty people walking across the field. We looked like a strange market procession, lines of men and women, boys and girls, all of us with heavy bundles on our shoulders or backs, making our way together.

I saw the girl who'd lost her possessions walking slowly ahead of me. I went more quickly to catch up. When I reached her side, I could see she was crying.

"I saw what happened," I said softly. "I'm sorry you lost your things."

She nodded to show she'd heard, but didn't answer.

"What's your name?" I asked.

"Naomi."

"I'm Dvora," I told her. "Are all those people in your family?" I asked, pointing to the men and women in front of us.

"No."

"Where are your parents?" I asked. "Are they in America?"

Naomi shook her head. "They're dead," she told me. "My father was in the army. He was killed before I was born."

"I'm sorry," I said. "What about your mother?"

"My mother and I lived with my uncle. Then she died when I was about five or six. I've been living with my uncle ever since. Now he's sending me to another uncle in New York."

I couldn't think of anything to say. "I'm sorry," I finally told her again.

"That's all right." Naomi had stopped crying by this time. "I was scared at first," she said, "but I think it'll be better for me there. My uncle wrote that there are lots of jobs. He's in a factory where they make dresses and coats. He says they can always use a good seamstress."

I thought of Rivkeh. She sewed beautifully.

"What about you?" Naomi asked. "Are you going to get a job in America?"

I shook my head. "No. I don't think so. My father promised I could go to school. I'd like to be a teacher, only I don't know if girls can be teachers there."

"Girls can be teachers there."

"How do you know?"

"My uncle sent all his children through school. They've had women teachers—even the boys!"

"Oh, Naomi," I said. "That makes me feel so much better about going." She smiled. "What was in your bundle?" I asked her.

"My other skirt—I was saving it to wear when I met my uncle—my good shawl—it used to be my mother's—and a gift, a cloth I'd embroidered for my uncle."

"It's too bad you lost it."

"I know. It's a good thing the money for my ticket was sewn inside my dress." Naomi looked up. "At first I thought I couldn't live without those things, especially Mama's shawl, but I guess I can."

We didn't talk for a while. I guess we were both thinking about America and what we'd find there. We walked through the field all night. Finally Peter stopped.

"What's the matter?" one of the men asked.

"Nothing," he said. "You'll be all right now. You're inside Poland."

People began to cheer and hug one another. The men crowded around Peter and shook his hand. They seemed almost happy to pay him their money.

"Town's that way," Peter told them, pointing the way we were going. "And the station's right on the main street."

Mama took out dry clothing for Yossel and food for all of us before we started off again. We were in Poland. The first part of the journey to America was over; the next part was about to begin.

1. How did the people feel about leaving Russia? What detail in the story tells you?

2. Name three of the hardships Dvora's family faced on their journey.

3. Find the sentence on page 106 that tells how Naomi felt about her mother's shawl.

4. What did you read that let you know that the people were happy to be inside Poland?

5. What important information did Peter give the people once they were inside Poland to help them continue on their journey to America?

Words such as *first,* *then,* and *next* and the number of hours or days that have passed are time clues. These clues help you follow a story's sequence. Find the time clues in "Dvora's Journey" that tell you how long each of the following parts of the journey lasted.

1. in the cart

2. in the hut

3. walking

Prewrite

This chart compares and contrasts the hut in "Dvora's Journey" with Dan's home in "Making Room for Uncle Joe." Copy the chart and add two more likenesses and differences.

The Hut and Dan's Home

Likenesses	Differences
Both are places to live.	The hut is dark.
Both have a door.	Dan's home has windows.

Compose

Write a paragraph comparing and contrasting the hut and Dan's home. Include the information from the chart above.

Revise

Check to make sure you have made your description clear. Also make sure you have compared and contrasted the two homes. Revise your work if necessary.

Homophones

Read the following sentence:

I won one of the grand prizes.

The words *won* and *one* sound exactly alike. Because they are not spelled the same, you know that they are different words. They also have different meanings.

Two words that sound alike but have different spellings and meanings are called **homophones.** The words *one* and *won* are a pair of homophones.

Read the following sentence from "The Amazing Voyage of the *New Orleans.*" Each of the underlined words is part of a homophone pair.

However, a steamboat can never make it through the terrible currents and snags and floating islands of our great river.

Do you know another word that sounds like each of the underlined words? The words *through* and *threw* are homophones. The words *currents* and *currants* are homophones (currants are small berries). The other homophone pairs are *our, hour* and *great, grate* (*grate* means "reduce to small pieces by rubbing against a rough surface").

When you read, you may find a word that sounds like a word you know. Yet the new word and its meaning may be unfamiliar to you. Read the following sentence:

The workers used a wrecking ball to raze the dangerous old building.

You may not know the word *raze,* but you know that it sounds like *raise,* a word meaning "move higher." From context clues in this sentence, you also know that the workers did not move the building higher; they knocked the building down. The words *raise* and *raze* sound alike but have different meanings. They are homophones. When there are no context clues to help with the meaning, you need to use a dictionary to find the meaning of the unknown word.

Read the following poem. It contains homophones. Some are correctly used. Others are not. Replace the incorrectly used homophones so that the poem makes sense.

Wood you believe that I didn't no
About homophones until too daze ago?
That day in hour class in groups of for,
We had to come up with won or more.

—George E. Coon

Look for homophones as you read. If you find a word that sounds like one you know but has a different spelling, it might be a homophone. Use the context of the sentence to help you figure out the word's meaning. If you still have difficulty, look up the word in a dictionary.

A boy's voyage home takes a detour when he is shipwrecked. Read to find out how he and a wild horse stay alive—and learn to trust each other—on a deserted island.

As you read, look for the details that make this selection realistic fiction.

The Black Stallion

by Walter Farley

Alec was returning to America on a ship from Bombay, India, when a storm struck. The ship was split in two! Alec stood in line for the lifeboat until he remembered that the black stallion was tied up in a stall. The horse would surely die if Alec didn't turn him loose.

The horse was a wild stallion. He had never carried a rider, and he hated being tied up. Most of the ship's crew thought the Black was a mean horse. Alec knew better.

Alec freed the Black in time. Together they jumped into the ocean just as the ship was sinking. After a very long swim, the Black pulled Alec ashore on a small island. There Alec made a rough shelter for himself out of wood he gathered on the shore. He found fresh spring water and food— some berries and fish. Alec also began to make friends with the wild black stallion.

Days passed, and gradually the friendship between the boy and the Black grew. The stallion now came at his call and let Alec pat him while he ate. One night Alec sat within the warm glow of the fire and watched the stallion eating moss beside the spring.

The flame's shadows reached out and cast ghostlike patterns on the Black's body. Alec's face became grim as thoughts rushed through his brain. Should he try it tomorrow? Did he dare try to ride the Black? Should he wait a few more days? Go ahead—tomorrow. *Don't do it!* Go ahead—.

The fire burned lower and lower. Yet Alec sat beside the fire, his eyes fixed on the black stallion.

The next morning Alec woke from a fitful sleep to find the sun high above. He looked for the Black, but the horse was not in sight. Alec whistled, but no answer came. He walked toward the hill. The sun blazed down and the sweat ran from his body. If it would only rain!

When Alec reached the top of the hill, he saw the Black at one end of the beach. Again he whistled. This time there was an answering whistle as the stallion turned his head. Alec walked up the beach toward him.

The Black stood still as he approached. Alec went cautiously up to him and placed a hand on his neck. "Steady," he whispered, as the warm skin quivered slightly beneath his hand. The stallion showed neither fear nor hate of him. His large eyes were still turned toward the sea.

For a moment Alec stood with his hand on the Black's neck. Then he walked toward a sand dune a short distance away. The stallion followed. Alec stepped up the side of the dune, his left hand in the horse's thick mane. The Black's ears went forward. His eyes followed the boy nervously — some of the wildness returned to them. His muscles twitched. For a moment Alec could not decide what to do. Then his hands gripped the mane tighter and he threw himself on the Black's back. For a second the stallion stood still. Then he snorted and plunged. Alec felt the mighty muscles heave. Then he was flung through the air, landing heavily on his back. Everything went dark.

Slowly Alec opened his eyes. The stallion was pushing him with his head. Alec tried moving his arms and legs, and found them bruised but not broken. Wearily he got to his feet. The wildness had once more disappeared in the Black. He looked as though nothing had happened.

Alec waited for a few minutes. Then once again he led the stallion to the sand dune. His hand gripped the horse's mane. This time he laid only the upper part of his body on the stallion's back, while he talked soothingly into his ear. The Black's ears moved back and forth as he glanced backward with his dark eyes.

"See, I'm not going to hurt you," Alec whispered. After a few minutes, Alec carefully slid onto the horse's back. Once again, the stallion snorted and sent the boy flying through the air.

Alec picked himself up from the ground—slower this time. When he had rested, he whistled for the Black again. The stallion moved toward him. Alec stepped on the sand dune and once again let the Black feel his weight. Gently he spoke into a large ear, "It's me. I'm not much to carry." He slid onto the stallion's back. One arm slipped around the Black's neck as he half-reared. Then, like a shot from a gun, the Black broke down the beach. His action shifted, and his huge strides seemed to make him fly through the air.

Alec gripped the stallion's mane. The wind screamed by and he couldn't see! Then down through a long ravine he rushed. Alec's blurred vision made out a black object in front of them, and as a flash he remembered the deep gully that was there. He felt the stallion gather himself. Instinctively he leaned forward and held the Black firm and steady with his hands and knees. Then they were in the air, sailing over the black hole. Alec almost lost his balance when they landed but recovered himself in time to keep from falling off!

The jump had helped greatly in clearing Alec's mind. He leaned closer to the stallion's ear and kept repeating, "Easy, Black. Easy." Alec kept talking to him.

Slower and slower ran the Black. Gradually he came to a stop. The boy let go of the stallion's mane, and his arms circled the Black's neck. Wearily he slipped to the ground. Never had he dreamed a horse could run so fast! The stallion looked at him, his head held high, his large body only partly covered with sweat.

That night Alec lay wide awake, his body aching with pain, but his heart pounding with excitement. He had ridden the Black! He had conquered this wild, unbroken stallion with kindness. He felt sure that from that day on the Black was his—his alone! But for what—would they ever be found? Would he ever see his home again? Alec shook his head. He had promised himself he wouldn't think of that anymore.

The next day he mounted the Black again. The horse half-reared but didn't fight him. Alec spoke softly in his ear, and the Black stood still. Then Alec touched him lightly on the side, and he walked—a long, loping stride. Far up the beach they went.

Then Alec tried to turn him by shifting his weight and gently pushing the stallion's head. Gradually the horse turned. Alec took a firmer grip on his long mane. He pressed his knees tighter against the large body. The stallion broke out of his walk into a gallop. The wind blew his mane back into the boy's face. The stallion's stride was effortless, and Alec found it easy to ride. Halfway down the beach, he was able to bring the stallion back again to a walk, then to a complete stop. Slowly Alec turned him to the right, then to the left, and then around in a circle.

Long but exciting hours passed as Alec tried to make the Black understand what he wanted him to do. The sun was going down quickly when he walked the stallion to the end of the beach. The Black turned and stood still. A mile of smooth, white sand stretched before them.

Suddenly the stallion bolted, almost throwing Alec to the ground. He picked up speed with amazing swiftness. Alec hung low over his neck, his breath coming in gasps. Tears from the wind rolled down Alec's cheeks.

Quickly the stallion neared the end of the beach. Alec thought that his breathtaking ride of yesterday was to be repeated. He pulled back on the mane. Suddenly the Black's pace slowed. Alec flung one arm around the stallion's neck. The Black shifted into his fast trot, which gradually became slower and slower, until Alec had him under control. Overjoyed, Alec turned the stallion and rode him over the hill to the spring. Together they drank the cool, refreshing water.

With the days that followed, Alec's mastery over the Black grew greater and greater. Alec could do almost anything with him. The wildness of the stallion disappeared when he saw the boy. Alec rode him around the island and raced him down the beach. Without realizing it, Alec was improving his horsemanship. He had reached the point where he was almost a part of the Black as they raced along.

One night Alec sat beside his campfire and stared into the flames that reached high into the air. He was deep in thought. The ship had left Bombay on a Saturday, the fifteenth of August. The shipwreck had happened a little over two weeks later, perhaps on the second of September. He had been on the island exactly—nineteen days. That would make it about the twenty-first of September. By now his family must think he is dead! He had to find a way out. A ship just had to pass the island sometime.

For the first time, Alec thought of the coming cold weather. The heat had been so strong upon the island since his arrival that it had never entered his mind that it would soon get cold. Would his shelter give him enough protection?

He rose to his feet and walked toward the hill. The Black, standing beside the spring, raised his head and whistled when he saw him. He followed Alec as he climbed to the top. The boy's eyes swept the dark, rolling sea. The stallion, too, seemed to be watching—his eyes staring into the night, his ears pointing forward. An hour passed. Then they turned and made their way back to camp.

A wind started blowing from out of the west. Alec built up the fire for the night, then crawled wearily into his shelter. He stretched out and was soon asleep.

He didn't know how long he had been sleeping, but suddenly the Black's shrill scream woke him up. Sleepily, he opened his eyes. The air had grown hot. Then he heard a crackling noise above. His head jerked upward. The top of the shelter was on fire! Flames were creeping down the sides. Alec leaped to his feet and rushed outside.

A strong wind was sweeping the island. Right away he knew what had happened. Sparks from his campfire had been blown upon the top of the shelter and had easily set fire to the dry wood. He grabbed a large shell and ran to the spring. Filling it, he ran back and threw the water on the flames.

The Black walked nervously beside the spring, his nostrils quivering. Alec rushed back and forth with his shell full of water, trying to keep the fire from spreading. But it had a good start and soon the whole shelter was on fire. Smoke filled the air. The boy and the horse were forced to move farther and farther back.

Alec knew that the fire could not spread much farther. The island was too barren of any real fuel. But right now the flames were burning everything in sight. They roared and reached high into the air. There was nothing that Alec could do. The one thing he really needed—his shelter—was gone. And there was no more wood.

The fire burned a long time before it started to die down. Then the wind, too, began to slow. Alec sat beside the spring, watching the flames, until the first streaks of dawn

appeared in the sky. He blinked his smoke-filled eyes and gritted his teeth. He wasn't licked yet! He'd find some way to make a shelter. If that didn't work, then he'd sleep outside like the Black.

His mind made up, he set out for the beach. Perhaps some wood had been swept onto shore during the night. The Black trotted ahead of him. Then Alec saw him snort and rear as he reached the top of the hill, and plunge back down again. Alec hurried forward. From the top of the hill, he looked down. Below him was a ship anchored four hundred yards off the island!

He heard voices. He saw a rowboat being drawn up on the beach by five men. Alec didn't believe what he saw. Unable to shout, he rushed down the hill.

"You were right, Pat, there *is* someone on this island!" he heard one of the men shout to the other.

The other replied, "Sure, and I knew I saw a fire reaching into the sky!"

Alec's eyes blurred; he couldn't see. He stumbled and fell and then jumped to his feet. Again he rushed forward. Then they had their arms around him.

Words jumbled together and stuck in Alec's throat as he looked into the five pairs of eyes staring at him. Then he found his voice. "We're saved!" he yelled. "We're saved, Black, we're saved!"

1. How did the horse and Alec help each other to get to the island?

2. What did Alec do to stay alive on the island?

3. What part of the story did you think was the scariest?

4. What was the first clue the author gave you that the Black was beginning to trust Alec?

5. Why did the ship come to the island?

1. Name four details from the story that help make "The Black Stallion" realistic fiction.

2. Words that are pronounced alike but have different meanings are called homophones. Find the homophone in each of the following sentences from the story:

   a. The ship was split in two!

   b. "See, I'm not going to hurt you," Alec whispered.

   c. The sun was going down quickly. . . .

   d. Alec stepped on the sand dune and once again let the Black feel his weight.

Prewrite

Imagine you are Alec and you are on the island with the black stallion. If the shelter had not caught fire, how would you have gotten off the island? The "ideaburst" below shows the problem in the center bubble. The other bubbles show some ways of getting off the island. Copy the "ideaburst" and complete it by thinking of two other ways to get off the island.

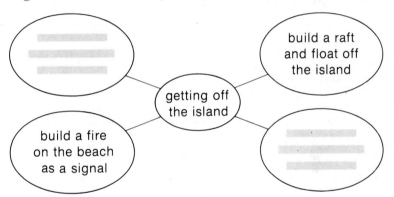

Compose

Choose one of the ideas from the ideaburst. Pretending you are Alec, write a paragraph telling how you would get off the island. Include enough details to make your idea believable.

Revise

Read your paragraph. Did you remember to pretend you were Alec? Does your paragraph make sense? If not, revise your work.

Roads

by Rachel Field

A road might lead to anywhere—
    To harbour towns and quays,
Or to a witch's pointed house
    Hidden by bristly trees.
It might lead past the tailor's door,
    Where he sews with needle and thread,
Or by Miss Pim the milliner's,
    With hats for every head.
It might be a road to a great, dark cave
    With treasure and gold piled high,
Or a road with a mountain tied to its end,
    Blue-humped against the sky.
Oh, a road might lead you anywhere—
    To Mexico or Maine.
But then, it might just fool you, and—
    Lead you back home again!

Characterization

Characters are the people or animals that appear in stories. The way an author tells you what a character is like is known as **characterization.**

Authors use several ways to tell about a character. Read the following sentences from a story about Carla. Each one tells about Carla in a different way.

1. Carla was the most cheerful person on the softball team.
2. When Carla's team lost a big game, she said, "Don't worry — we'll win next year!"
3. The softball coach said, "Carla sure knows how to cheer up the team."

In the first sentence the author describes Carla. What do you learn about Carla from the author's description? You learn that she is cheerful. In the second sentence you learn about Carla from her own words and actions. You learn that even when her team loses, Carla tries to make her team feel better. In the third sentence you learn about Carla from another character. The coach says that Carla knows how to cheer up the team.

Read the following paragraph. Think about what kind of characterization the author is using.

Hank Hippo was confused. He never knew which way to go. For this reason, he never went anywhere.

What is Hank Hippo like? The author describes him as confused and tells you that Hank never knows which way to go. You learn what Hank is like from the author's description.

Read this paragraph about Hank the Hippo.

Hank Hippo took three steps down the road to town. Then he stopped. "I don't think this is the right way to go," he said. Then he took three steps back toward the mudhole and stopped again. "Maybe I'll sit here and rest for a while," he said.

How do you learn about Hank in this paragraph? Hank's own words and actions tell you about him.

In what other way can you learn about a character? Read the following conversation.

"I've known Hank Hippo for two years now," said Tom Turtle. "He has never left this mudhole."

"I know," said Ruth Raven. "He's just too confused about which way to go."

In these sentences you learn about Hank from what other characters say about him.

Read and think about the different ways you can learn about a character. You can learn from

- the author's description of the character,
- the character's words and actions,
- what other characters say about the character.

Look for examples of the different kinds of characterization in the stories you read.

Author Profile

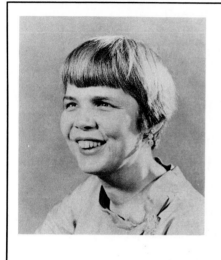

Jean Little

When Jean Little was young, she had a turtle that she named after the British poet Robert Browning. The name she gave her pet was an early sign of Jean's interest in literature. She may not have known then that she wanted to write books. However, she did know that she loved reading them.

Jean Little was born in Taiwan in 1932. Her mother and father were American doctors who had gone to Taiwan to live. Jean was blind when she was born, but she did gain some sight as she grew older. Jean was lucky because her mother, father, two brothers, and sister often read books to her. She listened to many stories. At an early age, Jean was able to read on her own.

When Jean was seven, the Little family left Taiwan and moved to Canada. There, Jean had some problems. The children at school made fun of her because of her poor eyesight. She just did not seem to fit in. Jean began spending more and more time in the library. She liked being around books better than she liked being with people her own age.

Jean's feelings about life changed the more she read. With each new book, she dreamed and thought about a career as a writer. Jean's love for literature grew.

Growing up with poor eyesight was not easy. Still, Jean has achieved a lot in life. She has chosen to make the most of the *ability* part of her sight dis*ability*.

Jean studied English language and literature at the University of Toronto. Then she began a career teaching children with handicaps. Working with these children led her to believe that she should be writing books in which disabled boys and girls could see themselves. Jean Little's first books, then, were for the children in her own classes.

Parts of Jean Little and her life are in her later books as well. She writes about children who have cerebral palsy. She tells about blind and mentally retarded children. The children in Jean Little's books are different. However, this does not mean that they are weak. They are true-to-life characters who learn to live with themselves as they are.

Jean Little's books have been translated into many languages. As a result, she is a pen pal to children across the world. Some of her books have won important prizes.

Jean Little has been brave as she faced life. She has not let her poor sight keep her from doing things. You will be reading a selection from Jean Little's book *From Anna*. As you read, think about how Anna, too, had to be brave to face her problems.

Read to discover how a girl gets a fresh start in a new country.

As you read, you will learn what kind of person Anna is. Watch for the ways the author helps you to know Anna better.

Anna's New Beginning

by Jean Little

Germany in 1934 had a new leader: Adolf Hitler. His hatred of the Jewish people was just beginning to change the country. The Solden family was not Jewish, but they sensed that soon all Germans might be in danger. Anna, the youngest of the Solden children, also faced personal challenges, both at school and at home.

At school, Anna was failing. When she tried to read, the letters jiggled on the page. At home, Anna's father and mother argued. Papa had once promised his "darling Anna" that she would grow up where thoughts are free. To keep his promise, he feared they might soon have to leave Germany. Mama did not think that they should leave.

Also, Papa had announced that everyone in the family must learn to speak English. Only Anna and her mother were slow to learn the new language.

It was a good winter, a lovely spring. Anna took for granted that the storm had blown over, that eventually Papa would even forget about the English lessons.

Then one morning early in June, 1934, a letter came from Canada. It was not from Anna's uncle in Canada, Uncle Karl; it was from his lawyer. And overnight, Anna's sometimes happy, often unhappy, but always familiar world turned upside down.

"Anna! You are going to be late for school," Mama called. "And there is a letter here for you from Canada, Ernst, which looks important."

They went to the table. The letter lay at Papa's place. He opened it and read it. Then his hands clenched, half crumpling the page.

"What is it?" Mama cried, hurrying to him.

Papa had to wait a moment. Anna saw him swallow.

"My brother Karl is dead," he said then. "He had a heart attack. He has left me everything he owned."

133

There was a babble of voices.

"Oh, Papa, how awful!" said Gretchen, who remembered Uncle Karl from when she was a small girl and he had visited Germany and stayed with them.

"Papa, are we going to be rich, then?" That was Rudi.

"Rich," Fritz echoed longingly, but he stopped there. Something in Papa's face silenced him.

"Poor Papa," Frieda chimed in, kicking Fritz.

It was then that Papa said the unbelievable thing. He did not ask anyone. He just made a statement, a flat, hard statement of fact.

"No, Rudi, we will not be rich. Karl was only a grocer with a small store, and Germany is not the only country that has been suffering from a depression. This is our chance. We will go to Canada."

"Canada!"

In every voice there was the same feeling that Anna had heard months before in Mama's. Canada was not a place to go to; Canada was a geography lesson.

"Mr. Menzies suggests we come in September." Papa went on as though he heard no outcry.

"Who is Mr. Menzies? What does he know about what we do?" Mama's words cut through the air as shrilly as a whistle.

"He is Karl's lawyer. I had written to Karl before, asking what our chances would be in Canada. He offered to take us in, but I wanted my own business. He said there was no place for a German English teacher. Now I shall be a grocer. I did not want Karl's

charity, but it seems he has given it to me after all."

Papa got up, letter in hand, and strode out of the room. There were tears on his cheeks. Anna saw the tears and could not move. She could not think. Mama, though, started after him, but at the last minute she saw the clock, gasped, and stopped to hustle the children off to school, refusing to answer any questions.

"Go! Go!" she almost screamed at them. "As though things aren't bad enough with this in your father's head!"

She whirled away then and left them without her "Good-bye." As Anna went out, closing the door behind herself, she could hear Mama right through the walls.

"Ernst, Ernst, I will not go. I tell you *I will not go!*"

Then, pausing, she heard Papa, not so loudly, but in a voice like iron. "We are all going, Klara. Whether you understand or not, whether you come willingly or not, we are going. You must start to get ready."

Papa bought their tickets. They were going by steam-ship. It should have been exciting. To Fritz and Frieda it was. They began to brag.

However, Papa even put a stop to that, the moment he found out about it. "I don't want you talking about the fact that we are going," he told the whole family.

"If you'd only explain, Papa," Rudi answered, "then we'd know what to say. People ask us questions, you know."

"You may tell people your uncle has died and we have been left a business in Canada. Say that I have to go and look after it. Say we have all decided to go. You don't need to say more than that. I do not want you to talk about it any more than you have to. It is not safe to say too much."

Papa sounded so serious. The children knew there was much he was not telling them. Mama thought he was wrong, but even Rudi believed Papa. He was too unhappy himself to be doing it for some foolish reason.

That was when Anna knew he did not want to go either, that he was going because of his promise to her that she should grow up where thoughts are free and because of his love for all of them — Rudi, Gretchen, the twins, even Mama, who was still fighting against him. Poor Papa!

Finally it was time. They were going tomorrow, away from their home, to a land where people spoke English.

Everything was packed. They sat on boxes to eat their last meal at home.

"It feels lonely here," Frieda whispered.

Papa laughed all at once. It was as though he had
been afraid but his fear was suddenly vanishing. He
could see where he was taking them, and it was a fine,
safe place.

"Let's not be lonely," he rallied them. "Why, we all
have each other. We can make a fresh start together,
we Soldens. We just need some courage. What's the
bravest song you know?"

It was Gretchen who said it, not Anna.

" 'Thoughts Are Free,' Papa," she cried.

Anna felt much braver as their voices chased back the
shadows and filled the emptiness with joyous sound.

Suddenly, Anna's voice faltered and broke off. Nobody else had seen, but Mama was crying again. Her
cheeks were wet with tears. As the others swept on
into the wonderful second verse and the triumphant
finish, Anna once more felt alone and afraid. Then she
saw her father smile at her mother, and she looked at
Mama again.

The tears were still there, but Mama was singing as
bravely as anyone.

The family stood in a huddle near the barriers in the waiting room at Toronto Union Station, in Canada. After leaving the ship in Halifax, they had come the rest of the way by train. There had not been money enough for berths. Anna had sat up for thirty-six hours, leaning against Papa whenever she dozed, and now she swayed on her feet. If only she could lie down somewhere!

"Mr. Menzies will be here any minute," Papa spoke again, anxiously scanning the faces of people near them.

Anna had let her eyelids close for just one second. Now she opened them wide in astonishment. Papa, who insisted that they all speak English, had spoken in German! He must really be worried.

Finally a man approached and spoke to Papa.

"Ernst Solden?"

"Yes, yes. You must be Mr. Menzies."

The men shook hands. Mr. Menzies was tall and his hair was gray.

"My wife, Klara," Papa began introducing them. "My oldest boy, Rudolf . . . Gretchen . . . Fritz and Elfrieda, our twins . . . and this is Anna."

Anna blinked at hearing Rudi and Frieda called by their real names. Mr. Menzies smiled politely.

"You two certainly look like your father," he told the older ones. "And the twins are very like you, Mrs. Solden."

Anna was startled again. She had never heard her mother called "Mrs." before. It made Mama seem a stranger.

Moving automatically, she followed the others out of the station, across the street, and into a restaurant. There she munched on a sandwich—something she had never eaten before—and sipped from a tall glass of milk.

"Franz Schumacher said he'd meet us here," Mr. Menzies was explaining to her parents. "He's a doctor and was a great friend of Karl's. We'll need two cars to get you and your bags to the house," Mr. Menzies said. "Dr. Schumacher is late. A last-minute patient, I suppose."

The words blurred in Anna's head. She dropped her sandwich half-eaten. By the time Dr. Schumacher came hurrying in, she was sound asleep in her chair. This time, she missed the introductions. She did not rouse until a deep voice, close beside her, said, "I'll carry the little one."

Mama objected. "She is much too heavy to carry. Wake her up. Anna . . . Anna!"

I can't, Anna thought groggily, keeping her eyes shut.

Strong arms gathered her up.

"She's not heavy at all," Dr. Schumacher grunted, shifting her to get a better grip. Anna flicked open her eyes for one split second, just long enough to see the big, friendly face. What had he said? Could she really have heard?

If the doctor knew she was awake, he made no sign. "Light as a feather—really!" he said to Mama.

Anna lay perfectly still in his arms. She kept her eyes tightly closed and she did not smile.

Yet she loved Franz Schumacher from that moment.

"When you get settled and a bit rested," the doctor said, "bring the children around to my office to have their medical examinations for school."

"School!" Fritz echoed, horrified.

The doctor looked back at the boy and laughed.

"Yes, school," he said. "It starts a week from Tuesday."

Dr. Schumacher's waiting room was shabby and crowded. When the Soldens arrived, the two boys had to stand up against one wall with their father because there were not enough chairs.

When he had finished examining Rudi, Gretchen, and the twins, Dr. Schumacher stretched out a broad hand to Anna. She slid off her father's knee at once and put her hand in the doctor's. Papa smiled. So someone else had discovered a way to reach his Anna!

"Let me hear you read the letters on this card," Dr. Schumacher said to Anna.

Anna froze. Reading! She couldn't . . .

She looked where he was pointing. Why, there was only one letter there. That was easy! She did know the names of the letters now.

"E," she told him.

"And the next line down?" Dr. Schumacher asked.

Anna wrinkled up her forehead. Yes, there *were* other letters. She could see them now, when she squinted. They looked like little gray bugs, wiggling.

"They're too small to read," she said.

Ten minutes later, when Dr. Schumacher was very sure about Anna's eyesight, he came out to the waiting room with Anna.

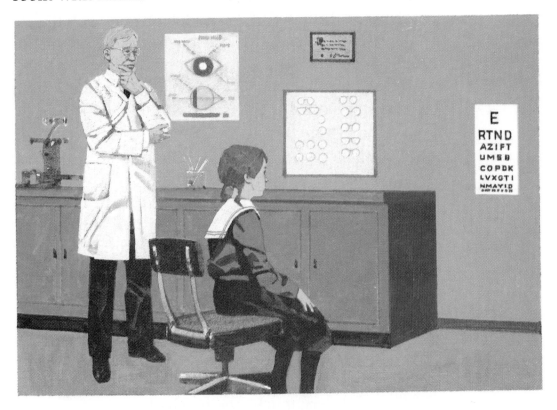

"She sees very poorly, very poorly indeed," he said. "She should be wearing glasses. She probably should have had them two or three years ago. Before we go any further, I want to have her examined by an eye doctor."

It was all like a nightmare to Anna. Once more, she had to read letters off a faraway card. Once again, she could only see the big E. The new doctor peered into her eyes with a small bright light. He made her look through a collection of lenses. All at once, other letters appeared.

"F . . . P," Anna read in a low voice. "T . . . O, I think . . . Z."

"Now read these," the eye doctor said, pointing to the next row of letters. These letters were too small for Anna to read.

Dr. Schumacher then took her to yet another room where she sat on a chair and was fitted for frames. When they were back in Dr. Schumacher's office, the grown-ups took the chairs.

"Even with the glasses, she will not have normal vision," Franz Schumacher explained. "She'll have to go to a special class, a Sight Saving Class," he went on. "Lessons are made easier there for children with poor eyesight."

"Not go to school with the others!" Mama wailed, hoping she was not understanding.

Dr. Schumacher switched back to German. He spoke gently, soothingly.

"It is a nice place. She'll like it there. You will, Anna. You'll like it very much," he finished.

Anna did not look up or answer. Dr. Schumacher had become part of the bad dream in which she was caught. She hardly heard what he said. What she did hear, she did not believe. How could she like school?

Then, three days before school was to begin, Anna's new glasses arrived. Perched on her nub of a nose, they looked like two round moons. She longed to snatch them off and hurl them into a far corner. Instead, she peered through them suspiciously.

For one startled moment, an utterly new expression came over her small, plain face, a look of intense surprise and wonder. She was seeing a world she had never guessed existed.

"Oh, Anna, you look just like an owl," Frieda laughed, not meaning any harm.

The wonder left Anna's face instantly. She turned away from her family and stumped off up the stairs to her alcove where none of them could follow without permission. Papa, though, came up alone a minute or two later.

"Do you like them, Anna?" he asked quietly.

She almost told him then. She nearly said, "I never knew you had wrinkles around your eyes, Papa. I knew your eyes were blue, but I didn't know they were so bright."

But Anna remembered Frieda's laughing words. How she hated being laughed at!

"Do I *have* to keep wearing them, Papa?" she blurted. Papa looked sorry for her, but he nodded.

"You must wear them all the time and no nonsense," he said firmly.

Anna reddened slightly. It was not right, fooling Papa like this. She was not ready to share what had happened to her. Even her father might not understand. She could hardly take it in herself.

"All right, Papa," she said, letting the words drag.

When he had gone, she lifted her right hand and held it up in front of her. She moved her fingers and counted them. Even though the light was poor, she could see all five. She examined her fingernails. They shone faintly and they had little half-moons at the bottom. Then she leaned forward and stared at her red wool blanket. It was all hairy. She could see the hairs, hundreds of them.

Everything, everywhere she turned, looked new, looked different, looked miraculous.

When Dr. Schumacher arrived to take Mama and her to the new school, Anna was ready with a bright bow on each of her thin braids.

"It is so kind of you to take Anna to this school," Mama fussed, getting herself and Anna into their coats.

"Nonsense," Dr. Schumacher said, "I know Miss Williams. I can help with the English, too. It won't take long."

The three of them found nothing to say to each other as they rode along. When they got out in front of the school, Anna marched along between her mother and the doctor. She tried to look as though this were something she did every day, as though her heart were not thudding so hard against her ribs it almost hurt. Franz Schumacher reached down his big warm hand and gathered up her cold little paw. His hand felt just like Papa's. She left her hand where it was and felt braver.

Miss Williams was the first surprise in what was to be a day of surprises.

"It's lovely to have you with us, Anna," she said when Dr. Schumacher drew Anna forward and introduced her and Mama.

The teacher had a low, husky voice, and her smile was so honest that even Anna could not doubt she meant it. She looked at Anna almost the way Papa did.

She doesn't know me yet, Anna reminded herself, not smiling in return. She hasn't heard me read.

"I've brought you a real challenge this time, Eileen," Dr. Schumacher said in an undertone.

Challenge.

Anna did not know that word. Did it mean "stupid one"? But no, it couldn't. Franz Schumacher still had her hand in his, and the kindness of his grasp had not changed as he said it. Anna kept the new word in her mind. When she got home, she would ask Papa.

Fifteen minutes later she sat in her new desk and watched her mother and Dr. Schumacher leave the classroom.

"Don't leave me!" Anna almost cried out after them, her courage deserting her. She must not cry. She must *not*!

"You can sit next to Benjamin," Miss Williams said. "Ben's been needing someone to keep him on his toes, haven't you, Ben?"

Quickly, she told Anna the names of all the other children in the class. The names flew around Anna's ears like birds, each escaping just as she thought she had it safely captured.

"You won't remember most of them now," the teacher said, seeing panic in the child's eyes. "You'll have to get to know us bit by bit. I think you and Ben will probably be working together," Miss Williams went on.

"Now you know us well enough to begin with," the teacher said. "It's time we got some work done in this room."

Anna, who had been relaxed while studying Ben, froze. What now? Would she have to read? She sat as still as a trapped animal while Miss Williams went to a corner cupboard. In a moment, she was back.

"Here are some crayons, Anna," she said. "I'd like you to draw a picture. Anything you like. I'll get the others started and then I'll be free to find out where you are in your schoolwork."

Anna did not take the crayons. She did not know anything she could draw. She was nowhere in her schoolwork. She wanted Papa desperately.

And what did "challenge" mean?

"Draw your family, Anna," Miss Williams said. "Draw your father and your mother, your brothers and your sisters—and yourself, too, Anna. I want to see all of you."

The feel of the box, solid and real, brought back Anna's courage. The crayons were big and bright. They looked inviting. The teacher put paper on the desk— rough, cream-colored paper. Lovely paper for drawing. Six pieces, at least!

"Take your time," Miss Williams said, moving away. "Use as much paper as you need."

Anna took a deep breath. Then she slowly picked out a crayon. She knew how to start, anyway.

She would begin with Papa.

A while later, Miss Williams came and bent above her.

"Who are they, Anna?" she asked.

Slowly Anna began to explain in German.

Miss Williams did not stop her and tell her to talk

English instead, but when Anna pointed and said *"Mein Papa,"* the teacher answered "Your father. My, he is tall, isn't he?"

"Yes," Anna replied in English, only half aware she was switching. She was intent on making sure Miss Williams understood her drawing.

"They are gone on . . . to the sea," she fumbled, looking in vain for an English word for "holiday."

"I thought they had," Miss Williams said.

It was not such a terrible day. Not once did the teacher ask Anna to read from a book. She printed the story of Anna's picture on another piece of paper. The letters were large and black. Anna read each line as it appeared. She did not panic. She did not think of this as reading.

"You like drawing, don't you, Anna," Miss Williams said, picking up the picture and looking at it again, smiling at the bright colors, the liveliness of the twins.

Anna did not answer. She was too startled, even if she had known what to say. She had always hated drawing in school.

"You like reading, too. I can see that. And your English! I can hardly believe you've been in Canada such a short time. You are amazing, Anna."

Miss Williams was not nearly as amazed as Anna Elisabeth Solden. She, Anna, like reading!

She wanted to laugh, but she did not. She still did not even smile openly.

All the same, Anna felt something happening deep inside herself, something warm and alive. She was happy.

When school was over, she walked past her own house and went on to the store where Papa was hard at work. She waited off to one side. When the customers were gone, she stepped up and leaned on the counter.

"Papa, what is a challenge?" She had said the word over and over to herself all day long so she would be able to ask.

Papa scratched his head.

"A challenge," he repeated. "Well, it is . . . something to be won, maybe. Something special that makes you try hard to win it."

Anna thought that over.

"Thank you, Papa," she said, turning away.

"But school," her father cried after her. "Tell me about it."

"It was fine," Anna said over her shoulder. Then she twirled around unexpectedly and gave him one of her rare half-smiles.

"It was a challenge," she said.

"Something special," she repeated, as she started for home. "Dr. Schumacher thinks I am something special, like Papa said. But why something to be won?"

She gave a little hop all at once. She would not mind going back tomorrow.

"It is a challenge," she said over again, aloud, in English, to the empty street.

She liked that word.

You can read the whole story of Anna Solden in the book From Anna *by Jean Little.*

1. What gave Anna a "fresh start" in Canada?
2. How did the character Anna change during the story?
3. What was the first clue the author gave you that helped you know that Anna might need glasses?
4. What unkind thing did Anna's sister say when Anna first wore her new glasses?
5. How did Anna's glasses change her feeling about school?

You can learn about a character in three ways: from the author's description; from what the character says and does; and from what other characters say about the character. Decide in which way you learn about the character Anna in each of the following sentences.

1. Anna once more felt alone and afraid.
2. "She sees very poorly, very poorly indeed," he said.
3. Then Anna twirled around unexpectedly and gave Papa one of her rare half-smiles.

Thinking About "Detours"

You have traveled far and wide in this unit. You have gone from Russia to Poland and from Germany to Canada. You have seen a part of New York City and a stretch of the Mississippi. You have been on a deserted island and locked in a library. The characters you traveled with were all taking detours. They were all going in new directions.

One character you traveled with was a real historical figure, Nicholas Roosevelt. You joined him on the *New Orleans* as he set out to prove that a steamboat could navigate on western rivers. However, most of the characters in this unit were not real people. Yet they *seemed* real. What they said and did could have been said and done by a real person. When Uncle Joe helped Dan learn to bowl, they acted like two real people. When Juan finally made some friends, you knew why he was so happy. When Dewey's raft plunged into the rapids of Trouble River, you could sense that the danger was real.

In a way, you went along with these characters on their detours. As a reader, you were allowed to travel everywhere that the writer's imagination could take you. Where do you think your reading might take you in the future?

1. Think about Juan in "How Juan Got Home" and Uncle Joe in "Making Room for Uncle Joe." Both had to get used to living in a new place. How were their problems alike? How were their problems different?

2. Dvora and Anna both took detours that led them away from their homes. Which detour do you think was more exciting? Why?

3. In which stories did the characters take an *unwanted* detour to escape from danger?

4. Two selections in this unit took place on a river. Which river do you think was more important to its story, Trouble River or the Mississippi River? Explain your answer.

5. Mary Rose and Jo-Beth were "prisoners" in a library. Alec was a "prisoner" on a deserted island. How were these two "prisons" alike? How were they different?

6. If you could be one of the characters in this unit, which one would you be? Why?

7. Which selection in this unit did you like the best? Why?

Read on Your Own

Anno's Journey by Mitsumasa Anno. Putnam's.
Follow the author's journey through drawings as
he travels in northern Europe. Drawings show not
only the lands but also the people—their art,
architecture, and folklore.

Little Tim and the Brave Sea by Edward Ardizzone.
Penguin. A boy becomes a deckhand on a ship
and has many exciting adventures at sea.

The Dastardly Murder of Dirty Pete by Eth Clifford.
Houghton. In this follow-up to *Help! I'm a Prisoner
in the Library*, Jo-Beth and Mary Rose travel with
their father to the west coast, where they get lost.
They wind up in a deserted town.

Help! I'm a Prisoner in the Library by Eth Clifford.
Houghton. Two sisters become trapped in a
library during a blizzard. They are frightened by
mysterious sounds as they try to find a way to
escape.

Smoke Above the Lane by Meindert DeJong. Harper.
Two unlikely friends, a tramp and a little skunk,
arrive in town just in time for the Labor Day
parade.

King of the Wind by Marguerite Henry. Rand
McNally. This award-winning story is about an
Arabian stallion who overcomes bad fortune to
become one of the most famous horses of all time.

A Button in Her Ear by Ada B. Litchfield. Whitman. A girl explains how her hearing problem was discovered and how it was corrected with a hearing aid.

From Anna by Jean Little. Harper. Anna has many problems growing up. When her family discovers that Anna can't see well, she goes to a special school where she makes some good friends. She surprises herself and her family, too.

Look Through My Window by Jean Little. Harper. Emily's family moves to a large house. Emily is used to being an only child and isn't happy to hear that her cousins are coming to stay with her family. As time goes by, she learns a lot about sharing.

There Are Two Kinds of Terrible by Peggy Mann. Doubleday. When Robbie breaks his arm on the last day of school, he thinks it is the most terrible thing that could happen to him. Then something terrible happens to his mother, and he realizes that there are "two kinds of terrible."

Mississippi Possum by Miska Miles. Little, Brown. When the river floods, a frightened possum hides in the tent of two children. The possum and the children gradually get to know and trust each other.

Skylights

What do you think of when you read the word *skylight*? You might think of a window in a roof that lets in light from the sky. You might think of one of the many lights you can see shining far off in space. By using your imagination, you might put these two ideas together. A skylight might be any kind of window that lets you look into the distance, into space, or even into the future.

In "Skylights" you will read about the sun and stars. You will read about other objects out in space. You will also find information that gives you a peek into the future: a "window" that lets you look beyond the present time.

As you read the selections, notice how many different kinds of skylights there can be!

Informational Books

Picture this. Your report about caring for a dog has to be turned in next week. Your class has been given time in the library to find information for the reports. You watch as your friends rush for the encyclopedias. Then you calmly walk over to the card catalog. You look for *dog* under the letter *D*. There you find cards for not just one but several books about dogs. You are sure that you will have lots of information from which to write your report.

Providing facts for school reports is one use of **informational books.** However, informational books do much more than that. They tell you about all kinds of things. In informational books you can find out what makes the wind blow, who invented the steam engine, and much more.

Informational books are nonfiction. They present facts. They tell about things and places that are real and events that really happened. They explain how something works or how to do something. Informational books do just what their name says. They inform.

Sometimes you can easily tell an informational book by its title. Sometimes you cannot. Read the following book titles. Which of these books are probably informational?

Riding the Wind   *Easy Bicycle Repair*
How to Use a Computer   *Catching a Ghost*

How to Use a Computer and *Easy Bicycle Repair* are clearly informational. The titles suggest that those books contain facts about real things. *Catching a Ghost* is probably fictional, because ghosts are not real. *Riding the Wind* might be fictional or informational. You cannot tell from the title whether the book contains a made-up story or real information. You would have to read some of this book to decide.

Either of the following two paragraphs could appear in a book titled *Riding the Wind*. Which paragraph would lead you to believe that the book is informational? Why?

Al was ready for his first balloon ride. He jumped into the basket, but nothing happened. So he grabbed the huge balloon and began to blow it up. Slowly, as the air filled the balloon, the basket began to rise.

Ballooning is a popular sport in the United States. A hot-air balloon follows the direction of the air currents. Many people find it exciting to sail along with the wind.

The second paragraph is informational, because it gives facts about something real. The first paragraph is probably fictional, because it describes a person doing something impossible.

Look for these characteristics of informational books as you read the selections in this unit.

- They are nonfiction.
- They present facts.
- They tell about real things, places, and events.

In this selection, you will read about one very special "skylight" and how we are learning to use its energy.

As you read, decide why this selection is informational. Does it tell you facts? Does it tell you how something works?

Putting the Sun to Work

by Jeanne Bendick

It's a hot summer day. You, your family, and some friends decide to drive to a park near the beach for a cookout.

When you walk over to the beach, the sand and the rocks are so hot that they hurt your bare feet. You put on sneakers in a hurry. The water is so bright and shining in the sun that you can hardly look at it.

While the charcoal fire is starting to burn in the cookout stove, you go for a swim. The water feels good. It is warm at the top, but cooler down around your toes. After you swim, you dry yourself with a towel.

For lunch there are hot dogs, corn, salad, rolls, and fruit. By the time the corn and hot dogs are cooked, all the towels are dry. You had spread them out on the rocks, in the sun.

While you were having fun at the beach, work was being done. Energy from the sun was doing the work.

Heat energy from the sun dried the towels. It heated the sand, the rocks, the water, and the air.

Light energy from the sun was working on the beach, too. It supplied the daylight. It made the sand bright and the water sparkling.

The sun also supplied the energy that grew the food you ate.

Making Energy

Plants use light energy from the sun to make food for themselves. The food itself is a kind of energy. Green plants change light energy from the sun into chemical energy.

Plants use some of that energy for everyday living and growing. They store the rest in their leaves and seeds and in their fruit, roots, stems, and berries.

The salad, corn, rolls, and fruit all came from plants. You—and all animals—need plants for food.

The charcoal you used for cooking began as a plant, too. Once, that charcoal was a living tree that used sunlight to make food and then stored part of the food it made. The energy in this stored food remained, even after the tree died. You used that energy when you burned the charcoal.

The gasoline you used for driving to the beach also began with energy from the sun. It was made from oil.

Oil was made from the remains of plants and animals that lived on earth millions of years ago. The remains of ancient living things are called fossils. This is why oil is called a fossil fuel. Coal and natural gas are fossil fuels, too.

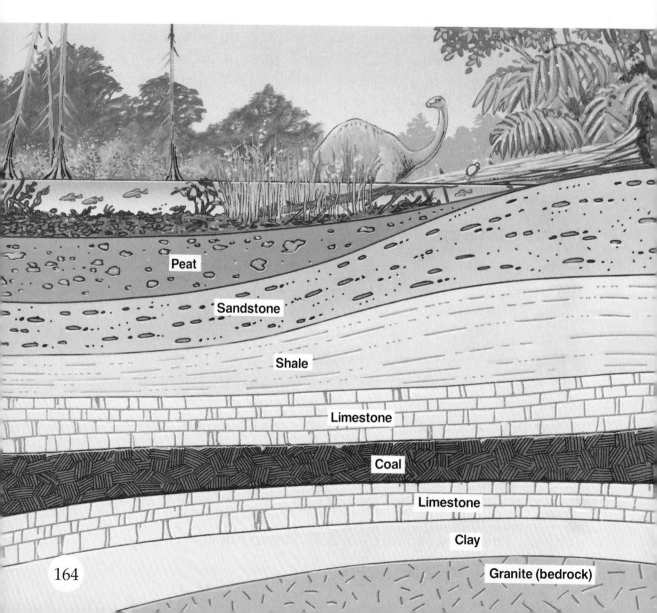

Peat

Sandstone

Shale

Limestone

Coal

Limestone

Clay

Granite (bedrock)

Fossil fuels are easy to use. They are easy to store. They are easy to change into other kinds of energy — heat, light, electricity. They are so handy that people around the world use fossil fuels to supply almost all the energy they need.

Now some fossil fuels are beginning to run out. However, as long as the sun shines, the earth will not run out of energy. The sun pours more energy onto earth than we can ever use. Most of that energy comes to us as heat and light.

Energy from the sun is called solar energy. Anything to do with the sun is called "solar." The word began with the Roman word for the sun, which is *sol* [säl].

Solar energy is a safe kind of energy. It doesn't cause pollution or have dangerous leftovers. That is why scientists and inventors are trying different ways to capture and use the sun's energy. They hope to find a way for the sun to do some of the jobs fossil fuels have been doing.

To make the sun do work like that, scientists have to solve some problems. They have to collect the sun's energy. Collecting sunshine isn't easy, unless you are a plant. Sunshine isn't easy to store, either.

Still, people have been using solar energy to help do their work for a long time. There are old ways and new ways of catching sunshine and putting it to work.

Catching Sunshine

If you were building a house in a place that had cold winters, would you build the house with the windows toward the sun or away from it?

You would probably build the house with the windows toward the sun. That way, sunlight could pour in to warm the house. People have been building houses that way for a long time.

Is it possible to catch even more of the sun's heat in a house? Yes, it is. Some houses also collect the sun's heat on the roof, move the heat indoors, and store some of it to use later. A house like that is called a solar house.

People who build solar houses have learned how to do those things by noticing how the earth itself uses solar energy.

Remember the beach we talked about earlier? Remember the hot sand and the hot rocks? Some materials take in heat energy from the sun and hold it. These materials absorb the heat. Sand and rocks do this. So do some other solid materials, such as metals. Water absorbs the sun's heat, too.

Color can also be important. Dark, dull colors absorb heat. Light-colored, shiny surfaces reflect heat. They bounce it back. That's why people wear dark clothes to stay warm in the winter and light-colored clothes to stay cool in the summer.

Storing Heat

The longer it takes something to heat up, the longer that thing holds the heat. Materials that heat up fast also cool off fast.

If you were to go back to the beach in the evening after sunset, the sand and the rocks, which heated up fast, would be cool. The water, which heated up slowly, would still be warm.

It takes a long time for the sun to heat the water in a big lake or the ocean. By the end of summer, however, a large body of water will have caught and stored enough heat from the sun to last for a long time.

Water stores heat very well. That's why land near a large body of water stays warmer in the winter than land far away from the water. The stored heat in the water helps warm the land around it.

Slowly, all winter long, heat from the water moves out into the cold air. Heat always moves that way—from a warmer place or thing to a cooler one. Once you know which way heat moves, you can understand how things get hot and how they lose heat.

Remember when the hot sand on the beach burned your feet? Heat from the sand was moving into your cooler feet! Once you understand how heat moves into things, through things, and out of things, it is easy to see how a solar house works.

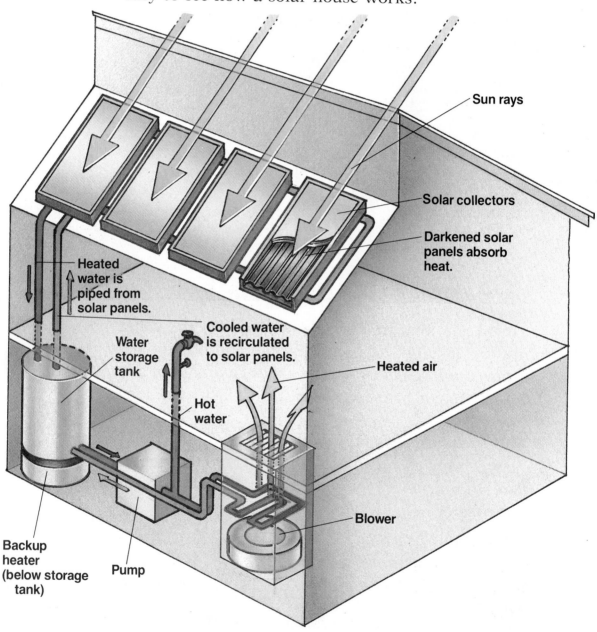

Sun rays

Solar collectors

Darkened solar panels absorb heat.

Heated water is piped from solar panels.

Cooled water is recirculated to solar panels.

Water storage tank

Hot water

Heated air

Backup heater (below storage tank)

Pump

Blower

In many warm places around the world, there is a lot of sunshine all year long. In those places, a solar house can supply all the heat and hot water most families need. A solar house in a cold climate often needs some kind of backup heater. The heater is used when the weather is very cold or if the sun does not shine for some days.

Keeping Heat in One Place

Once the house is warm, what keeps the heat from moving out of the warm house into the cool outside air?

Remember the sneakers you put on when the hot sand was burning your feet? They kept the heat from moving from the sand into your feet. The sneakers were insulation. *Insulation* is any material that keeps heat (or other kinds of energy) from moving from place to place.

Insulation in a house keeps heat from moving out of the house in the winter. It also keeps heat from moving into the house in the summer.

It does not take a lot of heat to make a house comfortable. Solar energy can do that job in many areas of the world. What about work that takes more heat, such as cooking dinner? Or still more heat, such as melting steel? Can the sun do work like that?

The sun can do these jobs and more. If you would like to learn more about how we can use the sun's energy, you might read the rest of the book Putting the Sun to Work.

1. What special "skylight" did you just read about? Why is it so special?

2. How can we put the sun to work?

3. Do you think we are using the sun's energy enough now, or should we be using it more? Explain your answer.

4. How did reading about a cookout at the beach prepare you to understand how solar heating works?

5. Why should we begin to use the sun for energy rather than using energy made from fossil fuels?

Informational articles present facts. They tell about things and places that are real and events that have really happened. They explain how something works or how to do something. Name three details from "Putting the Sun to Work" that show you that this is an informational article.

Prewrite

Think about all of the work the sun did in the selection. Copy the "sunburst" below and complete it by adding four more ways in which the sun was at work.

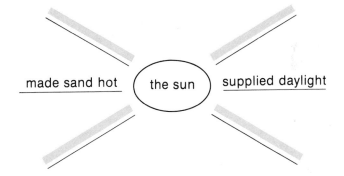

made sand hot   the sun   supplied daylight

Compose

Picnicking in a park and swimming at a beach are enjoyable activities because the sun has done its work. Choose either picnicking in a park or swimming at a beach as a topic. Then write a paragraph describing at least four ways in which the sun is at work to make the activity enjoyable.

Revise

Read your paragraph carefully. Does it list four ways the sun helped to make the activity enjoyable? Add more details if they are needed.

Kim is both proud and embarrassed about her family's energy-saving home. Read to find out how her family proves that "different" can be better.

As you read, decide whether this selection is informational or fictional.

Those Weird Wagners

by Bonnie Bisbee

Tom Barton leaned forward and tapped me on the shoulder. (Just my luck: He sits right behind me in class!) "What was that crazy thing I saw in your garage the other day, Kim?" he asked me in a loud voice. I didn't answer him or turn around.

"It looks like a big laser-gun for blasting something out of the sky. Ha-ha-ha-hee-haw!" Tom's laugh reminded me of a donkey's bray. A few kids sitting nearby snickered as Tom hopped up onto his chair.

"Are the weird Wagners going to fend off invaders from space? Zap, zap, zap!" he said, pretending to be shooting a gun into the air.

"That's not a laser!" I said hotly. "It's a solar mirror, if you want to know. It gathers the sun's energy and focuses it in one place for cooking. Next summer we'll be able to have a cookout without using any fuel at all!"

Tom sneered and shook his head as he climbed back into his seat. "You Wagners are hopeless energy nuts," he said. "First you put that crazy-looking wind thing in your backyard to make electricity. Then you put up those weird glass-covered boxes — what do you call them, 'solar water heaters' or some dumb thing. Now there's this hamburger and hot dog laser. What are you going to do next, get some hungry sheep to 'mow' your lawn so you won't have to use any gasoline? Ha-ha-ha-hee-haw!"

I blushed, because that's exactly what we'd do if we had more space. Then we'd be able to make nice warm, energy-saving sweaters from their wool.

Tom started to say something else, but our teacher, Mr. Huffler, came back into the room just then. He looked serious. The room stopped buzzing as everyone shut up.

"I have an announcement to make," Mr. Huffler said. "A bad snowstorm is coming, so the bus drivers want to get you home early."

I looked outside, and sure enough, the sky was heavy with dark gray clouds, and a few flakes were already falling.

"Now don't push and shove," Mr. Huffler said as we grabbed our books and coats. "You'll all be safely home before the storm hits. You can go now."

As we crowded out the door, Tom yelled above the noise, "Hey, Kim, I hope you don't want to take a shower when you get home. Those wonderful solar water heaters aren't going to do you much good during this storm. Ha-ha-ha-hee-haw!"

This time I think I did a pretty good job of ignoring Tom. But how I hated that stupid laugh!

As soon as I got home, I turned on the news. "The radio says this storm could reach 'blizzard proportions'!" I announced. "I hope that Mom gets home from work okay."

Just then the front door flew open. A snow-covered Mom came in, along with a blast of cold air. I ran to greet her.

"That storm is fierce!" Mom said, closing the door with effort. "I'm glad to be home."

Mom hung up her coat and walked over to our wood stove to warm up. I followed her.

"Tom Barton calls us the 'Weird Wagners'!" I blurted out. "He says lots of other people call us that, too."

My sister, Leslie, backed me up. "People think we're nuts," she said. "The other day Mr. Jacusi across the street asked me about our windmill. He called it another of our 'dopey gadgets.' "

Mom raised her eyebrows. "Lots of people are making their own energy these days. We're not the only ones."

"We're the only ones in our neighborhood who do!" I said. "And Tom's told the kids at school about some of our disasters — like the time we tried to make fuel from sugarbeets. He blabbed about how we goofed and how the mess could be smelled clear down the block."

Just then Dad walked in from the kitchen. "We've had our ups and downs, all right, and it cost us a bit to get started," he said with a smile. "But we've got some pretty good stuff working for us now."

"That's right," agreed Mom. "Now we don't have to depend on anyone for energy — not the electric company, not the oil company, nobody. So let 'em laugh."

Leslie joined in. "Who cares if people make fun, Kim? Our place is really neat!"

"I know, but sometimes I wish our house were a bit more . . . well, normal!"

"Don't pay attention to Tom and he'll give up his teasing," advised Dad.

"But I have to listen to that stupid laugh!" I said with a look of disgust.

Mom spoke up suddenly. "You know, all this talk makes me think of something. It was getting dark on my way home. But I didn't see any street lights or even house lights burning on our block — except here!"

Just then the doorbell rang. The wind sprang inside again as I opened the door. I was surprised to see who was there.

"Tom Barton! Mr. and Mrs. Barton and little Ann! Come in!"

Tom wouldn't look at me as I led the bundled-up family into the living room. For once he wasn't laughing.

Mrs. Barton looked around curiously at the cozy, well-lit room. "The wind and snow have knocked some power lines down," she explained. "No one in the neighborhood has electricity—except for you folks."

"At home we can't cook dinner, have hot baths, or watch TV," Mr. Barton said. "But the real problem is that we can't heat Ann's bottle, and she's getting hungry."

"We can easily heat her bottle on the woodburning cook stove in the kitchen," Dad said.

"Why don't you folks stay for supper?" Mom invited. "We'll make a big pot of soup. Our solar-heated greenhouse supplies us with lots of fresh vegetables. We won't have to worry about getting to the supermarket for more food."

"We'd love to stay. Thanks!" said Mr. and Mrs. Barton together.

"Anyone who wants to can have a shower," Leslie said. "Our solar water heater won't do much for us tonight. But our garbage will!"

The Bartons looked at each other kind of funny until Leslie started to explain. "We dump our garbage and other wastes into a big tank in the basement. The wastes digest, or break down, and we collect the gas that forms. And now we can use it to fire up our regular water heater."

I remembered what Tom had said earlier in the day — about our being out of luck when the sun wasn't shining. I looked over at him, but he was just looking at the floor.

"I wonder what the news is on this storm?" Mr. Barton said. Leslie ran to turn on the radio.

"Our wind machine and our sun-powered 'photo-cells' give us enough electricity for just about everything," Dad said.

"The power is stored in batteries in the basement, to use as we need," Mom added.

". . . *worst storm to hit Riverdale in years,*" the radio said. "*Half of the town is now without electricity.*"

Mrs. Barton suddenly said, "We always thought you were . . . well, different. But now I think I'd like to put some of your ideas to work at *our* house."

I glanced at Tom. He looked down at the floor some more. His face was turning a funny shade of red.

"Making power from wind, wood, wastes, and the sun can work for almost everyone," I said. "And it's pretty easy on the environment." (Our wood stoves were making too much smoke, but we were working on that.) "Besides," I continued, "with home-made energy you can smile when the power lines blow down!"

"We haven't smiled at our electricity bills lately," Mr. Barton said. "And they're going to go even higher. Your way of doing things makes pretty good sense, I guess."

Mom and Leslie went to warm the baby's bottle and to make hot cider for everyone else. Dad started the soup. I set the table while listening to the wind blow and our guests chatting by the stove. The snow piled up outside, but we were warm and happy.

"Can I help you?" a familiar voice offered. I whirled around. For the first time all evening, Tom's brown eyes looked straight at me.

"I'm sorry I teased you, Kim," he said with a sheepish smile. "I'm going to tell everyone at school how the Not-So-Weird Wagners saved my family from freezing in the dark! . . . Hey, do I smell gingerbread baking?" He sniffed like a hungry hound.

I smiled sweetly. "Yes, Tom," I said. "But why do you think you'll be getting some?" And then I added quickly, "Just kidding—ha-ha-ha-hee-haw!"

1. How did Kim's family prove that being "different" can sometimes be better?

2. Name three of the energy-producing gadgets the Wagners had in their home.

3. Which of the Wagners' gadgets do you think was the most interesting? Why?

4. When did you first begin to think that the Wagners were the only family to have electricity during the storm?

5. Why did the Wagners want to make their own energy?

Apply the Skills

Informational articles present facts. They tell about real things, places, and events. In realistic fiction, the characters and events seem real, but the story is not true. Is "Those Weird Wagners" realistic fiction, or is it an informational article? How do you know?

Prewrite

When Tom called the Wagners "weird," he meant they were "strange or odd." Really, the Wagners were just different. Copy the chart below and add three more ways the Wagners were different from others. Then make up three more statements that would mean the Wagners really were weird.

Different	Weird
The Wagners: • use a wood stove. • have a windmill.	The Wagners: • shovel with a spoon. • bathe in orange juice.

Compose

Study your completed chart. Choose the *Different* column and write a realistic paragraph describing the Wagners, or choose the *Weird* column and write an unrealistic paragraph describing them. Remember, a realistic paragraph is true to life; an unrealistic paragraph is not true to life.

Revise

Make sure you have written a good description of the Wagners. Your paragraph should be either very realistic or very weird. Revise your work if necessary.

Circle Graphs

You have learned many things by reading words and sentences. You have also learned many things from looking at pictures and drawings. A graph is a special kind of drawing that shows how two or more things are related. A graph can show some kinds of information more clearly than words can.

There are different kinds of graphs. Two of these are bar graphs and circle graphs.

Bar Graphs

You know that a bar graph compares one thing with another. In order to get information from bar graphs, you must learn to "read" the bars. Look at the bar graph below.

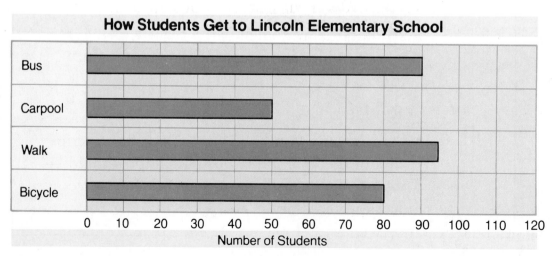

How Students Get to Lincoln Elementary School

Number of Students

The title tells you what the bar graph is comparing. The words at the left side of the graph tell you the different subtopics being compared. The numerals at the bottom of the graph give amounts. The label below the numerals tells what the numerals stand for.

From this graph you can find out how many students get to Lincoln Elementary School in each way shown. Look at each bar on the graph. Find the end of each bar, and follow it down to the numerals. The numerals will tell you the number of students who get to school in each different way.

Look at the subtopic *Walk*. Notice that the end of the bar is between the numerals 90 and 100 at the bottom of the graph. How many students walk to school? The answer is "about 95 students." You cannot know from this bar graph exactly how many students walk.

Circle Graphs

Another kind of graph is a circle graph. A circle graph shows clearly how a whole can be divided into parts. Circle graphs are often called pie graphs. Can you guess why? Read the following story:

Malcolm went to the county fair with his family. He took one dollar with him. He rode the roller coaster and the Ferris wheel. Each ride cost him 25 cents. Then he bought an apple. It cost him 20 cents. He played one game that cost 25 cents. He decided to save 5 cents for later.

Look at the circle graph on the next page. It shows how Malcolm spent his dollar.

How Malcolm Spent His Dollar

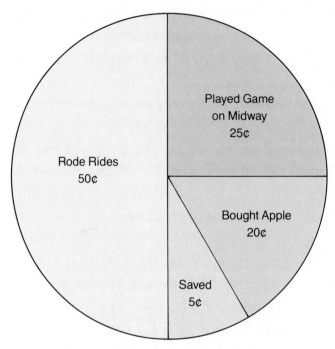

The circle equals Malcolm's dollar. A total of 50 cents was spent on the rides. Fifty cents is one-half of a dollar. So, the amount Malcolm spent on rides takes up one-half of the circle.

The game Malcolm played cost 25 cents. Twenty-five cents is one-fourth of a dollar, so the cost of playing the game takes up one-fourth of the circle.

The apple that Malcolm bought cost 20 cents. Twenty cents is one-fifth of a dollar. One-fifth is slightly less than one-fourth. The apple takes up a little less than one-fourth of the circle.

Malcolm had five cents left over. This is the remaining part of the dollar. If you add up all that Malcolm spent and saved, you will find that it equals one dollar.

Notice how long it took you to read the description of how Malcolm spent his money. Compare that with how long it took you to get the same information from the graph. Which way of getting that information was quicker?

Look at the circle graph below. Then read the two paragraphs that follow it. Which paragraph has the same information as the circle graph?

**Hair Color of Fourth Grade Students
at Lincoln Elementary School**

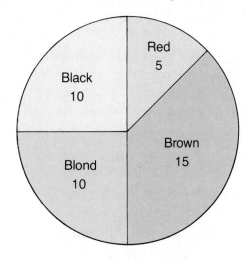

Lincoln Elementary School has forty students in grade four. Twenty of these students, or one-half, have brown hair. Ten, or one-fourth, have black hair. Five students, or one-eighth, have red hair. The remaining five have blond hair.

Lincoln Elementary School has forty students in grade four. Ten of these students, or one-fourth, have black hair. Another ten have blond hair. Five students, or one-eighth, have red hair. The remaining fifteen students have brown hair.

The second paragraph has the same information as the circle graph.

Textbook Application: Reading Circle Graphs in Social Studies

Read the following article about circle graphs. The sidenotes will help you.

Reading Circle Graphs

A circle graph shows how a whole is divided into parts. This circle graph shows how many Peruvians are in different age groups.

The title tells you what the graph is about.

This graph does not tell you the number of people in each age group. It does show you how the different age groups compare in size.

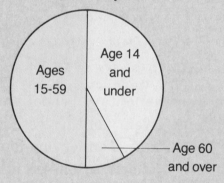

Peru's Population By Age Group

Ages 15-59

Age 14 and under

Age 60 and over

The blue part covers less than half of the circle. This age group has fewer people than the age group shown in the green part.

The green part of the circle graph stands for people between ages 15 and 59. This part is half of the circle. This means that half of the people in Peru are between the ages of 15 and 59. Does the blue part show more or fewer people than the green?

—*States and Regions*, Harcourt Brace Jovanovich

186

Textbook Application: Reading Circle Graphs in Math

Math books often have problems involving circle graphs. Look at the following circle graph. It shows how Jamie spent her day. The circle equals one day.

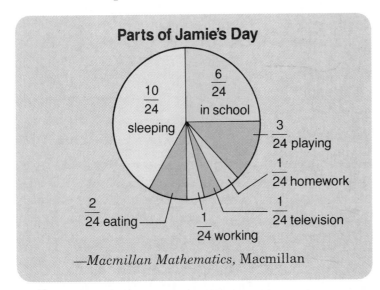

Parts of Jamie's Day

—*Macmillan Mathematics*, Macmillan

There are 24 hours in a whole day. The bottom number of each fraction tells this. The top number tells the number of hours the activity took.

The numbers in each part of the circle tell exactly how much time Jamie spent on each activity. She spent ten hours sleeping. She spent two hours eating. How much time did Jamie spend on homework?

The activities that took more time take up larger parts of the circle. By comparing the sizes of the sections, you can compare the amount of time Jamie spent on each activity. What did Jamie spend the most time doing?

Good readers read graphs as carefully as they read words in sentences. Knowing how a graph is organized will help you to get information from it.

In this selection, two brothers look at the night sky together and solve a puzzling question.

As you read, look for the puns that are part of this selection.

Einstein Anderson and the Night Sky

by Seymour Simon

Einstein Anderson was an average-size twelve-year-old boy in the sixth grade. Sometimes his light-brown eyes had a faraway look when he was thinking about some important problem in science. But Einstein was not always serious. He loved jokes of all kinds and liked to make puns, the worse the better.

Adam was Einstein's real name. But almost everyone called him Einstein, after the most famous scientist of the twentieth century. Adam had been interested in science for as long as he could remember. He talked about science, read about science, experimented in science, and even solved puzzles by using science. For years, even his teachers had called him by the nickname Einstein.

"Tonight is the big event," said Einstein. "I've finished my telescope's tripod, and we can go out in the backyard and do some stargazing."

"It's about time," said Dennis, his younger brother. "You've been working on that thing for months now. And you said the telescope was ready to use weeks ago. Why couldn't we look at the stars just by holding the telescope in our hands?"

"It wouldn't work," Einstein explained. "An astronomical telescope is too powerful to be hand-held. You'd never be able to keep it steady enough to observe anything."

"Then how come sailors are always looking through telescopes that they hold?" Dennis asked.

"That's not the same thing," said Einstein. "A ship's telescope may have a magnification of ten or fifteen. But even a small astronomy scope will magnify forty or fifty times. And the higher the magnification, the steadier the mounting you need. Wait till it gets dark—you'll see why the tripod is so important."

That night the boys ate dinner quickly and did the dishes in record time. However, it was dark by the time they carried the telescope and its mounting out to the backyard.

"That doesn't look much like a telescope to me," Dennis said after Einstein had set up everything. "Where's the glass lens at the front?"

"This is a reflecting telescope, not a refractor," Einstein said. "Refractors gather light by means of a glass lens at the front end of a tube. That's the kind of scope that most people recognize. But a reflector gathers light by means of a curved mirror at the bottom of a tube. A reflector is easier to build and much less expensive for the same size."

"Whatever you say, Einstein," said Dennis. "Let's look at some stars."

"Before we look," said Einstein, "let's wait a few minutes for our eyes to become dark-adjusted. Close your eyes for a little while. After your eyes adjust to the dark, don't look directly at my flashlight. If you look at a bright light, you'll lose your dark-adaptation quickly."

"Okay," said Dennis. He closed his eyes. "Are you thinking of becoming an astronomer?" he asked.

"I might," Einstein said. "Of course you know that an astronomer is a night watchman with a college education," he continued.

"Ha, ha," said Dennis, opening his eyes. "Could we look at some stars now?"

"Sure," said Einstein. He set up the telescope on the heavy tripod and pointed it at a spot in the Milky Way. Then he motioned Dennis to look through the eyepiece.

"Wow!" Dennis exclaimed, "I see so many stars I can't even count them. What am I looking at?"

"That's a small section of the Milky Way," said Einstein. "It's a huge mass of millions and millions of stars. They're so far away that without a telescope they just look like a band of hazy light. The Milky Way is a group of stars called a galaxy. Our sun is part of the Milky Way, out toward one edge. You're looking toward the center of the galaxy."

"Let's look at that bright star next," Dennis said, pointing.

"That's not a star. It's a planet," said Einstein.

"How can you tell without even looking through a telescope?" asked Dennis. "I thought planets move around in the sky so that they're in different spots all the time."

"That's true," Einstein admitted. "I'm not sure which planet it is, but I do know it's a planet."

Can you solve the puzzle: How can Einstein tell a planet from a star without using a telescope?

"It looks like a star to me," said Dennis.

"There's a difference," Einstein explained. "Except when they are high overhead, stars twinkle when you stare at them. Planets usually shine with a steady light."

"Why is that?" asked Dennis.

"Stars are so far away from us that they look like points of light even through the biggest telescopes. Planets are much closer than stars. A bright planet will look like a disk even through my little telescope. We get many light rays from a planet but only one ray from a star. The earth's atmosphere can interfere with a star's light much more easily than with a planet's light. When it does, the stars appear to be twinkling."

Einstein looked through his telescope at the planet. "I think the planet is Jupiter," he said. "The four faint points of light you can see nearby are Jupiter's moons. Just think. Jupiter's moons were first seen by the great scientist Galileo with a small telescope more than three hundred years ago."

Einstein paused and smiled. "You know that some people say Galileo would have been a great movie fan because he liked to watch the stars so much."

"Ugh!" said Dennis. "I think you should stick to being a night watchman."

1. How did Einstein tell the difference between a planet and a star without using a telescope?

2. What is the difference between a reflecting telescope and a refractor?

3. Why do you think that Adam didn't mind his nickname?

4. What did the boys do before they looked at the stars? Why did they do this?

5. Why did the boys wait for the tripod to be finished before they used the telescope?

1. A pun is a humorous play on words based on a word's double meaning. On pages 190 and 193, find the puns that use the words *night watchman* and *stars*. Explain the double meanings of the words.

2. One night, Dennis listed all the night-objects he saw in the sky: 22 stars, 9 birds, 3 planets, and 2 airplanes. Later, Einstein made a circle graph of the information for Dennis. Which objects did Einstein show as the largest and the smallest parts of the graph? Why?

Prewrite

Some nicknames describe people. Adam Anderson got the nickname "Einstein" because he was always studying science, like the scientist Albert Einstein. Copy and complete the chart below. Fill in possible reasons for the nicknames listed.

Nickname	Reason for the Nickname
Sunshine	always has a bright, sunny smile
Tadpole	loves the water and swims well
Encyclopedia	
Stormy	

Compose

Think about a nickname you know. Write a paragraph telling to whom the nickname belongs, how and when the person got the nickname, and who gave it to him or her.

Revise

Check your paragraph. Does it include all the information asked for? If not, correct your work.

Until We Built a Cabin

by Aileen Fisher

When we lived in a city
(three flights up and down)
I never dreamed how many stars
could show above a town.

When we moved to a village
where lighted streets were few,
I thought I could see ALL the stars,
but, oh, I never knew—

Until we built a cabin
where hills are high and far,
I never knew how many
            many
                stars there really are!

Maps

You may remember how information is given on a map. A compass rose tells direction. It shows where north, south, east, and west are on the map. A scale helps you figure out how far it is from one place to another. A legend uses symbols to show interesting or important places on a map.

Road Maps

Look at the following road map of Florida.

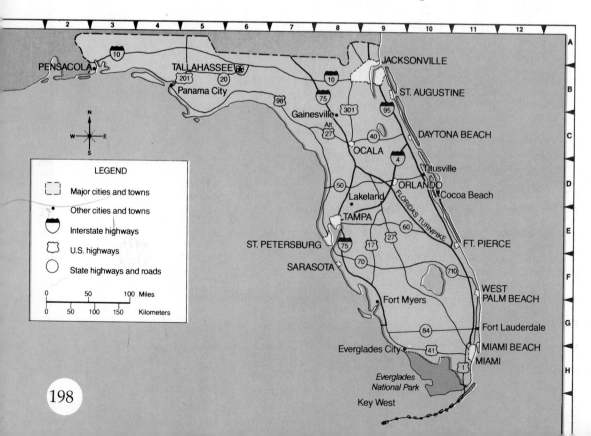

This map has a compass rose, a scale, and a legend. Use the legend to find out what the road map shows. Each highway and main road in the state has its own route number. Most of the cities and towns are marked with a small circle. The larger cities are shown as shaded areas.

You read a road map to learn which roads to take when you want to go from one place to another. Find Daytona Beach on the east coast of the state. Now find Tampa on the west coast. Which route would you take to go from Daytona Beach to Tampa? You would probably take Route 4. Why? Is there any other route you could take?

Coordinates

A map can also be used to help you find where a place is located. Look at the numbers across the top and the letters along the side of this road map. These are called map coordinates. You can use these coordinates to find cities and towns on the map.

Hold a piece of paper straight west from the letter *F* at the side of the map. Put another piece of paper straight south from the number *8* at the top of the map. You will find the city of Sarasota where the two pieces of paper meet.

Now look again at the letter *F*. Above and below the letter are arrows pointing west. The coordinate *F* covers the area between these two arrows all the way across the map. In the same way, the coordinate *8* covers the area between its arrows all the way down the map. The *F* and the *8* areas meet to form a square around Sarasota. This entire square is covered by the coordinates *F8*. All cities and towns inside this square have the coordinates *F8*.

Most road maps have a list of cities and towns and their coordinates. If you know how to use coordinates, you can find any city or town on the map. Next to Sarasota on the list for this map, you would find the coordinates *F8*.

St. Augustine is another city in Florida. Its coordinates are *B9*. Use the coordinates to find St. Augustine on the map.

Now find the area on the map covered by each of these coordinates: *B6, H11, D10.* Name at least one city or town in each area.

Street Maps

On a map of a city, street names help you find places. Some streets run north and south. Others run east and west. Look at the section of a street map at the top of the next page. The two avenues run east and west. The three streets run north and south. Find the *X* on the map. If you wanted some friends to meet you on that corner, how would you tell them its location?

You would probably say, "Meet me at the corner of Ocean Avenue and Main Street." However, there are four corners there. How would you tell them which one to go to?

Using the compass rose, you can see that the *X* is on the northeast corner. You could tell your friends to meet you at the northeast corner of Ocean Avenue and Main Street. Anyone looking at a map could then tell where to go.

Find the *Y* on the street map. If you were at corner *X*, how would you get to corner *Y*? Tell how you would go, using street and avenue names. Also use

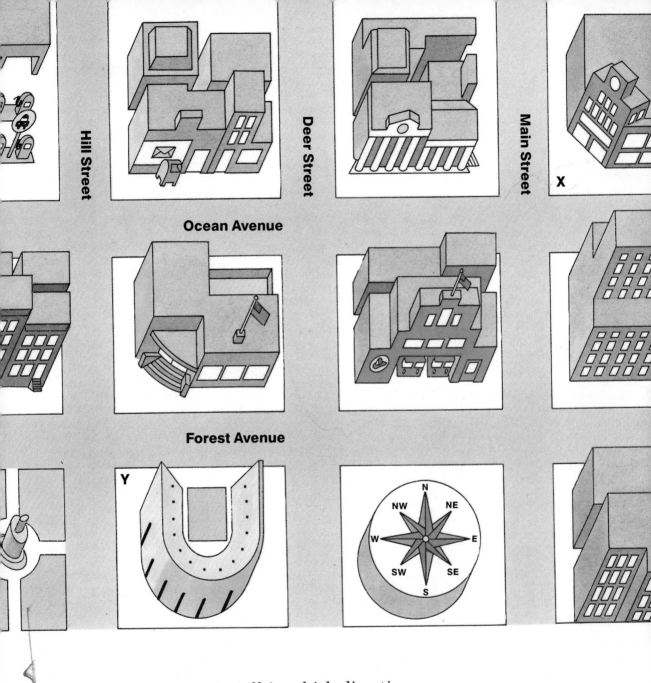

Hill Street

Deer Street

Main Street

X

Ocean Avenue

Forest Avenue

Y

N
NW   NE
W   E
SW   SE
S

the compass rose to tell in which directions you would go.

Knowing how to use maps will help you find cities and towns that you want to visit. It will also help you find your way around those places once you get there.

The skylight featured in this selection is a comet. Read to find out how one town reacts to the coming of the comet.

As you read, notice how the author describes one character's use of a map and how that character uses her imagination to make a location on the map seem real.

The Year of the Comet

by Roberta Wiegand

After her talk with Poppa, Sarah listened even harder whenever she heard Halley's Comet mentioned. Everybody in Ponder's Mill had been talking about it for weeks.

Ponder's Mill was the only place Sarah Lewis had ever lived. She'd been born there in 1900.

Sarah was able to find Ponder's Mill on only one map, because the town was so small. That was in the Goode's School Atlas. There was a big double page that showed the north central United States. Ponder's Mill was near the top edge of Nebraska. The day she found the map, Sarah moved the page closer and closer to her face. At first the heavy black lines around the different states became blurred. Next the red lines that were the railroads and the blue lines that were the rivers disappeared. Finally her nose was almost against the paper. All she could see was the small dark circle that stood for Ponder's Mill.

Then Sarah pretended she was going inside the circle. She pretended she stepped through the circle and was suddenly on the courthouse lawn at the bottom of Main Street. She pictured herself walking west between the elm trees.

In her game Sarah kept on walking up Main Street as it gradually began to climb the only hill in the county. She went past the livery stable and the General Merchandise Company, Inc., past Kirk's Bakery and Confectionery, and then past the hardware store that Poppa owned. It had a wide porch with wooden benches where people often sat and talked.

The old Opera House stood on the next corner. It was tall, with wooden lattices and curlicues.

Two-thirds of the way up the hill on the left was the Lewis house. That was where Sarah lived with Momma and Poppa, not to mention her brothers Harry, Charlie, and Georgie. There was also little Maryrose.

The tall Lewis house was surrounded by trees, because Momma loved them so. The house perched like a white dove in a green nest on the corner of Main Street and Old Mill Road. Main Street climbed on up to the new brick building where all twelve grades of children went to school. Old Mill Road curved down to the river.

Now when Sarah heard the talk about the comet, she thought of the small black circle on the page of the atlas. She wondered if Halley's Comet was already aimed at that black dot on the flat page of the prairie.

It didn't make her feel any better when she overheard Luke Pearson one afternoon. Luke was talking to several men on the corner.

"The comet's not going to hit the earth at all, you know. That's not what we have to worry about. It's when the earth passes through the comet's tail. There's cyanogen gas in that tail." The men looked impressed. "Do you know what could happen next?" Luke went on.

Certainly no one was about to leave that corner without finding out, especially Sarah.

"Well, maybe you know that in some places they use cyanide to poison gophers. The comet's gas is almost the same thing. Now you can see what could happen here." Luke nodded knowingly.

"When's that gonna be, Luke—that tail business?" someone asked.

"On May eighteenth. Just about a month from now. You won't be able to see the comet then because the sun'll hide it in the daytime, and the moon'll be too bright at night. But *if* we're all still here, we'll be able to see it in the evenings soon after that." Luke emphasized the *if*. Then Sarah could tell he noticed her for the first time, because he tried right away to make it sound less scary. "What I'm going to do is wear a face mask when we go through the gas in the tail. You'd all be smart to wear one, too."

Sarah trudged on up the hill. She mustn't forget to tell Momma and Poppa about the face masks. Maybe Halley's Comet wouldn't be so bad after all. She knew lots of folks who'd be glad to get rid of the gophers in their gardens.

The next day Sarah's fourth-grade teacher told her class something quite different. Miss Benedict said flat out that they shouldn't worry.

"Halley's Comet makes an orbit around the sun the way the earth does. Its orbit crosses ours approximately every seventy-five years. It's never hurt us before, and it won't now." Miss Elizabeth Benedict's whole body looked as starched as her clean white shirtwaist. When she spoke, even her words were crisp. It was hard not to believe Miss Benedict.

Still, all sorts of things did seem to be happening now that Halley's Comet was racing toward Ponder's Mill. Sarah kept hearing about them at home or in the streets and stores. (Momma said there was so much talk about the comet because it had been a dull winter and the town needed excitement.)

One night Grandpa Snow and Poppa were sitting in the front porch swing. Grandpa closed the weekly newspaper.

"It's a shame that that Mark Twain fellow had to die," he said.

Sarah, who was sitting on the top step, thought so, too. No one else would ever write books as good as *Tom Sawyer,* which Grandpa had read to her. Later somebody said Mark Twain's death was a "real sign." They said he'd been born right when the comet came the last time. It was almost as if it had circled the whole heavens and rushed back to get him.

Sarah had also heard about other things that were called "signs." A volcano near Italy had erupted and there had been an earthquake in Costa Rica. After all, there was a chance the world might end on May 18th. She guessed people thought these signs were warning them what could happen when they all went through the comet's tail.

Sarah didn't know for sure if it was the comet. But something was different these days in Ponder's Mill.

The eighteenth of May finally came. The day went slowly. Everything seemed to be waiting for night. Then it began—the quiet coming together of the people in Ponder's Mill, as if no one wanted to be alone. After dinner the Lewis family walked together down to the center of the town. Poppa unlocked the hardware store and lit the gas lamps. They all went out onto the porch where they could see anything that might happen. Kirk's Bakery and Confectionery was open, too. Many of the upper-grade students had come there to be with their friends on this night.

The banker's family was having a "comet party" in their house on top of the hill. Sarah could see all the lights. Colored paper lanterns were swinging like softly glowing fruit from the trees. She knew people were dancing up there. They were wearing their fanciest clothes. They were the ones who wanted to show how gay and unafraid they could be.

Eventually the full moon came up over the roof of the courthouse. Building by building its light crept up Main Street. Still nothing happened. Georgie curled up on one of the benches and went to sleep. Momma made a bed of gunnysacks in one of the new wheelbarrows for Maryrose.

Part of Sarah wished something would happen. Part of her was afraid it might. She noticed that her oldest brother, Harry, was starting to look bored. She wondered if he was half scared and half excited inside, too. Sarah never could tell what Harry was thinking.

"Herb, it's after one o'clock," Momma said at last. "I think we should take the children and go home." All at once Sarah felt the way she would if the circus poster went up on the side of the Opera House, and the circus never came. Maybe she'd been hoping for a chance to prove how brave she could be.

"I guess maybe you're right," Poppa decided. He looked as if he had been expecting the circus, too.

The colored lights still glowed up at the banker's house, but it was too far away to hear any party sounds. The confectionery was closed, and almost everyone was gone from the street.

The moon sailed peacefully overhead. Its pale silver spread gently over all of Ponder's Mill and the prairie around it. If Halley's Comet was hiding in the moon's light and sneaking toward them, Sarah couldn't see it. And if the tail was surrounding them with poison gas, she couldn't smell it either. All she could smell was the soft sweetness of honeysuckle and dust from the road.

Then, just as Poppa was scooping up the limp Maryrose, and Momma was locking the door of the hardware store, it happened.

Joe Robbins and several other men rushed down the street. They ran for the big old wagon in the shadows beside the building.

"C'mon, Herb! We need your help!" Joe yelled at
Poppa. "That crazy comet may have killed somebody
after all. Down by the river. It's Justin Hewitt!" Joe
jumped onto the wagon along with the others.

Poppa said, "Go inside, Hannah. Stay right there
until I get back. I'll come as soon as I can." Then Poppa
ran across the street. He leaped into the wagon beside
Joe, and they all went clattering up the hill toward the
Old Mill Road.

The children sat down or knelt on the floor by the front window of the store. It was as if the night had begun all over again. They watched the strip of sky that showed above the building across the way. At last Sarah realized that there wasn't a sound in town, not even a cricket or a barking dog. "Has everyone gone to the river?" she wondered.

"Maybe the old gas got 'em all," Harry said comfortingly, as if he had read her mind.

More than an hour went by. No one slept now except Maryrose. Then there was a low rumbling noise. They could hear it only because the town was so quiet. They looked at each other, but nobody spoke. In the empty night it seemed to come from nowhere in particular. Soon they could tell the noise came from the top of the hill and was getting closer and closer to them. Finally they knew it was the wagon coming back. It pulled up across the street.

Poppa jumped off the wagon and hurried into the store.

"Well, Justin's not dead," he reassured them as he pushed open the door.

"What happened, Poppa?" The children all crowded around him. "Did the comet hurt him?"

"It happened while he was going along that lonesome part of the road where it's steep over the river bank," Poppa said.

The children held their breath.

"He was watching the sky for any sign of the comet and drove his buggy right over the edge. Rolled all the way down into the river. Landed on top of him and broke his leg. Killed his horse. If old Everett Wagner hadn't happened by, no telling what would've happened to him."

A few nights later people were able to see Halley's Comet even without telescopes. Then it looked about as dangerous as the star on top of a Christmas tree.

So after all the waiting and wondering, a dead horse and a broken leg were the only damage the comet did to Ponder's Mill. The bravery Sarah had worked so hard to have ready wasn't even tested. The comet shone in the western sky for many nights—a beautiful soft yellow star with a greenish tail that trailed behind it. It reminded Sarah of a dragonfly like the ones that glinted their metallic wings in the reeds by the river.

Then it gradually disappeared.

Along with the other people in Ponder's Mill, Sarah put the sight and excitement of Halley's Comet away in her memory—at least for another seventy-five years.

1. How did the people in Ponder's Mill react to the coming of Halley's Comet?

2. What "signs" did the people think might be warning them about what would happen when the comet arrived on May 18?

3. What did happen on the night of May 18?

4. Who gave better information about the comet, Luke Pearson or Miss Benedict? Explain.

5. What did the author say about the moon that made you wonder whether anything was going to happen? Find those sentences on page 208.

6. When the comet finally did come, how did the people of Ponder's Mill feel about it?

Following Sarah's description of Ponder's Mill on page 203, draw a map of the town. Start with the courthouse and work westward. Include the other buildings on Main Street, as well as Old Mill Road. Add a compass rose to show direction.

Prewrite

Sarah described Ponder's Mill by pretending she was going inside the circle that stood for the town on the map. She added many details to her description so that readers could picture the town in their minds. The chart below lists places Sarah described and phrases that described them. Copy and complete the chart.

Place	Description
Hardware store	had a wide porch with wooden benches
Opera House	
Lewis house	

Compose

Write a paragraph describing a town or neighborhood that you know. Use detailed phrases to make your description complete.

Revise

Make sure your description is true to what you know. Be sure your paragraph contains enough detail so that your description is clear to the reader.

Join Kate and Vinny to find out why their class visited a planetarium.

As you read, look for an interview that appears in this selection. Try to decide what makes the interview different from the rest of the selection.

Indoor Stars

by Linda Beech

"Will the stars twinkle the way they do in the sky?" Kate wondered. "What will the planets look like?"

Kate and her partner, Vinny, hurried to catch up to the rest of their class. They were in New York City visiting the Hayden Planetarium, which is part of the American Museum of Natural History.

Kate knew that a planetarium is a place in which projectors and other machines show the Sun, Moon, planets, and millions of stars just as they look in the sky. Still, Kate was curious. What would these indoor stars be like?

At the planetarium Kate and Vinny found seats in the Sky Theater. The theater was round, and the seats were arranged in rows of circles facing the center. A large projector stood on a platform in the middle of the room. Blue and red lights surrounded it.

"That projector looks like a huge bug!" Kate whispered to Vinny. "I wonder how it works."

Just then the lights dimmed, and the show began. Kate and Vinny looked up in amazement. The ceiling of the theater was really a huge screen shaped like a dome. During the show the ceiling became the night sky. It was on this dome that the projector shone images of the stars and planets.

The program had several parts to it. The first part was about Halley's Comet. This comet was first seen sometime before the year 240 B.C. Like all comets, Halley's Comet travels along a certain path through the solar system. This path circles the Sun. Halley's Comet is well-known because it circles the Sun quite often—once about every seventy-six years. Also, as it moves closer to the Sun, the comet can be seen from Earth.

The program that Kate and Vinny watched showed that people had seen Halley's Comet many times in the past. A famous Italian artist, Giotto de Bondome, even showed the comet in one of his paintings in 1301. Kate and Vinny also learned that Halley's Comet last appeared in 1986.

As Vinny watched the show, he thought, "How do they make the comet move?"

Kate was thinking about something else. "I wonder if the stars look the same now as when Halley's Comet was first spotted," she said to herself.

The next part of the program honored the fiftieth birthday of the planetarium. Many people, events,

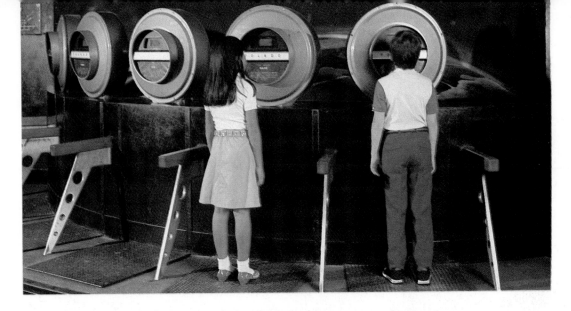

and inventions from the last fifty years were shown through pictures. The program also showed how people's ideas and knowledge about our world and space have changed.

Kate and Vinny's teacher talked to the class when the program was finished. "This planetarium is part of the American Museum of Natural History," she said. "The stars, too, are very much a part of natural history. Today, we know so much more about natural history because of what has happened in the last fifty years. Computers, rockets, and space flights have helped us learn a lot."

Then the class was allowed to look at the science exhibits in the planetarium. One of the favorites was called "Your Weight on Other Worlds." Vinny discovered that he would weigh 91 kilograms on the planet Jupiter and 980 kilograms on the Sun.

"How much do you weigh on Earth?" asked Kate.

"I won't tell you," said Vinny, "but I'll give you this hint. My weight on the Sun is 28 times what it is on Earth."

Kate laughed. "I'll figure it out and tell you how much you weigh later," she said. "In the meantime, here is a problem for you. I weigh 36 kilograms on Earth. How much do I weigh on Mars if my weight there is one-third of my weight on Earth?"

Vinny said he would think about it. Then they walked over to another exhibit. This one showed how old they would be on other planets. "Oh, look!" cried Kate. "If I lived on Mars, I would only be five years and five months old."

Vinny said, "You could move to Mercury. On that planet you'd be over forty-five years old!"

The exhibit explained that each planet rotates, or turns, at a different speed. This means that days are not the same length on every planet. Some days are longer and some are shorter than on Earth. Just as the days are not the same length on every planet, neither are the years.

It was now almost one o'clock. Kate and Vinny didn't want to be late. They had been chosen from their class to interview the head of the planetarium, Dr. William Gutsch. They were going to ask him questions about the planetarium and then share the information with the class. They rushed to his office.

Kate and Vinny found Dr. Gutsch easy to talk to as he explained his answers to their questions.

Vinny: How does the big projector work?

Dr. Gutsch: Inside each of the large balls is a light bulb, or lamp. Around these lights are lenses. Behind each lens is a glass plate. Part of the sky is on each glass plate. The light from the lamps shines through the lenses, which then project that part of the sky onto the screen.

Vinny: You mean that all of the stars are really inside the projector?

Dr. Gutsch: Yes, Vinny. The images for the stars, Sun, planets, and Moon are all in there. We don't have to change what is in this projector because the sky, or what we can see of it, has changed very little in ten thousand years.

Kate: Why does the projector move?

Dr. Gutsch: When the projector moves, the stars or planets on the screen move. In this way, it is possible to show how the sky looks at different times of the year.

Kate: I see lots of things around the sides of the dome. Are they projectors, too?

Dr. Gutsch: Yes. There are about a hundred small projectors that we use for different effects. Each has a special purpose. For instance, one projector shows how Halley's Comet moves along its path.

Vinny: Our teacher wanted us to ask about a laser light. Do you have one?

Dr. Gutsch: Yes, we do. It is a powerful thin beam of light that we use to write or draw things on the screen.

Kate: The show we saw about Halley's Comet was so interesting! Did you do it all by yourself?

Dr. Gutsch: No, not really. Putting together a planetarium show is something like making a movie. I write the scripts, hire people to read them, and work with artists, composers, sound engineers, and many others.

Kate: And you have real stars as the stars of your show!

Dr. Gutsch: I guess you're right, Kate.

Vinny: How do you get all the parts of a program to work together?

Dr. Gutsch: Much of this is done by computer. The computer tells each projector when to flash something on the screen and how long to keep it there. It also coordinates the sound track, the laser light, and the other parts of the show.

Kate: There were a lot of people here today. Is the planetarium always this busy?

Dr. Gutsch: The American Museum–Hayden Planetarium is one of the world's largest and busiest planetariums. More than one hundred and fifty thousand students come to see its shows each year. Thousands of other people, both New Yorkers and visitors, also come.

Kate: I'm glad we were some of your visitors.

Vinny: I am, too.

Kate and Vinny thanked Dr. Gutsch for his help and promised to return to see other shows.

"By the way, Vinny," said Kate as they got on the bus, "the answer to your problem is 35. You weigh 35 kilograms."

Vinny laughed. "That's right. And you would weigh 12 kilograms on Mars. But really, Kate, I hope you don't go there. There's so much we can still learn on Earth."

Kate agreed. "We sure learned a lot today," she said.

1. Why did Kate and Vinny's class visit the planetarium?

2. How is a computer used in the show at the planetarium?

3. What did you learn about planetariums that you did not know before you read this selection? Tell where you found the information.

4. What other questions would you have asked if you had been interviewing Dr. Gutsch?

5. Do you think Kate and Vinny learned all that they wanted to about the planetarium? Explain.

"Indoor Stars" is an informational selection. It tells about a trip to a planetarium. Kate and Vinny gained information by seeing a show, looking at exhibits, and interviewing the head of the planetarium. What information did Kate and Vinny learn at the interview that they could not have learned by just seeing the show and visiting the exhibits? Why is an interview an important way to gain information?

Prewrite

Vinny and Kate had the opportunity to interview Dr. Gutsch at the planetarium. The list of questions below could be used in interviewing an astronaut. Think of other questions to ask if you were going to do the interview.

Interview Questions
1. Why did you become an astronaut?
2. How does it feel to be weightless?
3. What kind of food do you eat in space?

Compose

Pretend you can interview one of the following people: an actor or an actress, a wildlife expert, the governor of your state, or another person of your choice. Write a list of at least six questions you would ask. Do not use the three questions listed above.

Revise

Check your work. Does each of your questions stick to the topic? Will your questions bring out all of the important information about the topic? If not, revise your questions.

Outlines

Understanding how an article is organized can help you remember what you have read. The writer of an article usually discusses one *general topic*. The topic might be a person, place, or thing. To explain the general topic, the writer breaks it down into *main topics*. In turn, the main topics are broken into smaller topics called *subtopics*. Each subtopic usually tells about only one part of a main topic.

For example, a writer might write about the general topic South America. Each of the writer's main topics might be a different South American country. Subtopics might be the different parts of one country. For Brazil, these subtopics might be small villages, cities, and the Amazon River Basin.

Also, there might be many *details* that tell more about these subtopics. Supporting details about the Amazon River Basin might include information about the Amazon River, the plants that grow near it, and how much rain falls there.

Making an Outline

An **outline** is one way to organize ideas about a general topic. An outline also helps to organize information when you want to write a report. Below is part of an outline a writer might make for a report on South America. On the right is the framework for this outline. A framework shows how an outline is organized.

South America	General topic, or title
I. Brazil	I. Main topic 1
A. Small villages	A. Subtopic 1
1. Found away from coast	1. Detail 1
2. Have one-third of people	2. Detail 2
B. Cities	B. Subtopic 2
1. Found on the coast	1. Detail 1
2. Have two-thirds of people	2. Detail 2
C. Amazon River Basin	C. Subtopic 3
1. Amazon River	1. Detail 1
2. Plants	2. Detail 2
3. Rain	3. Detail 3
II. Chile	II. Main topic 2

The main topics, subtopics, and supporting details are the important pieces of information needed to write a report. Notice how the outline shows the information. Which are the main topics? Which are the subtopics? Which are the supporting details? The main topics follow Roman numerals. Each subtopic follows a capital letter. The supporting details follow Arabic numerals. Did you also notice that each different part of the outline is indented, or moved to the right a certain amount of space?

Textbook Application: Outlining in Social Studies

Read the following article. Look for the main topics, subtopics, and supporting details. The sidenotes will help you.

The title of the article usually tells you what the general topic is.

GRASSLANDS AROUND THE WORLD

Savannas

A *savanna* (sə•van′ə) is a broad, grassy plain. The largest savannas are found in parts of South America, Africa, and Asia.

The writer identifies three types of grasslands: Savannas, Steppes, and Prairies. These are the main topics.

Savanna grass is tall. It sometimes reaches 2 feet (3.6 m). But this tall grass does not completely cover the ground like a lawn. Instead it grows in clumps.

Shrubs and tall trees are scattered throughout a savanna.

The paragraphs tell more about the main topics. The subtopics and details come from these paragraphs.

Steppes

Steppes (steps) are another kind of grassland. They are flat, dry plains covered with short grass. The largest steppes are found in parts of Asia, Africa, and Australia.

Plants on the steppes grow in clumps like plants on savannas. But steppes have shorter grass than savannas. Trees and shrubs are short and are widely scattered. Because the plants grow in clumps, much of the ground is bare.

Prairies

The third kind of grassland is called a *prairie* (prer′ē). A prairie is a large, flat or gently rolling grassland with few trees. Prairies are found in parts of North America, South America, and Asia.

Both tall and short grasses grow on prairies. The grasses grow close together.

Besides grasses, other types of plants grow on the prairies. These include trees, shrubs, and many kinds of wildflowers.

—*The Earth and Its People*, Macmillan

> The last three paragraphs describe prairies.

> This sentence is an important detail.

Each type of grassland is different from the others, but they are all examples of the general topic, *Grasslands*. In an outline, the three main topics would follow Roman numerals, as shown below.

I. Savannas
II. Steppes
III. Prairies

The writer describes different grasslands. The

writer also tells where each grassland is found. In an outline, what the grassland is like and where it is found would be subtopics. Each subtopic would follow a capital letter.

Any information that supports a subtopic is a detail. Each detail would follow an Arabic numeral.

Look back at the paragraphs about savannas. Can you find the details that describe savannas?

These details could be listed in an outline under subtopic A, as shown below.

I. Savannas
    A. What savannas are like
        1. Broad plain
        2. Tall grass that grows in clumps
        3. Scattered shrubs and tall trees

What are the details that tell where savannas are found? They could be listed under subtopic B of an outline.

    B. Where savannas are found
        1. South America
        2. Africa
        3. Asia

Look back at the paragraphs about steppes. We know that the writer has organized the information in the same way for each main topic. What do you think should be subtopic A under main topic II, *Steppes*?

If you thought the subtopic should be *What steppes are like,* you are right. The subtopics for each grassland are the same. Subtopic B under *Steppes* would be *Where steppes are found.* Now look at the outline for *Steppes.*

II. Steppes
   A. What steppes are like
      1. Flat, dry plains
      2. Short grass that grows in clumps
      3. Widely scattered, short trees and shrubs
   B. Where steppes are found
      1. Asia
      2. Africa
      3. Australia

Compare the outlines for *Savannas* and *Steppes*. Note that they have different details. The different details show the important differences between savannas and steppes.

Now make an outline for the paragraphs about prairies. The framework for *Prairies* should be similar to the one used for *Savannas* and for *Steppes*. Here is a possible framework:

III. Main topic
   A. Subtopic 1
      1. Detail 1
      2. Detail 2
      3. Detail 3
   B. Subtopic 2
      1. Detail 1
      2. Detail 2
      3. Detail 3

Outlining helped you compare and contrast the different grasslands. By organizing facts and information in this way, an outline helps make ideas clear. Compare your outline for *Prairies* with those of other students. Are there any differences in the outlines? Sometimes the same information can be outlined and organized in different ways.

In this selection, you will learn about a space station soon to be built. Read to find out why a space station is needed.

As you read, notice how the subheadings help you organize the information in the paragraphs that follow them.

A Giant Step into Space

by William Steele

When pioneers moved west across North America, they began by building small outposts. From the outposts, they went out to explore new lands. We are about to build an outpost in space: a space station.

The National Aeronautics and Space Administration (NASA) plans to build the space station early in the 1990's. It will be in orbit about four hundred kilometers above Earth.

It will not be the first space station, but it will be the first permanent one. An American space station called *Skylab* was launched in 1973. It stayed in or-

bit for six years. The Soviet Union put a space station called *Salyut 6* in orbit in 1977. It stayed there for almost five years. Another Russian space station, *Salyut 7*, was launched in 1982. The new space station will be larger and better equipped than any of these.

A Funny Shape

The station will probably look like a bunch of huge metal cans hanging on a long stick. The "cans" will be about fourteen meters long and five meters across. They will be that size and shape so they can fit in the space shuttle.

The crew of the station will live in one area of the station. They will work in other areas. The station will look as if it has wings. The "wings" will be panels that make electricity from sunlight. The "stick" will be a huge beam that holds it all together.

The station will be one hundred and twenty-two meters long and will weigh over two hundred thousand kilograms. Space shuttles will carrry it into orbit. It will take six shuttle flights or more to carry all the pieces up. More pieces may be added later.

Six or eight people will live in the station at first. Each person will have a "bedroom" about the size of a closet. A crew will stay on the station for about three months. Then another crew will take their place. Space shuttles will be visiting the station all the time, bringing food and other supplies.

The United States will build most of the station. Other countries will also work on it. In 1985, Canada, Japan, and the European Space Agency decided to help. (The European Space Agency is run by a group of countries.)

The station will be used as a factory and as a laboratory. It will also be used as a base from which to repair satellites. In time, it may be a starting place for trips to the moon and to other planets as well.

Factories in Space

Some products can be made better in space than on Earth because the space station will not feel the pull of Earth's gravity. Medicines, metal alloys, and electronic computer chips may all be made in space someday.

When medicines are made, the end product is sometimes a mixture. This mixture includes the needed medicine as well as substances that are not wanted. One way to make medicines pure is

with an electric current, which pulls the mixture apart. On Earth, the pull of gravity weakens the electric current. In space, this system works much better. It makes medicines that are much purer than any made on Earth.

Alloys are made when different metals are melted and then mixed together. The alloys are often stronger or better in some way than the metals from which they were made. The more smoothly an alloy is mixed, the better it will be. On Earth the heavy metals sink to the bottom and the light ones come to the top. In space they will mix together smoothly.

Electronic computer chips must be made out of material that is both very pure and very smoothly mixed. Space is the perfect place

to make them. Chips made in space may be better than any that have ever been made on Earth. These chips could make much faster computers.

It is important that these products can be made better in space. It is also important that they can be made for less money in space. Companies will have to pay NASA for letting them use the space station. Therefore, they will want to be sure that their products can be made cheaply. NASA needs to find companies that want to make their products in space. The money they give NASA will help NASA to pay for the space station.

High-Altitude Science

Some scientists want to study how plants grow and animals act without gravity. Some want to see how low gravity affects people. Other researchers in space want to find cures for some diseases.

Astronomers do not need to get away from Earth's gravity. They would like to get outside of Earth's layers of air. The atmosphere blocks light from stars far away. It also makes the view through a telescope fuzzy. Telescopes for studying the stars and planets will float near the space station. They will not be attached to it. This is so they won't shake every time someone on the station moves around.

An Orbiting Repair Shop

There are hundreds of small satellites in orbit around Earth. Sometimes they need repairs. Astronauts now use the space shuttle to fly up to a satellite to repair it. The people on the space station will be able to get to the satellites much more easily.

The space station may also be used as a base for workers. These workers will build huge satellites. The satellites will gather the sun's heat, turn it into electricity, and send the electricity back to Earth.

New Worlds to Explore

Once the station is built, it can be used as a base to send explorers out to other parts of space.

The spaceships we have sent away from Earth so far have been very small. They are small because the whole ship has to be

blasted free from Earth's gravity by one rocket. Out in space, we can build much larger ships. Also, less rocket fuel will be needed to launch a ship to another planet when the ship is already in orbit.

After the pioneers built their outposts in the Old West, more people came. The outposts grew into cities. Then people went out from those cities and built new outposts.

Someday, NASA's small space station may grow into a city in space. There may be more space stations in other orbits. The next project may be to build a base on the moon, or send a ship to explore Mars. The space station is just the first step!

1. Why is a new space station needed?

2. Name three ways in which the new space station will be used.

3. What would you like most about living and working on a space station? Why? What would you like least? Why?

4. Find the sentence that tells how the crew will get food and supplies during their three-month stay aboard the space station.

5. How is a space station like an outpost in the Old West?

Subheadings help organize information in an article. Below are the subheadings from the article "A Giant Step into Space." For each subheading, name a detail from the article that gives information about the subheading.

A. A Funny Shape

B. Factories in Space

C. High-Altitude Science

D. An Orbiting Repair Shop

E. New Worlds to Explore

Prewrite

Pretend that you have gathered information about life on a space station. Your next step is to write an outline based on that information. Copy and complete the following outline. Under each subtopic, add details from the selection and from your own imagination. Number each detail.

Life on a Space Station

I. Living areas
   A. Where the crew eats
   B. Where the crew sleeps
   C. Where the crew relaxes
II. Working areas
   A. Where research is done
   B. Where repairs are made

Compose

Use the completed outline to write two paragraphs about life on a space station.

Revise

Read your paragraphs to make sure each one states the main idea and lists supporting details. Revise your work if necessary.

In this selection, you will read the true story of a shuttle astronaut. As you read, think about how he set a goal for himself and worked to reach it.

Dates are given for the important events in this person's life. As you read, think about how these dates might be listed on a time line.

Space Challenger

by Jim Haskins and Kathleen Benson

Takeoff minus ten minutes and counting. Like a glowing monument, the space shuttle *Challenger* stood over five stories tall. It was 1:50 A.M. on August 30, 1983. At Cape Canaveral, Florida, the thunderstorms had passed, but the air was damp and hot. Just a few miles away, alligators went about their nighttime hunting in the Banana River.

On the shore of the Atlantic Ocean where *Challenger* stood, five men readied for takeoff. In minutes they would be the first shuttle astronauts to launch their craft at night.

The watching world knew that there was another "first" about this mission. One of the five astronauts was 40-year-old Lieutenant Colonel Guion S. Bluford, Jr. He would soon be the first black American astronaut in space.

President Ronald Reagan sent this message to the crew before lift-off. It said, "With this effort, we acknowledge proudly the first ascent of a black American into space."

Things That Fly

Guion Stewart Bluford, Jr., was born on November 22, 1942, in Philadelphia, Pennsylvania. His name is pronounced *Guy-on,* but he likes to be called Guy. Guy was interested in school, but he was much more interested in learning on his own. What he really wanted to learn about was how things work.

The oldest of three boys, Guy had lots of mechanical toys to take apart and put back together. What appealed to him most, though, were things that fly. Guy built model airplanes and collected pictures of real airplanes. When he played table tennis, he studied the way the light ball traveled through the air. He also tried different ways of hitting the ball with the paddle to make it fly differently. As a result, he became a great table tennis player.

Many young people are interested in model airplanes. More often than not, they want to be pilots. However, Guy Bluford didn't want to be a pilot. He didn't want to *fly* planes, he wanted to *build* them. "My room had airplane models and airplane pictures all over the place," he says. "My interest wasn't so much in flying them, but in designing them. I was fascinated with how they were put together, why they flew. I decided very early that I wanted to go into the aviation business, and I wanted to be an aerospace engineer."

An aerospace engineer works on the planning, building, and operation of spacecraft. Back in the 1950's, when Guy Bluford was in junior high school, aerospace engineering was still a very small, and very new, field. No one had yet gone up into space, but scientists and engineers believed it could happen. Scientists in both the United States and the Soviet Union were working on artificial satellites. The satellites would find out if human beings could indeed go up into space. Young Guy Bluford was interested in machines like these artificial satellites. When he grew up, he wanted to help build them.

Guy was accepted into the aerospace engineering program at Pennsylvania State University. He started taking classes at Penn State in the fall of 1960.

When Guy enrolled at Penn State, male students had to join a Reserve Officers Training Corps (ROTC) program for two years. Guy picked the Air Force ROTC. After his second year, he could have left the program, but he wanted to stay in it.

The Dream That Came True

In April 1961 the Soviet Union sent a man into space. Twenty-three days later, the United States launched its first man into space.

Most Americans were excited about the *man* who had gone up into space. Guy Bluford was excited about the *craft* that had taken him there. He wanted to learn how *Freedom 7* worked. He wanted to design a craft that would work even better.

In his last year at Penn State, Guy was a "full bird," or pilot, in the Air Force ROTC. In 1964, he graduated and was given the ROTC's Distinguished Graduate Award.

By the time Guy received his pilot wings, the United States was deeply involved in the war in Vietnam. Guy Bluford joined a fighter squadron and served in South Vietnam. Through his service, he collected some three thousand hours of flying time. He received ten Air Force medals, as well.

When Guy returned to the United States, he was thought of as one of the best pilots in the Air Force. Even so, Guy had not forgotten his dream of designing aircraft. Still hoping to become an aerospace engineer, he applied to the Air Force Institute of Technology. In 1972 he was accepted. Two years later he finished his studies in aerospace engineering at the Institute.

He then went to work at the Air Force Flight Dynamics Laboratory, at Wright-Patterson Air Force Base in Ohio. "We did a lot of testing of new airplanes and new aircraft designs," he says. "We looked for ways to make airplanes fly faster and higher. At last I had achieved the goal I'd had as a kid—I was an aerospace engineer."

New Goals to Explore

In 1978, 35-year-old Guy Bluford applied for the astronaut program. It seemed to him that NASA was the best place to learn new things about aerospace engineering. NASA is the National Aeronautics and Space Administration. NASA seemed like a wonderful place to put together his interests in both flying and engineering. However, he did not really expect to get into the astronaut program. That year alone, 8,878 other people also applied.

One day a few weeks after he had applied, someone from NASA called him. Guy couldn't believe it—he was being asked to become an astronaut!

The astronaut training program lasted for a year. Guy went to classes for about six months. Then he and his classmates went on field trips. "We went to a lot of the NASA space centers," he says. "We traveled around the country, meeting all of the people associated with the shuttle program."

When the year was up, Guy and the others in his class became full-fledged astronauts.

Guy spent the next few years flying in "shuttle simulators." Shuttle simulators are machines that have the look and feel of a space shuttle.

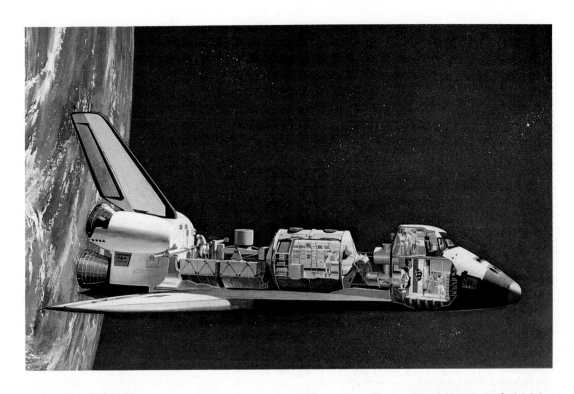

"Firsts" in Space

In 1972, NASA had started to build space shuttles. Shuttles are part rocket, part spacecraft, and part airplane. They are part rocket because they have rockets that move them. They are part spacecraft because they can navigate in outer space. That is something many rockets cannot do. They are part airplane because they have wings that can glide on air currents. Shuttles are the first spaceships that can be used over and over again.

The first space shuttle, *Colum-*bia, was launched in April 1981. On July 4, 1982, it finished its fourth flight. Then came *Challenger*, America's second space shuttle.

By May 1983, *Challenger* had made one flight. On its second flight, in June 1983, one of its three mission specialists was Dr. Sally K. Ride. She was the first American woman in space. In the early morning hours of August 30, 1983, *Challenger*'s third flight, and the seventh mission for the shuttle program, was launched. It carried the first black American into space.

Lieutenant Colonel Guion Stewart Bluford, Jr., was one of the three mission specialists on *Challenger*'s third flight. "I'm a strange bird because I'm equally as qualified to be a pilot as I am to be a mission specialist," he says.

Both pilots and mission specialists are needed to run the shuttle. The pilots fly the shuttle. The mission specialists carry out the work that the shuttle is up there to do.

A Place in History

Once in orbit, Guy Bluford and the other crew members unstrapped themselves from their seats. They then had to begin to get used to life in "Zero G" (zero gravity).

After they had gotten somewhat used to Zero G, the mission specialists went to work. They tested a new satellite communications link between the shuttle and Mission Control.

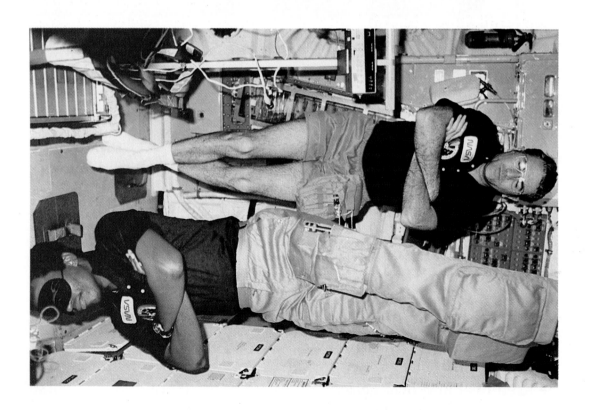

In the next five days, they carried out many experiments. The mission specialists also launched the *Insat-1B* satellite for India. The special launching of this satellite was the reason that the shuttle had taken off from Cape Canaveral at night.

When their work was finished, the crew of *Challenger* rested and got ready for their landing. The landing was to take place in the early morning hours of September 5.

Most people did not see *Challenger* until a few seconds before it landed. Its wheels touched the runway, and the shuttle rolled to a stop. Minutes later the hatch was opened. The five astronauts climbed out of the shuttle to cheers from the crowd.

For a while, the five *Challenger* astronauts had little chance to rest. Besides the official questions and doctors' examinations, there were interviews with the press and an appearance on a television special. After a few weeks, life for the five men returned to normal. Guy Bluford was glad. He had enjoyed going up into space. He was pleased to be a role model. He was someone for young people to look to and say, "Gee, if he could do it, maybe I can do it, too." However, he is a quiet man who doesn't like to be the center of attention.

Still, Lieutenant Colonel Guion Stewart Bluford, Jr., has a place forever in history as the first black American in space. He will be a hero both now and in the future. He is a source of encouragement for those who dare to dream big dreams. He gives hope to those who work to make those dreams happen.

Asked what he had to say to kids, Guy Bluford answers, "They can do it. They can do whatever they want. There really aren't any barriers to hold them back. They may find it difficult at times. But if you really want to do something and are willing to put in the hard work it takes, then someday—bingo, you've done it!"

1. What goal did Guion S. Bluford, Jr., set for himself when he was young?

2. Name three things that Guy Bluford did that helped him become an astronaut.

3. Why do you think NASA was so proud to have Guy Bluford in the astronaut program?

4. Guy Bluford was the *first* black American in space. Find the two other "firsts" mentioned in the selection.

5. What advice does Guy Bluford give to young people that will help them be successful?

Apply

the

Skills

Copy the following time line and complete it by filling in the missing dates and events of Guion Bluford's life.

		1972		1978	
Entered Penn State University	Received ROTC's Distinguished Graduate Award		Began work at Wright-Patterson Air Force Base		Became first black American astronaut in space

Prewrite

Guy Bluford has won each challenge he has faced in life. Copy the chart below and list how Guy worked through each challenge.

CHALLENGE	SOLUTION
1. playing table tennis	studied how the ball traveled through air
2. designing aircraft	
3. becoming an astro- naut	

Compose

Think about someone you know or have read about who has faced a difficult challenge in his or her life. Write two or three paragraphs to describe the person. Tell what the challenge was and how the person met the challenge.

Revise

Read your paragraphs. Do they include enough information? If not, add more details.

Clipped, Coined, and Portmanteau Words

As the world changes, so does our language. Words are created because there are new ways of thinking and new ways of doing things. When newly formed words are added to our vocabulary, they make it more interesting. Let's find out how some new words are created.

Clipped Words

One way of adding new words to our language is by clipping words. **Clipped words** are shortened forms of words that we already use.

A clipped word drops one or more syllables. For example, *math* is a clipped form of the word *mathematics*. The last three syllables of the word were dropped. Sometimes the remaining syllable of a clipped word is spelled the same as in the longer word, as with *math*. Other times, the spelling of that syllable will be changed when the longer word is clipped.

Think about the meanings of these words. Do *math* and *mathematics* share the same meaning? They both refer to the science that deals with the study of numbers. You can see that sometimes the meaning of a clipped word does not change. Often it means the same as the original word.

Read the following words:

laboratory   veterinarian   bicycle

What clipped words came from these longer words?

If you said *lab, vet,* and *bike,* you were right. Notice that when *bicycle* was clipped, the spelling of the first part of the word was changed from *bic* to *bike.*

A clipped form of a word may be used more than the word from which it was taken. You may see the longer form of the word used mainly in writing. The clipped word may appear more often in spoken language. Think about the words you use as you write and talk. If you were reporting on the different ways people travel, you would probably use the word *bicycle* in your report. If you were talking with your friends about what to do on Saturday, you might mention taking a *bike* ride.

Pay careful attention to the words you speak, hear, and read. You may notice other clipped words that have become part of our language.

Coined Words

Coined words are words that are made up to fit special needs. They are up-to-date words. They help to explain life in today's world. Scientists and inventors sometimes coin words to name what they have discovered or invented. It is hard to believe that some words we now use all the time were once coined. *Telephone* and *airplane* are words that were made up to name "new" inventions.

The space program has brought many new words into use. For example, a name was needed to describe the people who travel in space. Someone coined the word *astronaut* from the Greek words that mean "star" and "sailor."

Some coined words, such as *flashcube,* are made by putting two known words together as a compound. Other coined words, such as *debug,* are made from known words to which a word part is added. Still other coined words just seem to come out of someone's imagination.

Imagine that you discover a new type of plant. The plant's fruit looks like a tomato. However, the fruit tastes like a banana. Which of the following words might you coin to name the new fruit? Why would you call it that?

mudge   stendle   tomana

To describe a fruit that looks like a *tom*ato and tastes like a ban*ana,* you might have coined the word *tomana*. This word is a combination of the words *tomato* and *banana*. Of course, you might also have called this imaginary fruit a *banato*!

Portmanteau Words

A **portmanteau word** combines the beginning of one word with the ending of another. In this way, two known words are blended together to form a new word. The new word not only blends the letters of the older words. It also blends their meanings.

Read the following sentence. It has a portmanteau word in it. Can you tell which word is the portmanteau word?

The smog was very thick late in the day.

Smog is the portmanteau word. The word *smog* combines the words *smoke* and *fog*. The first two letters of *smoke* and the last two letters of *fog* are joined together.

Besides blending letters, a portmanteau word also blends the meanings of the words from which it was made. If you know what *smoke* means and what *fog* means, you can probably tell what *smog* means. Smog is a fog made heavy and dark from smoke.

Some portmanteau words are used as often as the words from which they came. Here are three pairs of words. For each pair, blend the letters of the two words to make a new word.

breakfast + lunch =
twist + whirl =
smack + mash =

You may have been surprised to see that the "new" words you made were words that you already knew. *Br*eakfast and l*unch* made *brunch*. *Tw*ist and wh*irl* turned into *twirl*. *Sm*ack and m*ash* became *smash*.

You can use the meanings of the older words to figure out what the new word means. *Brunch* is a meal eaten in place of breakfast and lunch. *Twirl* means "to turn around quickly." *Smash* means "to hit something and crush it at the same time."

In part, our language is what it is today because of clipped, coined, and portmanteau words. Our language is constantly changing. New words are created, and slowly we begin to use them. In time, these words become part of our everyday vocabulary.

This selection, presented in play form, gives information about the parts of a computer. Why do you think the parts of a computer are amazing?

As you read, notice the coined words that have been created especially as computer terms.

The Talking Computer

by Murray Suid

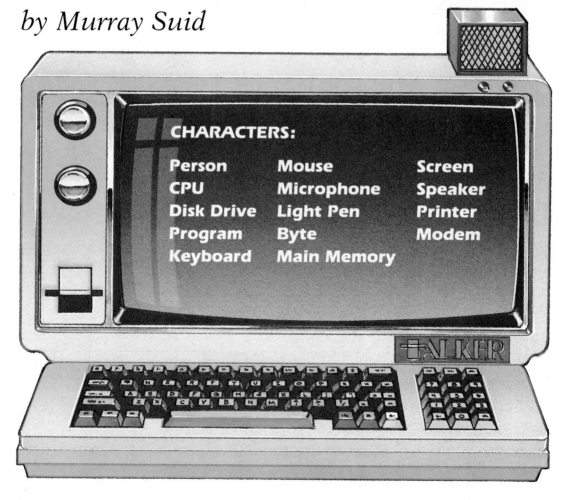

CHARACTERS:

Person	Mouse	Screen
CPU	Microphone	Speaker
Disk Drive	Light Pen	Printer
Program	Byte	Modem
Keyboard	Main Memory	

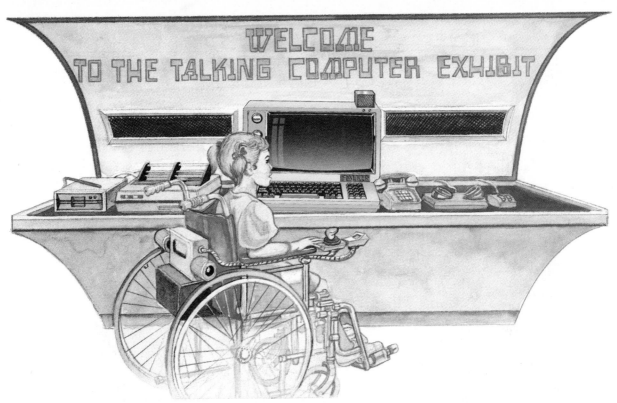

The scene is a science museum. A sign reading "Welcome to the Talking Computer Exhibit" hangs center stage. Note: **All Parts** *means that all characters except* **Person** *and* **CPU** *speak the given lines together.*

Person: This is the science museum's new talking computer. Since hearing is believing, I'll just turn it on.

All Parts: Hello. We are the parts of a computer. We're here to tell you what we do and how we work.

Person: That's great.

All Parts: (*All parts shout out.*) I'll go first because I'm the most important. You are not! I am! No, I am!

CPU: (*blows a whistle and everyone quiets down*) That's better.

Person: Who are you?

253

CPU: I'm the Central Processing Unit, or CPU for short. You might call me the computer's brain. I do the math and thinking work. I also tell the others what to do.

Person: I guess *you* are the most important part.

CPU: Not really. We're all important. Would your brain be much use without your heart, your skin, your . . .

Person: I see what you mean.

CPU: To know how a computer works, you have to learn about *all* of us. Isn't that right, everybody?

All Parts: Sure! We're all important!

Person: So, who goes first?

All Parts: Me! Me! Let me! Let me!

CPU: (*blows whistle again and waits for quiet*) You can see why a CPU is needed. Let's begin with you, Disk Drive. After turning the computer on, people often use you or your cousin Tape Drive.

Disk Drive: I knew I was the most important part.

All Parts: Boo! Hiss! That's not so! Boo!

CPU: (*blows whistle*) Cut that out. Our guest doesn't want to hear bragging and arguing. Now, Disk Drive, just tell what you do in plain English. Okay?

Disk Drive: Okay. I'm something like a record player, only I play magnetic disks. (*holds up a disk*) Disks or tapes store words, numbers, pictures, and programs. A program is . . .

Program: (*interrupting*) Stop! Don't tell what I do. I'll talk for myself.

Disk Drive: Excuse me, Program.

Program: You're excused. Now, a program is a list of instructions a computer follows in doing a job. It's like the script for a play. But in this case the actors are the computer's parts. For example, a checkers program tells the screen how to make a checkerboard pattern. It also tells the CPU how to make moves.

Person: Can that program play chess, too?

Program: Nope. Every time you ask the computer to do a different job, you need another program. There are thousands of ready-to-use programs for everything from doing mathematics to drawing pictures. Plus, you can always write your own programs.

Person: I see why computers are so popular! With different programs, one machine can be used in lots of ways. But how does it work?

Program: Put the disk or the tape into the drive. Then use the keyboard . . .

Keyboard: Did I hear someone say *Keyboard*? That's me. My keys can send signals directly to the CPU. After you put a disk into the disk drive, you type the name of the program.

Person: You mean like "Checkers"?

Keyboard: Yes. Then you push my *return* or *enter* key. That tells CPU what you want. Without me, nothing would happen.

Mouse: What about me, Keyboard?

Person: Who are you?

Mouse: I'm Mouse. I can do a lot of Keyboard's work, only faster. Plus, I can draw pictures. Some people think that I look like a mouse crawling around when I am doing my job.

Microphone: And what about me? Some computers let people use a microphone to tell CPU the job they want done. In the future I may be the main way people talk to computers.

Keyboard: We'll see.

Light Pen: Speaking about seeing, don't overlook me, Light Pen. (*holds up package with bar code*) I can read the bar codes used in stores and libraries. Keyboard, Mouse, and Microphone can't do that! So there.

CPU: No bragging! What matters is that each of you can let the user talk to me in electrical code. In most computers, the code is made up of messages called *bytes*. Each byte stands for a letter, a number, or a symbol.

Byte: I work the way a finger code works. Suppose you want to send a message to someone across the room. First you both agree that one finger up is C, two fingers up is A, and three fingers up is T. Then you could send the word *cat* in this way. (*Byte holds up one finger, then lowers the hand, then raises the hand and holds up two fingers, then lowers the hand, then raises the hand and holds up three fingers.*)

Person: But there are no fingers inside the computer.

Byte: That's true. Instead, I'm made up of eight electrical signals. By using different ones, I can send 256 different messages. (*Byte moves fingers up and down to make different patterns.*)

Person: I could never make sense of all these bytes.

CPU: I'm made so I can figure out this kind of message quicker than you can blink your eye. When a user asks for a program stored on a disk, I instantly send a signal—using the same electrical code—telling Disk Drive to send the program to Main Memory.

Main Memory: That's me. I'm the place where programs stay while being used. I also hold some of the data—words and numbers—that the computer is working with.

CPU: After Disk Drive has done its job, I send another signal, using different bytes, to Main Memory. I ask it for the program's first instructions.

Byte: (*running to Main Memory*) May I have the first instruction, please?

Main Memory: I send the first instruction, also in code, back to the CPU.

Byte: (*running to the CPU*) Tell the screen to print a message saying that the program is ready.

Screen: I'm something like a TV screen. Without me, the computer couldn't tell the user anything.

Speaker: Really? In some computers, a speaker like me can talk to the user in a voice that sounds almost human. Why, in a few years electronic speakers may replace screens completely.

Screen: I doubt it. Can you *show* pictures and colors the way I can?

Speaker: No, but can you play music the way I can?

CPU: (*blows whistle*) Cut it out! The point is that my job is to take the program's instructions from Main Memory one at a time. I then make sure they're carried out.

Person: Do you always have the other parts do the work?

CPU: No. Sometimes I do it. Part of me does the math and thinking work. In a way, I send messages to myself.

Person: What happens next?

CPU: After I deal with the first job, I ask Main Memory for the next thing to do. In some programs, thousands of little jobs have to be done before the big job is done. When the big job is finished, the result may be flashed on the screen or sent to the printer.

Printer: Like a typewriter, I put words and numbers on paper. I can even print pictures.

CPU: Sometimes, the information is sent to the modem.

Modem: My job is to change the code inside the computer into a different code that can be sent over phone lines to other computers.

CPU: But often the information will be stored for later use. In most computers, information can't be kept in Main Memory. When the computer is shut off, that erases everything. For safekeeping, information must be sent to the disk drive where it is put on a disk.

Person: Whew. You're really kept busy sending and receiving signals.

CPU: That's true. Most modern computers can move around a million or more messages each second.

Person: How do you do it so fast?

CPU: My main moving parts are electrical signals. Electricity travels at the speed of light. That's the fastest thing in the universe. Also, while I'm big in this play, I'm small in real life. I fit onto a tiny chip of silicon that's smaller than your fingernail. Many of the signals I send and receive travel less than a quarter of an inch. Since the trips are short, they don't take a long time.

Person: Well, all of you parts are amazing!

All Parts: Thanks. We like you, too.

Person: Shall I turn you off now?

All Parts: Yes, but before you do, we have one last message.

Person: What is it?

(*All Parts say nothing, but for three seconds they signal by rapidly moving their fingers up and down.*)

Person: Could you say it in English?

All Parts: Sure. This is *the end.*

1. Which parts of the computer do you think are amazing? Why?

2. How are the keyboard, the microphone, the mouse, and the light pen similar?

3. Which part of the computer in the play did you think acted like a teacher or a coach? Explain.

4. What is a byte made up of? How many different messages can be sent using different bytes?

5. What did you learn must happen for a computer to work best?

Scientists and inventors sometimes coin words. Coined words are words that are made up to fit special needs. Name five words from the play that have been created especially as computer terms.

Prewrite

Think about the parts of a computer. How are some of them like the parts of your body? Copy and complete the chart below, which compares the parts of a computer to the parts of the body.

The <u>CPU</u> is like the brain.
The <u>mouse</u> is like the fingers.
The <u>microphone</u> is like
The <u>light pen</u> is like
The <u>speaker</u> is like

Compose

Write a paragraph comparing parts of the body to parts of a computer. Tell how they are alike by telling what each part does. Then write another paragraph contrasting a computer with a person. List at least three ways in which a person differs from a computer.

Revise

Check your work to make sure you have compared and contrasted in separate paragraphs. Revise your work if necessary.

Robots can be used in many different ways. As you read, think about how a robot could be most useful to you.

Notice the information that is given in captions to explain the photographs.

Ready, Set, Robots

by Lisa Yount

The new workers are skilled, and they do many jobs. Some help put cars together. Others move packages in a warehouse. A team of them runs a supermarket in Japan. A few are learning to cut the wool from sheep in Australia. Some walk on the ocean floor. One has stood on the red sands of the planet Mars, where no human being has ever gone.

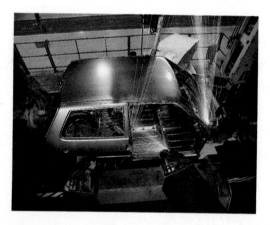

This robot is putting a car together. It works at a factory in Turin, Italy.

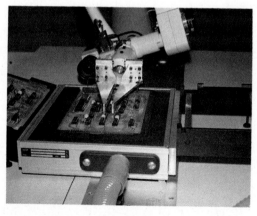

A robot's computer "brain" tells it what to do. This robot is making a part that may go in another computer.

The new workers are robots. Over twenty thousand are on the job worldwide—and that number is growing all the time. Robots can work all day and all night. They never become sick or tired. They do jobs that are too boring, dangerous, or difficult for people to do.

Of course, these machines cannot really think as people do. A robot's "brain" is a computer. People must plan every step of an action they want a robot to do. Then they write a set of instructions, called a program, for the robot's computer. The computer follows these instructions and makes the robot's body move. Television cameras act as "eyes" and send pictures to the robot's computer brain.

Most robots today work in factories. Many car factories in Japan, the United States, and other countries use robots. Almost all the workers in one Japanese factory are robots. One set of robots can paint a car after other robots have assembled the car. Another kind of robot can sort machine parts more quickly than people can. It pulls out any parts that are not made right.

You may soon see robots in stores, too. They already do most of the work in the big Seiyu market in Yokohama, Japan. A robot cart rolls along the market's aisles. Signs on it show what foods are on sale that day. A "butcher" robot slices meat, following orders that buyers give by pressing buttons. The robot then weighs the meat, wraps it, and shoots it out a slot. Other robots work at night, when the store is closed. They bring carts of food out of a warehouse behind the store. People put the food on the market's shelves.

Robots can go where people cannot. One kind of robot works on the bottom of the sea. It is guided by a person on a nearby ship. A television screen aboard the

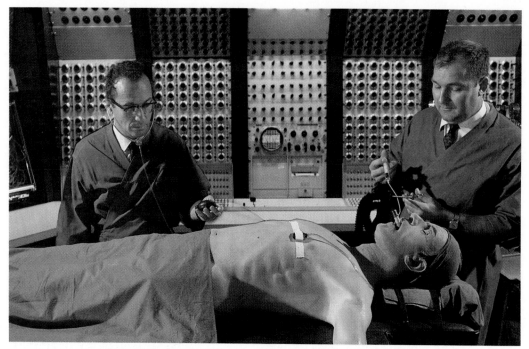

The "patient" on this operating table is really a robot. It is helping these people learn how to be good doctors.

ship shows the person what the robot "sees" below. To make the robot move, the person moves a robot arm on the ship. This sends a message to the robot on the ocean floor. That robot moves its arm in the same way that the arm on the ship was moved.

The two *Viking* landers that visited Mars in 1976 were also a kind of robot. Signals from Earth controlled them. The robots took pictures of the planet and tested its soil for living things.

Robots can help people become better doctors and nurses. Some robots are programmed to act as a real person would when given certain medicines. Other robots will really "bruise" or "bleed." By practicing with the robots, men and women learn how to help injured and sick people.

Robots can work for disabled people, too. People who cannot move their arms and legs may be able to move their heads to guide a robot that can feed or dress them. Some people may need to wear a robot arm and hand, which can pick up an egg without breaking it. A scientist in Japan is working on a robot "guide dog" for blind people. A talking robot that can read books to blind people is already in use.

Police and fire fighters use robots, too. Police departments use robots to take bombs apart. Robots can also act as guards. There are robots that visit classrooms to tell children about safety. Robots that can walk up walls may soon help fire fighters save people in burning buildings.

A robot "nurse" gives this disabled man a drink.

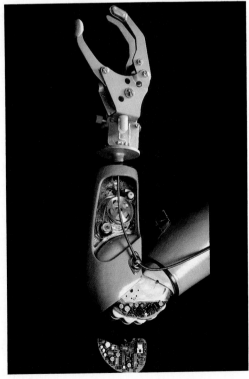

If someone loses an arm in an accident, a robot arm can take its place. This arm was made at the University of Utah.

This robot can help students learn about different languages.

OPD2 *belongs to the police department in Orlando, Florida. OPD2 is telling these children about safety.*

Robots can help children learn. A talking robot helped fourth-grade children in New York for several years. When a student gave the right answer to a question, the robot would tell a joke or a riddle. Children in a New Mexico classroom learned about computers by writing programs that told a robot how to do different jobs. Robots have been used to teach languages to children, as well.

People also use robots just for fun. Some amusement parks and restaurants have robots that sing, dance, play the piano, or tell jokes. A few even have robots that bring the food you order.

People even have robots in their homes. Today, though, most of these robots are just costly toys. Some can speak a few sentences. Some can roll across the room to greet a guest—if their owners tell them where to go. One day, perhaps, home robots may answer the door, cook the food, or walk the dog.

No one knows how robots will change our lives. Some people think that robots will take jobs away from those who need them. Others think robots will let people do more exciting jobs or have more free time. Whatever happens, you are likely to see more and more robots as you grow up. You may see them in stores or on street corners. You may work with them. Maybe someday you will even have a robot of your own!

WABOT-2 is a Japanese robot. It can read music and play the piano.

When this robot is finished, "he" may speak or sing. Robots like this can be found in some restaurants and amusement parks.

This robot was made by a Swiss clockmaker and his son in 1774. It writes messages.

1. If you could design a robot to work for *you*, what kinds of jobs would it be able to do?

2. Name four ways in which robots are being used to help people.

3. Do you think a robot would make a good friend? Why or why not?

4. Find the sentence on page 263 that tells *who* is responsible for making the robot a successful machine.

5. Why are more and more robots being used every day?

In this article, each photograph has a caption. The caption gives information about the robot that is pictured. Choose three of the photographs in this article. Copy the sentence in each caption that tells what the robot can do.

268

Prewrite

Imagine you have a robot of your very own. Complete the diagram below by listing five things you would like your robot to do for you or with you.

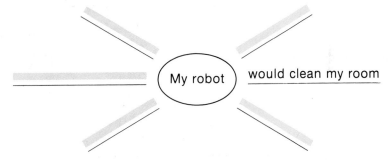

My robot   would clean my room

Compose

Choose one of the activities below.

1. Use the diagram above to write two paragraphs about your robot. Tell what you would have your robot do and why you would have your robot do these things.

2. Write a story about an adventure you and your robot could have. Remember to make your story interesting by adding details that describe the robot and what it does.

Revise

Read your paragraphs or your story carefully. Does your writing make sense? Did you include enough details? Revise your work if necessary.

Description

Using words to give information is called exposition. Using words to paint pictures in the reader's mind is called **description.** Read these two sentences:

1. It is raining today.
2. The tiny drops of rain beat against the window.

The first sentence simply gives the information that it is raining. The second sentence describes the rain.

"Sensory" words are often used in description. Sensory words appeal to, or ask you to use, your five senses of touching, tasting, smelling, hearing, and seeing. As you read the following sentence, let the sensory words make the sentence become real for you.

My teeth sank into the soft, fresh bread and crunched into the cool, crisp lettuce.

This description lets you imagine biting into a sandwich, using your sense of touch. The words *soft, fresh, crunched, cool,* and *crisp* create a picture of that sandwich in your mind.

Authors use description to make their stories interesting and enjoyable. By using description, an author helps the reader imagine what a character or place is like.

In "The Year of the Comet," the author describes

some of the buildings in Ponder's Mill by telling you interesting details. She describes the Opera House as being "tall, with wooden lattices and curlicues." The author mentions details that will help you "see" a fancy building.

The author also uses description to paint a picture of the comet for you. The comet "reminded Sarah of a dragonfly like the ones that glinted their metallic wings in the reeds by the river." In description, words may mean something different from the dictionary meaning. The author did not want you to believe that the wings were made of real metal. Instead, she wanted you to think of wings that were as shiny as metal.

Read and think about the following descriptions. To what senses do they appeal?

1. The clouds were puffy and white, like cotton.
2. The thunder rumbled as the wind screeched.

In the first sentence, the words *puffy, white,* and *cotton* help you "see" fair-weather clouds. The words *rumbled* and *screeched* in the second sentence help you "hear" the sound of the thunder and the wind.

Read and think about the following characteristics of description.

• It appeals to the reader's five senses.
• It helps to paint pictures in the reader's mind.
• It may use words to mean something different from the dictionary meaning.

As you read, notice how authors have used description to help you enjoy and understand their stories.

Author Profile

Alfred Slote

Alfred Slote, a well-known author, was first encouraged by his oldest son and a librarian to write children's books. Both his sports fiction and his science fiction are about young people, what happens to them, and how they handle it.

Alfred Slote's career has taken many interesting turns. After attending the University of Michigan, he served in the Navy during World War II. After the war he returned to the university to finish his studies. Later he went back to school, this time in France. There he wrote his first book. When he returned to the United States, he became an English teacher at a Massachusetts college.

Alfred Slote has strong feelings about reading. He believes that reading is the most important thing a child can do. "You only know what your eyes can see and your ears can hear," he says. "This firsthand knowledge is good, but it is not enough to cope with the world we live in." He believes that books go beyond firsthand knowledge to help us see life from other points of view. "If you read," he says, "you have a better chance to understand human relationships."

Alfred Slote likes to visit schools to talk with students who read his books. He says, "Children really keep you on your toes. They make you think."

One day he was with a group of fourth-grade students. One boy asked him, "Why did you write *My Robot Buddy?*"

Mr. Slote began very slowly to answer. He said, "I think I wrote it . . ." Then he paused to think about why. While Mr. Slote was pausing, the boy tried to help him. He said, "Oh, you wrote it all right. Your name is on the cover."

If he had been given enough time, Alfred Slote could have answered that question. *My Robot Buddy* was different from the sports fiction he had written. It was a type of science fiction that allowed him to use more of his imagination. He says, "The *Robot Buddy* books are mysteries set in the future. They are not pure science fiction. I use the future because nobody knows exactly what it's going to be like, and my guess is as good as any. It gives me a lot of freedom as a writer."

When children ask him how to become a writer, he tells them to read. "Not every reader becomes a writer," he says. "But no one ever became a writer who wasn't a reader."

Alfred Slote has written many children's books. Two of his sports books are *Jake* and *Hang Tough, Paul Mather.* Other titles in the *Robot Buddy* series are *C.O.L.A.R., Omega Station,* and *The Trouble on Janus.*

As you read "My Robot Buddy," think about what Alfred Slote's picture of the future is.

In this science fiction story, read to find out how a ten-year-old boy gains a new friend on his birthday.

As you read, notice how the author uses description to create a picture in your mind of the place that Jack visits.

My Robot Buddy

by Alfred Slote

I had no business wanting a robot for my birthday. My folks weren't well off. My father needed the mobile telephone for his solar car. He needed the mobile telephone for business. I needed a robot for pleasure.

My folks and I live out in the country, and after school there was no one my age around. On the Read/Screen I had seen pictures of kids who had robots that acted like brothers and sisters to them. They could talk with them, play ball with them. I wanted someone like that, someone I could talk with, throw a ball with, go fishing with, climb trees with.

So I bugged my parents about a robot for a long time. If they talked about the latest line of solar cars, I talked about the latest line of robots. "You know," I'd say, "I saw on the Read/Screen that the newest robots look more like people than people do."

"Is that so, Jack?" Mom would say, and change the subject.

When that didn't work, I'd march around the room pretending I was a robot. Robots have that stiff-in-the-knees walk, and I got so I could robot-walk perfectly.

"Hey, look at me," I'd shout, and march around until Dad would ask me to remember that I wasn't a robot, and couldn't become one no matter how hard I tried, and to please stop shaking the house. When I wouldn't stop, he would say I looked sleepy.

That was a cue for bed.

About a week before my tenth birthday, I put on a big "look-at-me-pretend-I'm-a-robot" show, and I got sent up to bed early again. I lay in bed and knew I was being a pest, but I also knew I had to have someone to play with after school, or I'd go nuts.

I guess Mom thought the same thing. I heard her saying downstairs, "Frank, I think we're going to have to get him his robot."

"We can't afford it, Helen," Dad replied. "Nor does he really need one. If *you* wanted a robot to help us with the housework, I could understand that, but just because Jack is bored . . ."

"Couldn't we get one robot that would do both?" Mom was thinking that she could kill two birds with one stone.

"I don't think so," Dad said. "My guess is that it's fairly simple to program a robot to do jobs, whether they're housework, gardening, or factory work. But to show emotions, hold a conversation, think, be a companion—those are complicated responses, and programming a robot to do things like that must be expensive. I don't think we can afford that kind of robot, Helen."

"All right, Frank, then I think we ought to move back to the city where Jack can have other children to play with."

Now Mom was hitting Dad where it hurt. He hated cities. He hated the feeling of people crowding him. He hated driving in traffic. Dad had grown up in Metropolis III in the northeast, and after college he had worked as an engineer on a space shuttle. When he'd made enough money, he had bought our house in the country, away from modern life and other people. He said people who lived in cities were growing soft. He wanted me to chop wood and dig gardens and climb trees. I didn't mind country life, except that I was lonely. I didn't want a robot to do my chores for me. I just wanted someone to play with.

"Helen," Dad said, and I could tell from the way he said Mom's name that he was weakening, "buying an expensive robot means no mobile telephone for my car. It means my business won't get bigger. That means constant trips to the home office to report in orders, which means less time that I can spend at home."

"Frank," Mom said, "measure your business against your son's happiness."

Dad was silent for a moment. "You're right," he said at last. "We'll buy him his robot."

I clapped my hands and started to shout with happiness, but I had the sense to shut up.

"What was that?" Mom asked.

"Probably a branch falling on the roof," Dad said.

The next day Dad asked me if I wanted to take a tour of a robot factory on Saturday. Saturday was my birthday.

"A tour?" I asked innocently. "What for?"

"Well," Dad said casually, "you're always talking about robots. Perhaps it'll cure you to go through a place that makes them."

"Suppose it doesn't cure me."

"I'll take that chance," Dad said.

On Saturday, Mom, Dad, and I drove in Dad's solar car to Metropolis VII. Metropolis VII is a small satellite city that had been moved down from the northeast after a pollution crisis and rebuilt by the river. Mom liked it. She liked the shops and the parks and the theaters and the art we saw along its moving sidewalks. Even the industrial section was pleasant to drive through. Trees had been planted everywhere.

Dad drove up one ramp and then another, and in a few moments we saw a big sign that said: *Atkins Robots, Inc., The Very Best in Robots.*

Behind the sign was a circular white building.

"Here we are," said Dad.

It didn't look the way I thought it would. I had expected something much larger and straighter, like the factories where solar cars and spaceships are made.

We drove up the ramp right into the building and came to a sign that blinked:

Stop.

Dad stopped the car.

The sign then blinked:

Leave your motor on.

Blink:

Now leave the car.

"Why, they're treating us as though *we* were the robots," Mom said with a nervous laugh.

"It looks pretty efficient," Dad said.

As we got out of the car, a door to the building opened and a man in a chauffeur's uniform came toward us. He had that stiff-in-the-knees walk. He was a robot.

"You may go inside, if you please," said the robot-chauffeur. "I will park your car."

We watched the robot-chauffeur get in our car and drive it away smoothly.

"I would never have known except for how he walked," Mom said. "Now what do we do?"

"We go inside, just as he told us," Dad said. He looked at me. "Excited, Jack?"

"Yes, aren't you?"

Dad nodded. "I'm curious, I'll confess."

We went through the door the chauffeur had come out from, and we found ourselves inside a green room. There was a desk in the middle of it, and behind the desk was a blond lady in a white uniform. On her uniform was a small label that said: *Atkins Robots, Inc.*

She smiled brightly at us. "May I help you?"

"We're the Jameson family," Dad said. "I made an appointment for a tour."

"Of course. Won't you be seated? Dr. Atkins himself will give you the tour."

She checked our name on a list, took a piece of paper out of a drawer, and then left the room, walking stiff in the knees. "Hey," I whispered. . . .

"We know," Mom said.

"There probably isn't a human being in the place," Dad said.

"I wonder if Dr. Atkins will turn out to be a robot," I said.

"It's scary," Mom said.

"I like it," I said.

Dad smiled. "Well, it's a form of living advertising."

"If you can call it living," Mom said.

"I can, and I do," said a voice behind us. We all turned. Standing there was a tall, thin man wearing a green smock and carrying a clipboard with papers on it.

"When robots are well-built and well-programmed, they have lives of their own," the man said. "And who is to say really whether a human being in his humanness is any more alive than a well-programmed Atkins robot in his robotness?"

He looked right at me as he asked that, but I wasn't
going to answer him. For one thing, I didn't know if
he was a robot or a human.

"A human," he answered my unspoken thought,
and that gave me goose pimples. "I am Dr. Atkins.
And you, I take it, are the Jameson family. If you will
please follow me, we will begin our tour of the factory."

We followed Dr. Atkins into a small room in which were three chairs facing a blank white wall.

"Please sit down."

Dr. Atkins stood next to a side wall that had a panel of buttons on it.

The lights in the room grew dim.

"Our factory is made up of five *P* departments: Production, Programming, Physiognomy—"

"What's that mean?" I whispered to Mom.

"*Physiognomy* means 'face,' " Dr. Atkins said. He had good ears all right. "The fourth *P* is Personality, and finally there is the Power department. We will now begin the tour."

He pushed a button. It was completely dark in the room now. Suddenly the wall in front of us began to move. What kind of tour was this? I had thought we would go through the factory. But here the factory appeared to be moving while we were sitting still. The wall now seemed to be melting in front of our eyes. We were looking right through it into a long room. In the middle of the room was a conveyor belt with robots lying down on it. Standing above them, working on them, wiring them, soldering connections, attaching terminals, were other robots. Robots were manufacturing robots!

"In Production," Dr. Atkins's voice rang out, "we construct the outer shells and the inner hardware. Atkins Robots, Inc., produces fifteen robots per day. Not many compared with the output of large factories, but we take pride in the quality of our custom-made, long-lasting, lifelike robots."

Suddenly Production disappeared. The wall was dim again, and the factory once more appeared to move behind the screen.

"We are now coming to our second *P* department— Programming."

A scene lighted up in front of us. Seated at a row of machines with keyboards were a dozen older people punching out computer data cards.

"These people are your computer experts, I take it," Mom said.

"You are half-right, Madam," Dr. Atkins said. "They are computer experts, but they are not people. They are robots. Our most expensive robots. We have programmed them to program other robots. These Programming robots are never allowed to leave the factory. We keep them under lock and key at all times. The ransom we would have to pay a robotnapper to get a Programming robot back would be exorbitant."

Dr. Atkins paused. "That means 'very expensive,' young man."

"Thanks," I said.

Programming disappeared. The factory appeared to glide along behind the wall again.

"Now we are coming to Physiognomy—which means, young man?"

"Faces," I said.

"Very good. Suppose you wanted a robot as a companion. What kind of face would you like your robot to have?"

I knew what was going on. I was going to pick out a face for my birthday present.

"Can I see some?" I asked.

I saw more than some. So many faces flashed on the screen, I couldn't keep up with them. There were boy faces and girl faces, funny-looking faces and good-looking faces. There were faces with pug noses, long noses, big ears, little ears, buckteeth, little teeth, no teeth; redheads, blondes, dark-haired kids. Freckles, pimples . . . it was as if every face you ever saw in your life was passing in front of your eyes, and never the same face twice.

"Do you see any face you like, Jack?" Mom asked.

"Lots," I said. "Hey, there's a swell face."

The face that I liked held still on the screen. It was a boy who looked about my age. He had red hair and freckles. He was grinning. It was a friendly face.

A light flashed on the screen and then a voice said, "Physiognomy pattern A-1-Y17."

"Is that his name?" I asked. The screen went black.

"That is his facial pattern," Dr. Atkins said. "The person who buys him names him."

The factory views began moving across the screen again.

"What kind of name would you give to that face, Jack?" Mom asked.

"I don't know. 'Bob' . . . no, he doesn't look like a Bob. Red-haired, freckles, grinning . . . I've got it—'Danny'! That's a good name for a redhead with freckles. Danny!"

"Danny One," said Dr. Atkins.

"One?"

"In case he gets rebuilt. The owner may want a similar model.

"We are now arriving at our Personality department." We were looking into another room. This one had a gigantic computer in it.

"Young man, if you were to have a robot for a friend, what kind of personality would you like him to have?"

"Like mine," I said.

"That is not very helpful," Dr. Atkins said. "How would you describe your personality?"

I glanced at my folks, but they didn't say anything. My dad's eyes were twinkling.

"Nice. . . . I think."

"And what exactly does 'nice' mean?"

"Well," I said, looking at the computer where a single light was going on and off, "I'm happy . . ." Suddenly a whole battery of lights went on and cards started going through the machine. "I like outdoor things. I like baseball and football and I like to fish. I'm a good tree climber and a pretty fast runner. Gee, I guess I like most everything."

I thought the computer would go wild. Green lights, yellow lights, red lights, cards going in and out, and bells sounding.

"Hmmmm," said Dr. Atkins, "you are a happy, all-around boy. Happiness is very difficult to program, and a robot who liked to do all those things would be as close to a real ten-year-old boy as possible. That would make Danny One a very expensive robot."

The screen went dim. The factory started moving again.

Dad cleared his throat. "I . . . uh . . . don't suppose there's any inexpensive way you could program for happiness."

"No, Mr. Jameson," Dr. Atkins said. "I'm afraid you have to be born a human being to be able to feel happiness for free: a nice day, a pretty sunset, a birdcall . . . enjoyment like this, people get just by being alive. But a robot must be programmed to enjoy things like that, and I'm sorry to say, that is very costly. Ah, now we are arriving at our final *P* department: Power."

We were looking into a dark room that had a solid screen at the end of it. In the screen were hundreds of small holes with light bulbs above and below them. Looking up at the screen were stiff, shadowy figures. They were holding wires in their hands.

"The bulbs you see on the screen stand for voice calls from Atkins robots in the field. The hum you hear in the background comes from nuclear generators stored below this level. In this room we can monitor the energy cells of every Atkins robot no matter where on

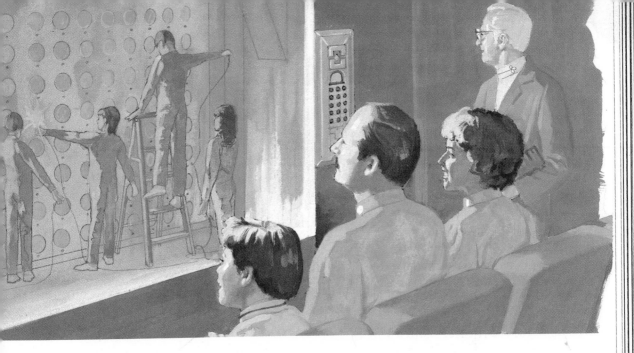

earth it is. If an Atkins robot needs an emergency charge, it can radio in to our Power department and receive one. Of course, you can recharge an Atkins robot by merely plugging it into your home nuclear power core. But should your robot run out of energy on the road or should your home nuclear core be damaged, the robot itself can call in and request a charge."

A bulb began flashing. Instantly, the low-pitched hum grew louder. A robot figure moved quickly.

"There are earphones below your chairs," Dr. Atkins said. "You can hear a robot calling in for an emergency charge if you put them on."

We did, and this is what we heard:

"Vic II. Vic II. Code 89C1, located in Agricultural Region 14. I have been working all night in the fields and need an emergency charge."

"All right, Vic II," said a Power department robot. "You'll be plugged in immediately."

A Power department robot climbed a little ladder and plugged a wire into the hole below the flashing light.

"When this happens," Dr. Atkins explained, "a bill is sent to the owner. Naturally, emergency charges are not included in the original price of our robots."

"Naturally," Dad said with a sigh.

"However, if you look after your robot, this should not happen."

"You are receiving now, Vic II," said the Power department robot in our earphones.

"I am receiving now. Thank you, Power department," said Vic II.

"Every Atkins robot has a built-in two-way radio so it can communicate with Power in emergencies. The radio is a simple affair with an on-off button located on the robot's belly."

"A belly button!" I exclaimed.

"Precisely," Dr. Atkins said. "In robots, it is a communication source. Our tour is now over."

The images behind the walls stopped. The lights went on. The room was the same as when we had started—which was no surprise, since we had never left it.

"Are there any questions about Atkins robots?" Dr. Atkins asked us.

I had a question all right, but it wasn't for Dr. Atkins. It was for Mom and Dad. It was: When do I get my robot? But I was afraid to ask. These were really expensive robots. Now I understood why. And Dad really needed a mobile telephone for his solar car.

Suddenly there was a knock on the door. .

"Come in," Dr. Atkins said.

The door opened. A red-headed kid with freckles was standing there. He had a paper in his hand.

"Happy birthday, Jack," Mom said.

"Happy birthday, Jack," Dad said.

They were both smiling at me. I stared at the red-headed kid.

"Happy birthday, Jack," the kid said, grinning. "I'm Danny One. Here's my printout, Dr. Atkins. I hope he likes me."

"I'm certain he will, Danny One," Dr. Atkins said. "After all, it isn't given to every ten-year-old boy to create a friend. Now, let's check this over . . ." Dr. Atkins examined the paper Danny had given him. "According to the printout Danny One is programmed to play baseball. He bats right and throws left. In football, he can punt, kick, and throw a pass. He knows how to tackle and block. He is not a fast runner."

"I'm a little stiff in the knees, Jack," Danny said apologetically.

I laughed. "Hey, he's for real."

"He is a real robot," Dr. Atkins corrected me. "Programmed also to play basketball, climb trees, fish, and carry on general conversations. He has been programmed for a fourth-grade education in geography, arithmetic, history, and spelling. He can also do light chores around the house"—Dr. Atkins looked at me severely—"like any well-mannered ten-year-old boy. Ahem.

"Happy birthday, young man. May you enjoy your robot friend Danny One. Take good care of him."

Danny One and I stood there grinning at each other. This was both our birthdays.

To find out about Jack and Danny One's adventures, read the rest of the book My Robot Buddy.

1. How did Jack get his new friend?
2. Why was Danny One such an expensive robot?
3. Name the five *P* departments of Atkins Robots, Inc.
4. Do you think that Jack might want to rebuild Danny One in the future? Explain.
5. What sentence on page 287 tells you that the homes in this story used nuclear energy?
6. Why did Jack's parents decide he needed a robot friend?

Read the following descriptions from the story. Tell whether the author is painting a picture in the reader's mind or appealing to the reader's senses (or both). Then explain, in your own words, what each description means.

1. Robots have that stiff-in-the-knees walk.
2. That gave me goose pimples.
3. My dad's eyes were twinkling.
4. Looking up at the screen were stiff, shadowy figures.

Thinking About "Skylights"

Through the skylights in this unit, you have looked in many directions. You have looked to the past, to an earlier visit of Halley's Comet. You have looked at the present, with its interest in solar energy, computers, and space exploration. You have also looked toward the future, in which newer computers and robots and spacecraft will continue to change our world.

Some of the selections in this unit were about real lights in the sky. "Einstein Anderson and the Night Sky" is one. It is fiction, yet it gave you information about the stars and planets. "The Year of the Comet" is fiction, too. Yet it presented you with a realistic picture of what life was like in the early 1900's in a small midwestern town.

This unit presented you with many other interesting facts about our world. However, there is much, much more to be learned. Where can all this information be found? Nearly all the information in the world is stored in libraries, and most of it is available to you. Remember, books are skylights, too. They give you the opportunity to look into the distance, into space, or even into the future.

1. In "Those Weird Wagners" you read about how Tom Barton made fun of the Wagner family partly because they used solar energy. Do you think Tom Barton would have acted differently if he had read "Putting the Sun to Work"? Why or why not?

2. If Einstein Anderson went to the Hayden Planetarium, what do you think he would find most interesting? Why?

3. In "The Talking Computer" you learned that the different parts of a computer must work together. There are computers in the robots that paint cars. What do you think might happen if the computer parts in one of these robots did not work together correctly? What might the car look like?

4. The author of "My Robot Buddy," Alfred Slote, likes to write stories that take place in the future. Imagine that he wrote a story that takes place on the space station you read about in "A Giant Step into Space." What do you think his story would be about?

5. Name three facts about space that you learned or that interested you while you were reading this unit.

Read on Your Own

Computers by Neil Ardley. Watts. This book includes a history of computers as well as information about how a computer works and how to program a computer.

Putting the Sun to Work by Jeanne Bendick. Garrard. The principles of solar energy are explained in this book, which includes experiments and many diagrams.

Energy from the Sun by Melvin Berger. Harper. Readers of this book learn how the sun gives us energy and how we use energy. They also learn why everything that grows or moves or changes needs energy.

Sally Ride: America's First Woman in Space by Carolyn Blacknall. Dillon. In this biography of Sally Ride, we learn the story of the first woman astronaut.

A Book of Stars for You by Franklyn M. Branley. Harper. This book tells how stars are born, what they are made of, what happens as they are formed, and much more.

One Hundred and One Questions and Answers About the Universe by Roy A. Gallant. Macmillan. Using actual questions asked by children at a planetarium, this book tells about stars, planets, and outer space.

That Game from Outer Space: The First Strange Thing That Happened to Oscar Noodleman by Stephen Manes. Dutton. Oscar's fascination with the new video machine at a pizza parlor leads him into an unusual adventure with aliens from outer space.

Robots A Two Z by Thomas H. Metos. Messner. This book is about the history of robots, robots today, and robots in the future. It also has chapters on robots in movies and television and robots around the house.

Find the Constellations by H. A. Rey. Houghton. Readers of this book will learn how to recognize stars and find constellations throughout the year.

Einstein Anderson Sees Through the Invisible Man by Seymour Simon. Viking. A twelve-year-old solves ten puzzling cases involving science. One concerns an invisible man, and another concerns an allergic monster.

The Long View into Space by Seymour Simon. Crown. This book about space has information about planets, moons, comets, and our solar system. It includes many good photographs.

My Robot Buddy by Alfred Slote. Harper. Jack gets a robot for his tenth birthday, and then the adventures begin!

Unit 3

Symphonies

A symphony is a piece of music written to be played by an orchestra. To play a symphony well, the musicians in the orchestra need to work as a team. The many different sounds of the instruments must *blend* together to make one complete and beautiful sound. Such blending can be found in other forms of expression, too. For example, some paintings have been called "symphonies of color."

In "Symphonies" you will read about people who have found their own special forms of expression. Some of these people enjoy music; others dance, write, or paint. Through practice and with great determination, all have learned how to do something that is important to them.

As you read the selections, think about how all these forms of expression are alike and different.

297

Biography

A **biography** is the true story of a real person's life. Most often, the subject of a biography is a person who is well-known or has done something important. Biographies have been written about famous presidents, such as George Washington and Abraham Lincoln. These people were chosen because of their important place in American history. Biographies have also been written about people who are well-known in sports, science, medicine, and the arts.

The author of a biography must learn everything possible about the subject, or person being written about. If the subject of a biography is living, the author may try to interview the person. If the subject has died, the author has to use other ways of learning about the person.

Imagine that you wanted to write a biography of Abraham Lincoln. How would you find information about him? You might read the letters he wrote or diaries he kept. You might also read other books written about him. You would probably visit the places in which he lived when he was growing up. You might also visit museums that have samples of Lincoln's clothes and other things that belonged to Lincoln.

Biographies are nonfiction. They tell a person's life story by using what is known to be true about the person. However, an author may use dialogue in a biography to make it more interesting. Usually, no one knows exactly what a person said long ago. So the author has to make up the dialogue based on known facts about the person.

Sometimes an author writes a short description of a real person's life. Such a story may be called a sketch or a profile. A profile may tell about just one part of a person's life, or it may briefly tell about the person's whole life. You can find a profile of the writer Jean Little on pages 130–131 of this book.

An **autobiography** is a special kind of biography. It is a true story about a real person. However, the author of an autobiography tells the story of his or her *own* life. If Abraham Lincoln had written a book about his own life, that book would have been his autobiography. Only *you* can write your autobiography.

Read and think about these characteristics of a biography:

- It is a true story about a real person.
- It gives information about the person's whole life.
- It often tells about a person who is well-known or has done something important.

As you read biographies, keep these characteristics in mind.

Read to find out how one woman began her music career as a young piano student and later became one of the world's greatest singers.

As you read, decide what makes this selection a biography.

Leontyne Price: Opera Superstar

by Sylvia B. Williams

"Leontyne!" No answer.

"Leontyne, time to practice your piano lessons."

"Coming, Mother!"

Six-year-old Leontyne Price did not mind leaving her friends and their game. She did not mind coming inside to practice her music lessons. In fact, she loved playing the piano.

When Leontyne was a young child in Laurel, Mississippi, it was clear that she had musical talent. Leontyne's mother wanted to do everything she could to develop her daughter's talent. She involved Leontyne in music at home, at school, and at church. Music soon was Leontyne's life.

Leontyne began taking piano lessons when she was five years old. She was six when she played in her first piano recital.

Until this time Leontyne's father had had little interest in her music lessons. But after hearing Leontyne perform, he helped Leontyne in every way he could.

A big surprise was waiting for Leontyne on her sixth birthday.

Her parents had saved enough money to buy a used piano. Finally Leontyne had a piano of her very own!

When Leontyne was nine years old, her mother took her to Jackson, Mississippi, to hear Marian Anderson. Marian Anderson was the first black singer to appear at New York City's Metropolitan Opera. Leontyne thought that Marian Anderson was wonderful. She decided that she wanted to be a singer like Marian Anderson.

When Leontyne entered Oak Park Vocational High School, she quickly became a leader at the school. Leontyne sang with the Oak Park choral group. She also played in many programs at school and at church. Before she finished high school, Leontyne gave a recital by herself, singing as well as playing the piano.

Leontyne was a part of many school activities. She was well liked by her teachers and classmates. She graduated with honors and was presented with a special music award.

Leontyne's mother and father

wanted Leontyne to continue her education. So plans were made for her to go to Wilberforce College in Ohio.

It was a day to remember when Leontyne boarded the train. She was leaving home for the first time to go to college. It was hard leaving her family, friends, and home. But Leontyne knew that she could not stay in Laurel and still hope to follow the plans she had made for her future.

When Leontyne began college, she had no idea of just how wonderful her voice really was. Her plan at that time was to finish school so she could teach music.

Her first voice coach at Wilberforce was pleased by how quickly Leontyne learned. She helped Leontyne get the special training needed to develop her voice in the right way.

During college Leontyne sang more and more. The college president thought she should try for a career in singing. Music teachers at the school also hoped that Leontyne would carry on with her training. After graduating from college, Leontyne won a scholarship to the well-known Juilliard School of Music in New York City.

Leontyne's parents were very happy when they heard about the scholarship. They were glad that Leontyne had been given such a chance. But they wondered how she could use it. With Leontyne's brother George now in college, they just did not have the money needed for their daughter's music career.

Help, however, came from some friends in Laurel. They gave the family enough money so that Leontyne could go to Juilliard to study music.

Shortly after entering Juilliard, Leontyne became very interested in opera. For four years she studied with her first formal voice teacher, who became her friend as well as her teacher.

Leontyne was in many of the school's concerts and operatic productions. During one of these performances, the composer Virgil Thomson heard her. He then asked her to sing in his opera *Four Saints in Three Acts*.

This short Broadway appearance went so well that Leontyne was signed for another part. She was asked to sing the role of Bess in George Gershwin's folk opera *Porgy and Bess*. After appearing in *Porgy and Bess*, Leontyne wanted more than ever to succeed in opera.

The next step in her career was to perform in an opera on television. She sang the lead in a television production of *Tosca*. Leontyne was picked for this role because she was the best singer for the part.

Leontyne made successful first-time appearances in operas in Europe. She won over audiences in Paris, Vienna, and London, as well as in the United States. Following these successes, Leontyne was invited to star at the Metropolitan Opera in New York City. The Metropolitan Opera is one of the greatest opera houses in the world.

That night at the Metropolitan Opera, Leontyne sang the role of Leonora in Verdi's *Il Trovatore*.[1] When she finished, she was given the longest round of applause in the Metropolitan Opera's history. The clapping lasted forty-two minutes. It must have been quite a thrill for the beautiful young black singer.

After her wonderful performance at the Metropolitan, Leontyne added another "first" to her list of accomplishments. She became the first black singer to have the honor of opening a Metropolitan Opera season.

Not very often in musical history has there been such an important event as the opening night at the new Metropolitan Opera House at Lincoln Center. One of America's greatest composers, Samuel Barber, wrote a new opera, *Antony and Cleopatra*, just for the occasion. Tickets quickly sold out. Many singers wanted the part of Cleopatra in this new work. But there was no question as to which singer

would be given the role. The choice was clear—Leontyne Price of Laurel, Mississippi!

Singing a leading role in one of the world's most famous opera houses on opening night is the hope of all singers. An even greater honor is to be chosen to open a new opera house. Few singers receive either honor. Fewer still receive both. Receiving both of these honors marked Leontyne Price as one of the greatest singers of all time.

Leontyne has been successful offstage, too. She has been given many awards and honors. In 1964 the Presidential Freedom Medal was given to her by President Lyndon B. Johnson. She

_____

[1][ĕl trō•vä•tôr′ä]

was the first opera singer to be so honored. In addition, she was given the Spingarn Medal for high achievement by a black American. She has also received many honorary degrees from leading universities.

Leontyne has been written about in magazines. Her recordings have won eighteen Grammy Awards from the National Academy of Recording Arts and Sciences. She also has three Emmy Awards for her work in television.

Leontyne gives many concerts to help other people. One of her concerts helped her mother's old school, Rust College in Mississippi, build a new library. To show its thanks for Leontyne's help, the college named the new library after her.

Leontyne Price had a strong wish to become a successful opera singer. This wish, along with her wonderful voice and personality, has led to her great success. The strength of character she has shown during her career marks her as one of America's great women.

1. Why did Leontyne Price decide to become a singer rather than a pianist?

2. Name three honors that Leontyne Price received for her musical ability.

3. Who do you think most helped Leontyne Price become a great singer?

4. What details on page 304 tell you that the opening of the new Metropolitan Opera House was an important event?

5. After she became a star, what did Leontyne Price do that showed she was grateful to her mother?

Apply

the

Skills

Which of the following sentences about Leontyne Price are characteristic of a biography? Look back at page 299 for help.

1. The Metropolitan Opera is one of the greatest opera houses in the world.

2. In 1964 the Presidential Freedom Medal was given to her by President Lyndon B. Johnson.

3. She also has three Emmy Awards for her work in television.

Prewrite

Often, before an award is given, someone delivers a short speech of introduction. Copy the following list and give other details of Leontyne Price's life that might be included in a speech introducing her.

1. born in Laurel, Mississippi
2. attended Oak Park Vocational High School
3. _____
4. _____
5. has sung in operas throughout the world
6. _____
7. is thought to be one of the greatest singers ever

Compose

Write a short speech introducing Leontyne Price. Use details from your list. Add other details that you need to complete your speech.

Revise

Read your speech to be sure that you have included all the details you need. If possible, read your speech aloud to a classmate. Revise your speech if changes are needed.

The Snow Has Come at Last

a Navaho poem selected by Flora Hood

The snow has come at last,
Coming down in soft flakes,
Caressing my face with tenderness
As if it were telling me,
You are the first I've touched.

And as I walk along,
The snowflakes seem to sing
A song that has never been heard,
A song that has never been sung,
Unheard, unsung, except in my heart.

A Central Eskimo Chant

selected by James Houston

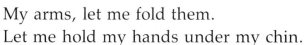

Ayii, ayii, ayii,
My arms, they wave high in the air,
My hands, they flutter behind my back,
They wave above my head
Like the wings of a bird.
Let me move my feet.
Let me dance.
Let me shrug my shoulders.
Let me shake my body.
Let me crouch down.
My arms, let me fold them.
Let me hold my hands under my chin.

This selection tells how a symphony with a surprise ending came to be written. Read to find out what the surprise was.

As you read, think about what makes this selection historical fiction.

The Boy Who Loved Music

by David Lasker

Karl was a young musician who played the horn in an orchestra. The orchestra entertained in the great European castle of Esterhaza [es′tər•hä•zä], which was owned by a wealthy Prince. The musicians were really the servants of the Prince. They had to do whatever the Prince wanted them to do. This was the way it was in the eighteenth century. If they wanted to leave the castle for any reason, they had to get permission from the Prince.

One year, the Prince decided to keep his orchestra at the castle longer than usual. This story tells how Karl and the other musicians felt when this happened. Based on a true story, it also tells how Joseph Haydn came to write the *Farewell* Symphony, in 1772.

Prince Nicolaus Esterhazy, the richest man in Hungary, owned many acres of land and dozens of castles. The largest was Esterhaza, the most beautiful castle in the Austrian Empire. The Prince liked it so well that even though it was a summer palace, he stayed there later and later each year. Summer ended and fall began. Yet the Prince would not return to Vienna, capital city of the Empire.

While the Prince stayed, Esterhaza's musicians, singers, actors, dancers, and painters stayed, too. They were lonely. The Prince did not let them visit their families. Only during those few months when he returned to his winter palace could they see their families.

Joseph Haydn, the famous composer, was the music director at Esterhaza. At a rehearsal one day in October 1772, he spoke to his musicians. "Gentlemen," he said, tapping his violin bow against his music stand, "I know you are all tired and homesick. This time the Prince has kept us here longer than ever before. But you know why: the Empress Maria Theresa will visit Esterhaza for a few days. We must play well for her during her visit. When she returns to Vienna, Prince Nicolaus will surely follow, and then we will go with him. Now, let us tune our instruments and begin the rehearsal."

Xavier, the bass viol player, was a tall man, but his instrument was taller. He winced as he turned the tuning pegs. The long strings were stretched so tightly that the pegs always slipped loose. He took longer to tune than anyone else, and the other musicians liked to joke about it.

"I'll bet you wish you played the piccolo," teased Karl, the young horn player.

Xavier was mad. "I've heard that one before, Karl, at least a hundred times," he said.

Suddenly cannons fired in the distance.

"The Empress! The Empress is coming!" said Haydn. "No time to rehearse now. Quick, gentlemen, to the gate."

The musicians took their instruments and rushed to their places near the gate that led to the Vienna road. Prince Nicolaus, in a golden chair carried by footmen, held a piece of lace cloth in his right hand. When he saw the Empress's party coming, he waved the cloth in the air. The great spectacle began.

The trumpets and drums played a rousing "ta-ran-ta-ra." One hundred and fifty grenadiers fired their muskets into the sky. People from the villages around Esterhaza crowded both sides of the road and cheered.

The royal coach stopped at the gate. Out stepped her Imperial Majesty, the Empress Maria Theresa. Her jewel-laden dress was so wide that she had to turn sideways to fit through the door of the coach.

The Prince led his guests to the palace, where they took time to rest from their trip. Later he entertained them with an opera. The musicians, led by Haydn, were placed between the audience and the singers on the stage.

As they played, they thought: Each note brings us closer to the end of another day. Each note brings us closer to Vienna and to our families and friends.

The following morning a servant shook Karl awake. "Get up," he said. "The Prince wants to go on a fox hunt."

"I wish I were home in Vienna instead of chasing a silly fox," Karl said sleepily.

"Don't argue with the Prince's orders," said the servant as he left.

Karl was angry at the Prince for staying at Esterháza so late into the fall. He was angry at himself for being a horn player.

Karl was the huntmaster, who rode at the head of the pack as it charged out of the castle grounds. He was needed to blow loud horn calls to the hounds, not to make music.

Karl used a small horn for hunting. Unlike his larger orchestral horn, it could sound only a few notes. Like many horn players of his time, Karl was afraid that someday his horse would leap forward, bang the horn's mouthpiece against his teeth, and knock them out. If that happened, he could never play the horn again.

After the hunt, Karl rushed to join the other musicians at lunch. He was dusty, sweaty, and out of breath. Xavier called out, "I'll bet you wish you played the bass." Everyone laughed, but Karl was angry.

"It's not fair!" he yelled, stamping his feet. "Prince Nicolaus has no right to keep us here this long!" The laughing stopped. Everyone felt as Karl did.

"It's late October," said Xavier. "I haven't seen my family for seven months."

Karl sat down and looked out the window. Toward the west was Vienna, where he and his father had played their horns together. There he had sung songs with his sisters and mother. "Oh," he said. "I wish I could say farewell to this place."

The Empress left, and only a few guests remained. After many days of activity, Esterhaza was quiet. A week passed, then two weeks. The days grew shorter and colder. The leaves dropped off the trees. But Prince Nicolaus was still at Esterhaza.

At last Haydn spoke to the Prince. He walked into the Prince's chamber and bowed deeply. "Exalted Prince, I kiss your noble hands. I beg you to hear this plea: When would it please Your Majesty to depart?"

The Prince, himself a musician, liked Haydn very much. When Haydn's house in Vienna had burned down, Prince Nicolaus had built him a larger one right away. He had never before kept his musicians away for so long; he knew how they felt. But to leave his lovely Esterhaza now? The peaceful gardens? The splashing fountains? He thought a moment and said quietly, "Haydn may tell our musicians that we shall leave Esterhaza when we wish it."

Haydn answered in the formal way that was expected of him. "Gracious lord and sire, I thank you for your kindness. I am now, and for my whole life will be, your most humble and obedient servant."

Karl met Haydn after Haydn's meeting with the Prince. Karl asked if the Prince was ready to leave. "Ready? I'm afraid we'll never get out of here," replied Haydn.

Then Karl noticed Baron von Scheffstoss, the Prince's secretary, at the head of the staircase. Without thinking, Karl ran up the marble steps.

"Honorable Baron, please ask the Prince to let us go home," Karl said breathlessly.

The Baron became stiff as a statue and red with rage. "How dare you!" he shouted. "Who do you think you are? I'll have you thrown into the dungeon! Now get out!" With that, he pushed Karl, who fell backward down the stairs.

Haydn, trying not to laugh, helped Karl up. "Don't you know better than to approach a nobleman like that?"

Karl brushed himself off. "Just trying to help," he said.

"That's not the way, Karl. Prince Nicolaus won't be won over by rudeness. We've got to do something that will amuse him. He'd like that."

"If all the musicians got up in the middle of your next performance and marched off to Vienna, *I'd* be amused," said Karl.

"Hmm. That's not bad! I like your idea, Karl. Let's give it a try."

A few days later the orchestra performed for Prince Nicolaus and his few remaining guests. They played the symphony Haydn had just written. It had a surprise ending.

Karl played a solo. Then, while the others went on playing, he blew out the candles alongside his music stand. He packed up his horn under his arm and walked off into the side room. Xavier did the same and carried off his heavy bass viol. They waited by the door and watched the Prince's surprised face.

One by one, the musicians left. Only a few violinists and cellists remained. The sound of this small group was much softer than that of the full orchestra. A great stillness settled over the room. The music told the Prince how the musicians felt: homesick and lonely.

More players finished and joined the others. Soon only Haydn and Tomasini, the first violinist, were left. Finally they, too, put out their candles and withdrew. The symphony was over.

Prince Nicolaus stood up. "What a wonderful symphony! Congratulations, Haydn," he said. Then he turned to his guests and announced, "If they all leave, we may as well leave, too."

"Bravo! Hooray for Haydn!" the musicians cheered, shaking hands and slapping backs. Xavier and Tomasini lifted Haydn onto their shoulders.

Karl blew a loud horn call and they happily marched back to their rooms.

They all left for Vienna the next day.

1. What was the surprise ending to the *Farewell* Symphony?

2. Why did the musicians want to leave Esterhaza?

3. Where on page 317 does the author give a clue to how the selection will end?

4. Which did Karl enjoy more, being the hunt-master or playing in the orchestra? Explain.

5. How was Haydn responsible for Prince Nicolaus's decision to return to Vienna?

Historical fiction helps us understand what life was like in the past. Which of the following sentences from "The Boy Who Loved Music" help us understand what life was like in Hungary during the eighteenth century? Explain each answer.

1. The musicians were really the servants of the Prince.

2. Karl sat down and looked out the window.

3. "I'll have you thrown into the dungeon."

4. "The Prince wants to go on a fox hunt."

Prewrite

Karl probably thought of different ways to return home to Vienna. Pretend you are Karl. What might you do to get back to Vienna? Copy the list of ideas below and add at least two more ideas.

Ways to Get Home
1. run away from Esterhaza
2. play the horn poorly and be asked to leave
3.
4.

Compose

Write a paragraph describing one of the ideas you have listed. Include each step that would be needed to turn your idea into a plan that could really work.

Revise

Read your work carefully. Make sure you have enough details to support your idea. If your work needs revision, make any changes that are needed.

Advertisements

Advertisements have two main purposes. One is to **inform,** and the other is to **persuade.** An advertisement that informs tells you facts about a product or service. An advertisement that persuades tries to convince you that you need what is being offered. Many advertisements both inform and persuade.

Advertisements, sometimes called *ads,* can be very helpful. They can help people to find jobs and places to live. They can also help people to locate products and services that they need. Ads also give people more choices. If you read several ads from different companies for the same product or service, you can make a better decision about what to buy.

Read the following ad. Notice the information it gives.

Variety Brings the Birds!

Our new Variety Bird Feeder is made of strong materials top and bottom. The feeder has three separate compartments to allow for three different kinds of seed. Each compartment will hold a liter of seed. The feeder is 40 centimeters high. It can be either hung from a tree or mounted on a post.
Old Country Store. $24.95

Through reading the ad for the bird feeder, what information did you learn? You were told the name of the product, and you were given a description of it. What else were you told? You were told where you could buy it and how much it costs. This kind of advertisement mainly informs the reader.

Some advertisements do more than give you information. They also try to persuade you to buy or use the product. This happens especially when there are a number of products in competition with each other.

Read this ad for True-View Binoculars. Look for the information it gives. Notice how it tries to persuade you.

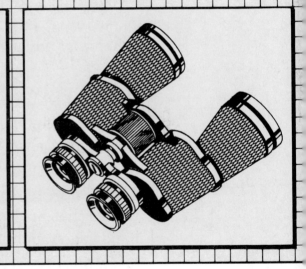

True-View Binoculars!

True-View Binoculars, made of the finest quality materials, will make your world a close-up. Amazing high-powered lenses will zoom you up to the details of a leaf on a distant tree. You will be delighted! A handy carrying case comes with every pair.
Only $99.95 at Dell's Camera Shop.

This advertisement does give information. It tells you a little about the binoculars. It says you get a carrying case. It tells you where you can buy the product and how much it costs. However, this ad does more than that. It also tries to persuade you to buy the binoculars.

How Advertisements Persuade

How can an advertisement try to persuade you to buy something? One way is by using descriptive words such as *finest, amazing, zoom,* and *handy,* as in the True-View Binoculars ad. An item made of "the finest quality materials" sounds more impressive than an item made of "quality materials." An "amazing high-powered lens" sounds better than a "high-powered lens." It is probably not any better.

The ad for True-View Binoculars also says that you will be delighted with the binoculars. How can anyone know that you will be delighted? This is the advertiser's opinion, and it may not be a fact.

While this ad does give information, it does more persuading than informing. Now let's look at another way advertisers try to persuade you.

The Bandwagon Approach

You may have heard the old expression "get on the bandwagon." To get on the **bandwagon** means to join in with what everyone else is doing. Advertisers know that people want to be in step with things that are going on. That is why they use the bandwagon approach.

Do you need a Robot Pen or a Rocket Recorder? Do you even know what they are? You probably do not, but imagine that you see these headlines on two different ads:

Don't Be the Last One to Get a Robot Pen!
You Mean You Still Don't Have a Rocket Recorder?

If these headlines make you feel as if you are going

to be left out of things unless you have a Robot Pen or a Rocket Recorder, then you are being persuaded by bandwagon advertising.

Advertisers sometimes use bandwagon advertising in another way. Instead of trying to make you feel left out, they suggest that you should have something because everyone else does. An ad with this approach might say: "All your friends have Robot Pens" or "Everybody records with a Rocket!"

Sometimes an ad praises one product at the expense of another. Look at the following example:

In our recent test, 88% of the students in the fourth grade chose Robot Pens over Ever Writers.

This is an example of the bandwagon approach because it tells you that a great number of people have chosen one product over another.

Remember that advertisements are useful and important to people who need products and services. Because many similar products are competing for your dollars, advertisers try to persuade you to buy *their* product or service instead of the others. Read every advertisement carefully to be sure you are getting all the information you need to make a good decision. Notice whether or not you are being persuaded, and if you are, notice how. If you read ads carefully, you will not be persuaded unless you *want* to be.

Read to find out why audiences especially enjoy performances by this famous musician.

As you read, try to decide what makes this newspaper article different from the other selections in this unit.

Center City Post

Itzhak Perlman: Violinist for All People

by Stephen Wigler

OF THE CENTER CITY POST STAFF

CENTER CITY, MAY 7—Every year Itzhak Perlman travels around the world to play his violin. No matter what country he is in, many people want to hear him play. When Itzhak Perlman appears in concert, every seat in the hall is filled.

This does not surprise anyone who knows the Perlman story. For many years, people have lined up to hear him. After he plays, halls echo with loud cheers. No other violinist in the world gets such cheers.

Part of the reason for the cheers is that people love Itzhak Perlman. When Perlman plays, he makes people think that he's playing just for them. They react to him the way they would to a close friend. He brings joy to his listeners.

Itzhak Perlman first appeared in the United States as a thirteen-year-old prodigy on television's *Ed Sullivan Show.* Millions of people watched that night. They fell in love with the Israeli boy on crutches who played so beautifully. They have never stopped loving him.

Even if people did not love him so much, Itzhak Perlman would still be one of the world's greatest musicians. He plays everything wonderfully. He can play short, crowd-pleasing pieces or long, difficult ones.

It is hard to say why Itzhak Perlman has such extraordinary appeal. Perlman himself says that there are violinists who play as well as he does, or even better. However, no other violinist seems to be as lovable. With his short, rounded build and thick, curly hair, he looks like a teddy bear. He has been a favorite on TV talk shows, and he has appeared in several TV advertisements. Some people think that Perlman is the world's most popular violinist because he appears on TV so much.

However, that is not the real reason. Itzhak Perlman shows something to an audience that other violinists do not: love of playing the instrument.

The violin is one of the most treacherous instruments to play, yet it does not seem to be hard for Itzhak Perlman. Violinists who may have as much skill as Perlman just do not seem to enjoy playing as much.

Itzhak Perlman seems to be having a good time onstage, and he wants his audience to have a good time, too. When he plays with an orchestra, he always works out a *shtick* with the concertmaster, or head

violinist. A *shtick* is a planned joke.

The joke goes like this:

Perlman hands his violin to the concertmaster before walking offstage. When he returns to play an encore, or extra piece, Perlman asks for his violin. The concertmaster hands Perlman his own violin. He keeps Perlman's priceless Stradivarius for himself. Perlman looks as if he is about to play. Then suddenly he sees that the violin is not his. Perlman makes believe he is angry, and grabs his violin back from the concertmaster. The audience always claps and cheers.

Perlman once explained why he plays jokes on the stage that do not have anything to do with music.

"When I go out to play," Perlman said, "I never say to myself that I have to make this audience love me. I love to play music, and people catch that and enjoy it.

"The thing is this: The minute there is something not normal, like a joke, it makes the audience feel good. And it makes me feel good to make people have a nicer time. I talk to people at concerts; I try to reach them. A lot of people think they are not supposed to have a good time at a concert. I think they should. I like to make people feel, 'Hey, I've gotten to know this man.'"

Even when Perlman gives concerts without an orchestra, he makes his audience feel at home. He makes jokes with his old friend, Samuel Sanders, who accompanies him on the piano. He loves to make people laugh. He even jokes about the problem that makes him walk on crutches.

Once, after agreeing to meet with a newspaper writer, he stood the writer up. When Perlman called the writer the next day, he said he was sorry. Then he joked, "I never really stand anyone up. I *sit* them up."

Perlman developed polio at the age of four. Only in the last few years has he been able to joke, or even talk, about his disability.

The same strong will that kept Itzhak Perlman playing the violin when he was a very sick little boy still shows now when he plays. He walks across the stage leaning on crutches. It is not easy for him. His legs are in braces. When he plays, he does so sitting down.

People wrote about Perlman in the 1960's and 1970's when he first came to this country. They always talked about what a great player he was even though he had a disability. This made Perlman angry.

"All the writers talked about how brave I was," he once said. " 'He walked across the stage barely able to move,' they said." After a while, however, the writers didn't talk about his disability anymore.

"Then I got mad that they had forgotten. I realized that I had become so well-known that I could do some good. Now every time I speak to a writer, I bring up the problems that the disabled face. I've come full circle."

A lot of people, Perlman said, are afraid of disability. "People don't like to look trouble in the face. It's not pretty. But it's human."

Perlman has done a lot more than talk about the problems of the disabled. Everywhere he plays, he tries to make concert halls easier for disabled people to enter and move around in. He doesn't like the halls in which someone has to take his wheelchair up the steps. He talks to friends who are architects about how to make things easier for the disabled. He wants disabled people to be able to take elevators from floor to floor.

Of course, Perlman does not think about these problems when he is onstage. When Perlman sits down to play, his face shows nothing but happiness.

It is hard to believe that any human being could be so happy. "Sure I am," Perlman has said. "You can't fake that. And if I'm very happy, why should I hide it?"

That may be why people love Perlman so much. During the two hours that his concerts last, audiences share his joy in being alive.

There is one thing in his life that most of Perlman's audiences cannot share: his disability. To help them understand disability better, he wishes that they could experience it.

"They should spend a week on crutches or in a wheelchair," he has said, "and try to do their work."

In spite of the difficulties, Itzhak Perlman will keep on working. He loves playing music too much to stop.

1. Give three reasons why audiences enjoy Itzhak Perlman's performances.

2. How did Itzhak Perlman begin his career in the United States?

3. How does Perlman help other disabled people to enjoy his concerts?

4. Why do you think Perlman was upset when writers stopped talking about his disability?

5. What did you read that makes you think that Itzhak Perlman might make a good actor?

Apply
the
Skills

1. What makes this newspaper article about Itzhak Perlman different from a biography?

2. Read the following advertisement for a television appearance by Itzhak Perlman. Which words are used to persuade?

Tonight, the amazing violinist Itzhak Perlman will be a guest on *Music Hour*. Tune in to watch a lively interview with this master musician. Don't miss it!

Prewrite

Interviewing is one way to get firsthand information about a person. Before an interview, a good reporter prepares a list of questions to bring out all the needed information. The questions below might be used to interview someone who wants to be President of the United States. Add two more questions to this list.

1.	Why do you want to be President?
2.	Why should people vote for you?
3.	
4.	

Compose

Write a list of questions that you might ask Itzhak Perlman if you were a reporter. You might choose to interview him about his disability, his childhood, how he pleases an audience, or some topic of your own.

Revise

Be sure each question you have written fits the topic you have chosen. Revise any question that does not fit the topic.

Sequence

Read the following paragraph. Something is missing. What is it?

Most of the people in California were American Indians and Mexicans. Gold was discovered. People from all over the United States rushed to California. One hundred thousand miners were living in California.

The paragraph mentions several events, but it does not tell you when these events took place. Therefore, you have no clues to the **sequence,** or time order, of the events. Knowing the time order would help you understand how the events are related.

Now read the same paragraph rewritten with time-order clues. Notice how the clues connect the events.

In the early 1800's, most of the people in California were American Indians and Mexicans. Then, in 1848, gold was discovered. Suddenly, people from all over the United States rushed to California. By the end of 1849, one hundred thousand miners were living in California.

The time-order clues in this paragraph include dates and time words. Both kinds of clues help explain how events are connected.

Clues to Time Order: Dates

Writers often use dates to show time order. A date may be general, such as *Thursday* or *September* or *1606,* or it may be specific, such as *Saturday, August 26, 1978.*

Read the following paragraphs. As you read, think of the dates as clues to what you are reading. Notice how the dates help to connect the events and show how things happened.

There are many interesting stories about baseball. One story is about Johnny Vander Meer, a pitcher for the Cincinnati Reds.

The story takes place in 1938. In a game against the Boston Bees on Saturday, June 11, Johnny pitched a no-hit game. Not one Boston batter made a hit.

Four days later, on June 15, Johnny was pitching again. His team was playing against the Brooklyn Dodgers. This was a special game. It was the first baseball game to be played in Brooklyn at night. This game was also special for another reason. Johnny Vander Meer pitched his second no-hitter in a row.

The paragraphs you just read contain several dates. These dates give clues about things that happened. For example, in what year did Johnny Vander Meer pitch his two no-hitters? The answer, of course, is 1938. You read that his first no-hit game occurred on Saturday, June 11. Can you figure out what day of the week his second no-hitter occurred? Since it was four days later, the answer must be Wednesday.

Clues to Time Order: Time Words

In addition to dates, writers often use time words to show how events are related. Some of these time-order word clues are *before, after, then, next, now, at first, suddenly, earlier, while, during, already,* and *today.* These words do not give exact times, but they do help you figure out the time order.

The following paragraph contains both dates and time words. As you read it, use both kinds of time clues to help you understand the time order.

Most people today remember Babe Ruth as a famous baseball player. Only a few people remember that he was once in the movies. In 1942, Babe Ruth played himself in *Pride of the Yankees,* the first big baseball movie ever made. Babe had played himself in a few earlier movies, but none of these did as well as *Pride of the Yankees.* The second big baseball movie was about Babe Ruth himself. Babe did not act in the movie, but he did see it in July 1948. A month later, while *The Babe Ruth Story* was still playing in theaters, Babe Ruth died.

Notice how the time words and dates in the paragraph help you follow the order of events. Was *Pride of the Yankees* the first movie in which Babe Ruth acted? What time clue helps you find the answer?

Knowing the time order of certain events can help you discover other information that is not given directly. Use the dates and time-order clues in the paragraph to answer this question: In what month and year did Babe Ruth die?

Textbook Application: Time Order in Social Studies

Read the following article about how a young American Indian woman helped a group of explorers. As you read, use dates and time words to follow the order of events. The sidenotes will help you.

She was only 16 years old at the time of her greatest adventure. She was a **Shoshone** (shuh SHOH nee) Indian. At her death in 1812 only a few people knew her name. Today we know **Sacajawea** (sa kuh juh WEE uh) as an American hero who helped our country grow from coast to coast.

> This date gives you a general idea of the historical time period in which Sacajawea lived.

Why was Sacajawea important? Let's go back hundreds of years before she was born. People from Europe were exploring America then. They could travel only as far as the Rocky Mountains. The high, rugged mountains were a huge wall blocking the way. It would take many years before the region could be settled.

> This is a clue that you are about to be given some background information.

The Spanish came first. Spanish settlers pushed north from Mexico in the 1700's. Next came French fur traders from Canada. They found many Indian tribes living here. Yet Americans in the

> Notice how the dates and time words in this paragraph tell you the order of events.

East knew very little about the Rocky Mountains in the early 1800's. Was it possible to take a wagon through the mountains? Could a person go by river from the Atlantic to the Pacific? No one could say for sure.

Lewis and Clark

President Thomas Jefferson sent two men to find out. Their names were **Meriwether Lewis** and **William Clark.** Lewis and Clark with a small group of men left St. Louis, Missouri, in May 1804. They spent the summer and fall going up the Missouri River. In November they stopped at an Indian village to spend the winter. The village lay at the edge of the Rocky Mountains. The hardest part of their journey was just ahead.

Sacajawea now enters our story. She was the slave of a trapper staying at the village. Lewis and Clark hired the trapper to help them find a way through the mountains. Sacajawea joined them because she could speak to the Indians.

Across the Rockies

In the spring the party started up the Missouri again. One day one of their

This time clue tells you when Lewis and Clark's group started up the Missouri River. Use clues from earlier paragraphs to figure out what year it was.

boats tipped over. All their goods fell into the icy water. Sacajawea did not waste a moment. She jumped in and saved almost everything.

Now the party was in the mountains near Shoshone country. Lewis and Clark set up a meeting with the Shoshones to buy horses from the Indians. The Shoshones did not want to sell their horses. Sacajawea stepped forward. The Shoshone chief gasped in surprise. Sacajawea was his sister! He had not seen her in five years.

Sacajawea persuaded her brother to sell the horses. The Shoshones also helped guide the group through the mountains.

Lewis and Clark reached the Pacific after much suffering. Then they turned around and made the same trip back. They traveled 8,000 miles (about 12,900 km). The trip took them nearly three years! They had gone from the Mississippi River to the Pacific Ocean, opening up the land to Americans. Sacajawea had helped them do it.

—*States and Regions*, Harcourt Brace Jovanovich

You read earlier that the starting date of the trip was in May 1804. Use the time clue in this paragraph to determine about what year it was when the group finished their trip.

Reading about a series of events can sometimes be confusing, especially when the events are not described in order. As you read, remember to use time clues to help you place events in their proper order.

As you read this autobiography, notice how some of the artist's early life is reflected in her artwork.

Time-order clues will help you follow the order of events as you read about the artist's experiences as a child and as a young adult.

Self-Portrait: Trina Schart Hyman

by Trina Schart Hyman

The author, Trina Schart Hyman, is a well-known artist. She has won awards and honors for her illustration of children's books. She drew the pictures in this selection.

Trina Schart Hyman usually expresses herself through her colorful drawings. In this selection she also paints pictures with words. As you read, you will see that the author's language and her art are both colorful.

The Farm

I was born forty-two years ago in Philadelphia, Pennsylvania. We lived out in the country about twenty miles north of the city. Our house was in one of the very first housing "developments" built during the Second World War. It was a little square brick house on a corner of new green grass. My father planted a tiny willow tree and a golden ash in the front lawn. My mother made a big garden in the backyard.

Those six blocks of new houses seemed out of place. The rest of the landscape was open, grassy fields, some thick patches of woods, hidden rocky streams, and just a few old houses. The old houses had lawns so richly green and soft, and trees so big and gnarled and ancient, that I knew that they all belonged rightfully in their places.

The farm was the oldest of the old places. It was set back from the road. You could see it from the corner of our yard. Even so, you had to walk the length of two fields and then down a long avenue of trees before you could get to the house.

A WALK TO THE FARM TO BUY EGGS, IN 1942

It was a long, low, stone farmhouse with at least forty rooms, three chimneys, and a slate roof. It had an enormous stone barn, a mossy spring house, and a hidden rock garden. It also had several flower gardens, a large vegetable garden, and a lovely pond fed by ancient springs. It had horses, cows, chickens, geese, sheep, goats, and lots of dogs and cats.

The barn was always filled with hay. It was a dark, sweet, dusty landscape that reached four stories high. The deep, rich smell of animals and drying clover was so thick it seemed touchable, like velvet. The people who owned the farm were the King and Queen to me.

The Queen wore farmers' overalls, heavy boots, faded shirts, an old sailor's hat, and beautiful old rings on her long fingers. She was always darkly tanned. She had a bony face and a smile with long white teeth. She was an artist. She painted pictures of people who were as mysterious as she.

I can remember one of the first drawings I worked on. It was of the Queen with a big basket of eggs on her arm. I didn't think her overalls were pretty. So I drew her in a beautiful long dress with lots of little egg-shaped polka dots.

I never saw the King. I learned later that he was a farmer and an archaeologist. He spent most of his time in faraway countries.

One spring, years later, when I was in art school, the farm was sold. Men and machines came and tore it down. They ripped up the grand old trees and burned them in a big fire. They smashed the old stone walls. They beat on the solid old barn, with its families of rats and birds, until it finally collapsed and died. Then they plowed it under with their bulldozers.

I SHOW THE QUEEN MY DRAWING.

I learned something that day. I learned that everything changes, and nothing is safe. I still have dreams about the farm. It was my first kingdom and, in a way, my first real home.

Little Red Riding Hood

I was a really strange little kid. I was born scared of anything and everything that moved or spoke. I was afraid of people, especially. I was afraid of all people — kids my own age, all grownups, even my own family. I was afraid of dogs (until my parents bought me a puppy of my own), horses, trees, grass, cars, and streets. I was afraid of the stars and the wind. Who knows why?

My mother is a beautiful woman with red hair and the piercing blue gaze of a hawk. She never seemed afraid of anyone or anything. It was she who gave me the courage to draw and a love of books. She read to me from the time I was a baby. Once, when I was three or four, she was reading my favorite story. Suddenly the words on the page, her spoken words, and the pictures in my head fell together in a blinding flash. I could read!

The story was *Little Red Riding Hood*. It was so much a part of me that I really became Little Red Riding Hood. My mother sewed me a red cape with a hood that I put on almost every day. On those days, she would make me a "basket of goodies" to take to my grandmother's house. (My only grandmother lived in Rhode Island, three hundred miles away. That didn't matter, though.) I'd take the basket and carefully walk through the backyard, "going to Grandmother's house." My dog, Tippy, was the wolf.

My Father and the Museum

My father worked as a plumbing and heating supplies salesman. He loved music and singing, walking quietly in the woods, and fly-fishing. He could play almost any musical instrument. The one he played most often was a concertina. A concertina is like an accordion. It was beautiful, with inlaid pearl and wood designs on it. He played the harmonica, too. Sometimes he played both at once, holding the harmonica on a brace around his neck.

He also told the best stories. When I was a tiny little girl and still afraid of the stars, he sometimes took me for walks at night. He told me long, magical stories about the stars and of the many gods who created the universe.

I had to have braces on my teeth for nine years. So my father drove me into the city to the dentist every Saturday morning. I'm sure he would much rather have spent the time fishing the quiet backwaters that he loved. But for me, those city trips were journeys into a magical kingdom.

Some Saturdays, after the dentist, I got to go to the Philadelphia Art Museum. I should have been afraid of that grand building, but I wasn't. I loved it. I loved the halls full of paintings. I loved the tapestries and glass and wood. I even loved the furniture that the artists who had done the paintings must have used or known!

There's a little painting by Brueghel [broō'gəl] in a corner of a hallway. It shows a fat man with red stockings, running, running. His hands are clutching at his hat and his satchel. He is running away from a hillside full of sheep! Why?

There is a dark tree to the far right of the painting. A bird is perched on the only branch in a yellow sky. I could feel his fear. Why is the man so afraid? If you look closely, there is a wolf in with the sheep, sneaking closer and closer. Oh no! He's really Little Red Riding Hood! Oh, Brueghel, I love you.

School

In school, I couldn't ever concentrate on what I was supposed to be learning. All I wanted to do was to be left alone. I wanted to read books or listen to music, or to draw pictures of witches and princesses. I should have been learning fractions.

After I finished high school, I went to art school in Philadelphia. Then everything changed. Suddenly, I was not only *allowed* to draw all day long, I was *expected* to! I was surrounded by other artists all day. We talked, ate, lived, and dreamed about art. It was as though I had been living, all my life, in a strange country. There I could never quite fit in—and now I had come home.

THE PIGEON LADIES: 1958

After the first year of basic drawing, painting, print-making, and design classes, I majored in illustration. My best friend, Barbara, was an illustration major, too. Barbara and I went everywhere together. We'd walk all over the city. We'd draw everything we would see: people, streets, doorways, subways, trees, piles of trash. If we discovered a "new" street, we were as excited as if we'd found a new world.

Whenever we had any free time, we'd walk to the art museum. We'd wander through its miles of beautiful rooms and quiet halls, looking at paintings and drawing from them. And every day for lunch, rain or shine, we went to Rittenhouse Square. We took our sketch books, hamburgers, and a big box of saltines for the pigeons. We were comrades. We were *artists*. Everything was exciting and beautiful. We loved it all.

1. What important people in Trina's early life are reflected in her drawings?

2. What would Trina rather have been doing in school instead of learning fractions?

3. Why do you think Trina liked the painting by Brueghel so much?

4. Find the sentence in the story that tells what Trina learned the day the farmhouse was torn down.

5. Trina Schart Hyman began drawing at an early age. How does she use this talent today?

Read the following paragraph from the selection. How many years pass in this paragraph? What are the clues to time order?

"My mother . . . read to me from the time I was a baby. Once, when I was three or four, she was reading my favorite story. Suddenly the words on the page, her spoken words, and the pictures in my head fell together in a blinding flash. I could read!"

Prewrite

On pages 345-46, Trina Schart Hyman describes a painting by the artist Brueghel. Using her description, you can imagine what it might look like. Copy the chart below. Fill in other descriptive words and phrases about the painting.

Painting by Brueghel
1. fat man with red stockings running
2. hillside full of sheep
3.
4.

Compose

Choose one picture from the selection and write a paragraph describing it. Describe characters, location, and events shown. Use details to make your description as complete as possible.

Revise

Read your description. Does it give a clear idea of what the picture looks like? If not, add more details.

Wind Circles

by Aileen Fisher

Without a pen,
without a hand,
without a pair of glasses,

The broken stalks
so bent and tanned
among the scattered grasses

Draw curves and circles
in the sand
with every wind that passes.

And *I*
can't draw them half as grand
in school, in drawing classes.

A pan of gingerbread and a slide trombone cause problems between the king and queen in this folktale. Read to find out how the problems are finally solved.

As you read, think about what makes this folktale so humorous.

The Queen Who Couldn't Bake Gingerbread

by Dorothy Van Woerkom

King Pilaf of Mulligatawny was having a very bad day. To begin with, he bumped his head against the Lord Chamberlain's upon getting out of bed. Then he discovered a hole in the heel of his stocking that was the size of a marble. And he knew without asking that his breakfast gingerbread would be crumbly again.

The King sat on the edge of his bed with his thumb through the hole in his stocking.

"It is time," he said to the Lord Chamberlain, "that Mulligatawny had a Queen and I a wife. She must be beautiful enough to please me. She must be wise enough to help me rule—and to find me a tailor who knows how to *mend*."

The Lord Chamberlain slipped the King's stocking over the Royal foot.

"A splendid idea, your Majesty!" he said. "By happy chance I was thinking the very same thing myself. As a matter of fact . . ."

The King wagged his foot under the Lord Chamberlain's nose and sighed loudly. "Not one of your speeches so early in the day, my Lord. Just help me into my boots, and let's have some breakfast."

So they drank their lime juice and ate cheese omelets, with gingerbread that crumbled. The King frowned at the crumbs on his plate and said, "My Queen must be *more* than just wise and beautiful. She must also know how to bake gingerbread."

Now it was the Lord Chamberlain who sighed. For when Pilaf became King, he had turned Mulligatawny inside out to find a gingerbread baker.

"There isn't one in my kingdom who can bake it to a turn," the King was saying. "It should be neither too hard nor too soft, but just properly crisp."

Then the King called for their horses, and away they rode to the kingdom of Ghur, where there lived a princess as wise as she was beautiful. Her name was Madelon.

"No, I cannot bake gingerbread," Princess Madelon said. "But I make perfect little almond cakes."

King Pilaf thought about that: a Queen both wise and beautiful, who could make pretty cakes. But at last he shook his head sadly, and kissed Princess Madelon's hand.

"I'm sorry to say that it must be gingerbread," he said.

Then off he galloped with the Lord Chamberlain to the kingdom of Shoggen.

Here lived a Princess who was not as wise as she was beautiful. Her name was Jebelle.

"No, I cannot bake gingerbread," said Princess Jebelle. "But I can bake the best zwieback that you will ever taste."

Princess Jebelle would make a beautiful Queen. But *zwieback*—no, the King could never like zwieback at all.

"I'm sorry to say that it must be gingerbread," he said.

King Pilaf kissed her hand and rode away with his Chamberlain to the kingdom of Tintinnabulum.

Here lived a Princess who was not as beautiful as she was wise. Her name was Calliope.

"Ah, King Pilaf!" Princess Calliope cried, as the King strode into her chamber. "You are, I suppose, seeking a wife?"

"I am, indeed, your Highness. A wife who can bake gingerbread and who . . ."

"Oh no, I *never* bake gingerbread. But I am seeking a husband. He must be as kind as he is handsome, and he must know how to play the slide trombone."

For a moment the King's mouth made an "O" like the hole in the heel of his stocking.

"I cannot play the slide trombone," he said at last. "But I can shoot an arrow as straight as the tail of a comet." He took a deep breath.

"Then I'm sorry to say," said the Princess, "that the husband for me is the man who can play the slide trombone."

Her smile made him wish he could say, "Yes, I can!" But all he could do was bow himself out, and take to his horse once again.

Now, in every single kingdom it was the same: no one at all could bake a proper gingerbread. King Pilaf kissed the hand of the very last Princess. He called for his horse and rode home with his Chamberlain, to brood.

After quite a long while (a hole had now appeared in the heel of his other stocking—and he had never felt so lonely, besides!) he said, "Lord Chamberlain, it is plain to see that I must do without gingerbread. Go back to the kingdom of Ghur and ask the Princess Madelon if she will marry me. She is as wise as she is beautiful, and perhaps in time I can learn to like almond cakes."

When the Lord Chamberlain arrived in Ghur, he found the kingdom prepared for a wedding. The Princess was going to marry the King of Rocky Knob Island!

"Well," said King Pilaf, when he heard about this, "you must go to the kingdom of Shoggen. Princess Jebelle is not as wise as she is beautiful, but perhaps in time I can learn to like zwieback."

The Lord Chamberlain soon returned with news that Princess Jebelle had left a note on her crown for her father. She had run off to marry a sourdough baker and was baking miles of zwieback.

King Pilaf surprised the Lord Chamberlain by dancing a jig when he heard about Princess Jebelle.

"To tell you the truth, my Lord," he said, "I like Princess Calliope best. She is not as beautiful, of course, as she is wise. But then what chance have I, since I cannot play on the slide trombone?"

"As a matter of fact," the Lord Chamberlain said, "I was thinking of Princess Calliope, too. She is, as you say, very wise. Perhaps she knows what can be done."

"Excellent advice!" cried the King. "I shall go to see her at once."

When Princess Calliope heard why King Pilaf had come, she said, "Let me think about this. I am sure we can come to some sort of agreement."

He paced up and down outside of her chamber, until at last she came to the door.

"It seems to me," she said with a bow, "that a husband who is as kind as he is handsome is more to be loved than one who can play on the slide trombone."

"And a wife who is wise," the King said quickly, "as well as—er—beautiful, does not need to know how to bake gingerbread."

They clasped hands together, and Calliope said, "Then let us add this to our marriage vows: We must never again mention *slide trombone* . . ."

"Or *gingerbread!*" he finished, with a laugh that shook the walls of the castle.

They lived happily together for nearly a year, and ruled their kingdom as well as anyone could.

Then one day, everything went wrong. The King dropped the crown on his foot, and the Queen awoke with a headache. The Lord Chamberlain was ill, and the cook slept late. The court painter put his head through their Majesties' new portrait, and the Queen's dog chewed up all the paintbrushes. Outside, it snowed one minute and rained the next.

The King was angry; the Queen was cross. They quarrelled all day.

"I wish," the King shouted, "that you could bake gingerbread! Then *something* would be right about this terrible day."

"And why," cried the Queen, "can't *you* play on the slide trombone? It would certainly help to calm my nerves!"

They glared at each other with anger and spite. The forbidden words had been said, their marriage vows broken.

They both turned around and swept from the room, to the opposite ends of their castle.

They stayed there for days, feeling grumpy and sorry for themselves. Servants left food on trays near their doors, then scampered away before the doors might open.

The citizens of Mulligatawny began to ask each other, "What has gone wrong at the castle?"

At last, Queen Calliope looked at herself in her mirror. "The King married me because I was wise, not beautiful," she said. "Now, was it wise to shout *slide trombone* at him?"

It was not. She sent for the Lord Chamberlain.

At the other end of the castle, King Pilaf was trying to shave himself. "With that nose and those eyes," he said to the King in the mirror, "you are not nearly so handsome as you like to believe."

He wiped blood from the cut on his chin. "Why, the Queen married me because she thought I was kind! Was it kind to shout *gingerbread?*"

He struck off the last whisker and sent for the Lord Chamberlain.

Before very long, from one end of the castle came the odor of scorched pots. From the other came sounds like an elephant blowing its nose. The servants rushed in one direction holding their ears; in the other they rushed holding their breath.

The citizens of Mulligatawny thought the world was coming to an end.

But then, in the middle of one night, the smells grew sweeter. At the very same time, the sounds became more tuneful. The servants hurried about with noses high in the air to smell the delicious smells. They paused in their work to hear the sweet sounds.

The citizens of Mulligatawny began to hope for the future.

At last, the Lord Chamberlain announced that their Majesties would come from their opposite sides of the castle and meet in the Great Hall.

With a blast of trumpets, the door at one end of the Great Hall swung open. In marched the King, with an apron around his middle, a baker's hat on his head, and flour on his nose. He carried a pan of the most perfect gingerbread that had ever been baked in his kingdom — or in any other.

Without any sound at all, the doors at the other end of the Great Hall opened. Through them stepped the Queen. She raised a slide trombone to her lips, and played such a melody that even the nightingales hushed.

From that day, the first sound heard each morning in Mulligatawny was Queen Calliope's slide trombone. The first scent was that of King Pilaf's fresh gingerbread. It became the custom of the citizens to awake at sunrise, to sniff, and to listen. Their noses and their ears would tell them if all was still well in the kingdom.

To the end of their days, they were never disappointed.

1. How did the King and Queen finally solve their problem?

2. What was King Pilaf looking for in a Queen?

3. Name three things that happened on the day that everything went wrong at the castle.

4. Do you think the Lord Chamberlain was an important character in the story? Explain.

5. When did you first begin to think that Queen Calliope was sorry that she and the King had quarreled? What did the Queen say to make you think that?

Apply

the

Skills

Folktales are a very old type of fiction. As storytellers have passed these stories on, more and more details have been added and new versions invented. Many folktales are humorous, such as "The Queen Who Couldn't Bake Gingerbread." Name three things in the story that you think are humorous, and explain why you think so.

Prewrite

The chart below lists the qualities that the King wanted his future Queen to have. Copy the chart and complete it by listing the qualities that Princess Calliope wanted in a husband.

The King wanted:	The Princess wanted:
1. a wise queen	**1.**
2. a beautiful queen	**2.**
3. a queen who could bake perfect gingerbread	**3.**

Compose

Think about the qualities listed on your chart. Write a paragraph to answer the following questions: Which of these qualities were the King and the Princess willing to do without? Which qualities were the most important? Why?

Revise

Check your work carefully. Be sure that your paragraph has a main idea and you have answered all the questions. Revise your paragraph if necessary.

SQ3R

Would you be surprised to learn that there is a study plan that works well and doesn't take a long time? You might even be surprised to learn that it works well for many students in all of their subjects. This plan will both give you good results and help you to use your study time in the best way. The plan is called SQ3R.

What is SQ3R? **SQ3R** is a five-step plan that will help you to organize your study time and remember more of what you study. The *S* and *Q* stand for *survey* and *question.* The three *R*'s stand for *read, recite,* and *review.*

What can SQ3R do for you? This plan will help you to set a purpose for reading *before* you begin to study. Setting a purpose will make it easier for you to understand and remember the material *after* you have read it.

Here are the five steps of the SQ3R plan. Read each step carefully.

1. Survey

Survey means "to look over." When you begin to study, take a few minutes to get an idea of how the material is put together. Look at each page that you will be reading. Look for headings that divide the material into sections. If there are pictures, look at them and read the captions that go with them. While you are looking over the material, try to predict what it will be about.

The survey step is meant to be a short activity. It should take only a few minutes of your study time.

2. Question

Question yourself about the kind of information you want to get from the study material. The best way to do this is to read the title and any headings and try to turn them into questions. Ask yourself, "Who? What? Where? When? Why?" and "How?" For example, if you were surveying a science text and you saw the heading *Plant Life,* you might ask yourself these questions: "What is plant life?" or "Where can plant life be found?" or "Why is plant life important?" By asking yourself questions such as these, you are establishing a purpose for reading the material. Trying to answer the questions as you read will help you to understand and remember more of the selection.

3. Read

Read the material carefully. You have already surveyed the material and have an idea what it will be about. You have also prepared some questions to be answered. Now you need to do a careful, close reading. Read all the details as well as the main ideas. As you read, try to understand all the important points the author is making. You may want to reread some paragraphs or sections to be certain you understand them fully.

You should allow the largest part of your study time for this step.

4. Recite

Recite, in SQ3R, means to put the facts and ideas you read into your own words and say these words out loud to yourself. Putting the facts and ideas into your own words will help you to remember them.

When you get to this step, you should be able to answer the questions you prepared in step 2. If other questions are asked at the end of the section or chapter, try to answer them also. If you have trouble answering any questions, go back and read the material again.

5. Review

Review the material by looking back over it. Reviewing the material will help to remind you of what you have studied. Look back at the headings and answer again the questions you asked yourself in step 2. Look back at any boldface words or any notes that you may have taken.

You will find this step more helpful if you allow some time to pass between step 4 and your review. If you have done steps 1 through 4 well, you should be able to do a quick review an hour, a day, or even several days after you have studied.

When you use SQ3R, first *survey* the material. Then ask yourself *questions*. Next, *read* carefully to find the answers. Then put the important facts and ideas from the material into your own words, and *recite* these words to yourself. At a later time, *review* the material. Remember, you should give steps 2, 3, and 4 the most time as you study.

Textbook Application: Using SQ3R in Health

Read the following selection, using the SQ3R plan. Remember, do *not* start reading right away. First survey the selection and predict what you will find in it. Then ask yourself some questions based on the headings you see. Use the sidenotes to help you practice your new study plan.

How Muscles Help You Move

When you move, you use both bones and muscles. Muscles connect to bones by tough bands called **tendons** (TEN dunz). Your bones move when your muscles contract (kun TRAKT) and relax. Many muscles work in pairs. When one muscle contracts, the other one relaxes. To **contract** means to become smaller. When a muscle contracts, it becomes shorter and thicker. The two ends of the muscle come closer together. When a muscle contracts, it pulls on the bone to which it is attached. This will cause the bone to move. When a muscle relaxes, it stretches and becomes longer. See Figure 7–7.

A muscle does not completely relax. Your muscles are made of fibers. Some of these fibers are always contracted. These

> Noticing the title is part of the *survey* step. In the *question* step, you would change this heading into a question, such as "How do muscles help you move?"

> Pay attention to the boldface words. Why do you think these words appear this way?

> This reference is keyed to the caption for the drawing on the next page. The drawing illustrates what is explained in the paragraph.
>
> After you study the picture, *recite* the main ideas of what you have read so far.

fibers help keep your muscles ready for quick action. Your muscles will feel firm. When your muscles are firm while relaxed, you are said to have good muscle tone. Good muscle tone helps you keep healthy. You get good muscle tone by exercising and eating healthy foods.

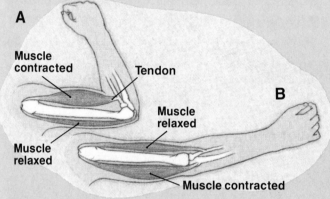

A

Muscle contracted

Tendon

Muscle relaxed

Muscle relaxed

Muscle contracted

B

Reading captions is something you can do in the *survey* step. It will help you make predictions.

Figure 7–7. When your arm bends, your muscle contracts (A). When your arm is straight, your muscle relaxes (B).

Figure 7–8. Playing hopscotch requires strong, healthy muscles and improves muscle tone.

Try to answer this question. Did you look at the caption of Figure 7–8 for help?

Have you heard the saying "Healthy muscles make a healthy body"? <u>What do you think this means?</u>

Muscle Injuries

Often, textbooks are divided into sections to set apart major ideas.

What question did you ask yourself after you read this section heading?

What parts of these paragraphs will you read most closely? What parts will you use when you review?

Many people your age are very active. They may jump and run for long periods of time. This is healthy. But sometimes young people can injure their muscles. There are different types of muscle injuries.

One type of muscle injury is a strain. A **strain** is muscle soreness caused by too much use. For example, you may shovel a lot of snow. You used your back muscles for a long period of time. Perhaps it was the first time in many months that you used a shovel. Your back muscles felt sore the next day. They were strained. Often, no harm is done. The soreness can be relieved with a hot bath and rest.

Many people your age get muscle bruises. A **muscle bruise** is an injury to a muscle caused by a blow. Have you ever been kicked while playing? Did you ever bump your leg against a hard object? If you did, you had a muscle bruise. The blow to the muscle caused some blood vessels to break. Blood under the skin made a black-and-blue spot.

—*Health: Focus on You,* Charles E. Merrill

As you study, use the SQ3R study plan. It can help you get the most out of what you read.

In this informational selection you will find out how different sounds are made.

As you read, use the information you learned about SQ3R to help you remember important facts about sounds.

High Sounds, Low Sounds

by Franklyn M. Branley

Listen. What do you hear?

You hear bangs and shouts, pops and roars, music and noise.

Every sound you hear is made by something that is moving. To make a sound, something must move back and forth rapidly. It must vibrate.

When things vibrate very fast, you cannot see them move. When they vibrate more slowly, you can see the motion.

Slow Vibrations

If you vibrate a rubber band, you can see it move. Loop a rubber band over a doorknob.

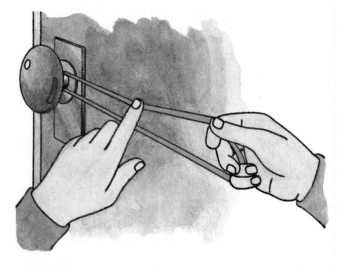

Stretch the rubber band and then pluck it with your fingers.

You hear a sound, and you see the rubber band vibrate back and forth. When it stops moving, you don't hear any sound.

370

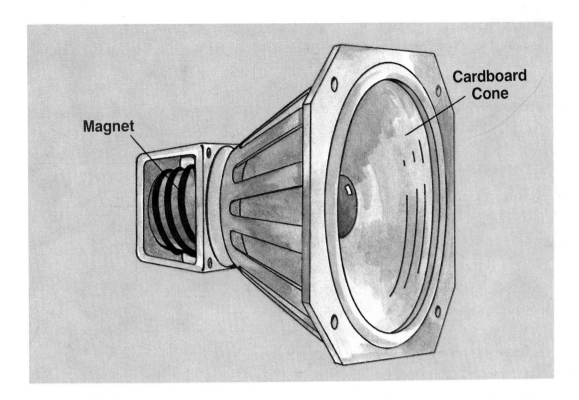

Magnet

Cardboard Cone

Fast Vibrations

You can hear a radio, yet nothing seems to move. You cannot see anything vibrate.

The whole radio does not move. But inside the radio there is a speaker that does move.

The speaker is a piece of cardboard shaped like a cup or a cone. It is fastened to a magnet. When you turn on the radio, electricity goes through the magnet. This makes the magnet move. The cardboard moves, too, because it is fastened to the magnet. The cardboard vibrates.

All radios, even tiny ones, have speakers in them. Big radios have both big and little speakers. The big speakers move slowly. They make low sounds, and are called woofers. The little speakers vibrate very fast. They make high sounds, and are called tweeters.

When things vibrate slowly, they make low sounds. When they vibrate fast, they make high sounds.

371

Vibrations in a Piano

A piano has long strings and short strings. The long strings vibrate slowly. They make low sounds. The short strings vibrate fast. They make high sounds.

Look inside a piano. Strike one of the low keys. Watch the string that makes the note. You can see it vibrate.

Strike a high key on the piano. You can hear the sound, but you cannot see the string move. That's because it vibrates very fast.

Sounds from a Straw

You don't need a piano to make high sounds and low sounds.

You can make them with a drinking straw. Paper straws are the best to use.

Flatten the last half-inch of one end of the straw.

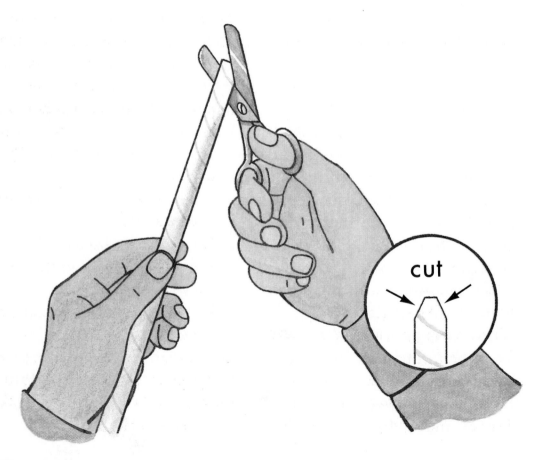

cut

With scissors, cut both sides of the flattened end. Taper the cuts so that the narrow part is at the end of the straw. The top and the bottom are then free to move up and down.

Hold the flattened end of the straw between your lips and blow through the straw.

You should make a sound. If you do not, try blowing harder. If you still get no sound, blow softer. Also, move the straw a little farther into your mouth, or out a little. After some practice you will be able to make a steady tone.

When you have learned how to make the sound, try this. Take the straw out of your mouth. Hold the straw in one hand and a pair of scissors in the other hand. Snip an inch or so off the end of the straw with the scissors. Try blowing into the straw now. What happens to the sound? Cut off another inch — and another.

The more straw you cut off, the higher the note becomes. That's because the straw and the air in it vibrate faster. The shorter something is, the faster it vibrates and the higher the sound.

Sounds from a Spoon

You can make a sound like a bell with a spoon and a piece of string. You can also see one way that vibrations can travel.

Here is how to do it:

Tie a metal spoon to the middle of a piece of string. The string should be three feet long.

Hold the ends of the string in your ears. Swing the spoon back and forth. You will hear no sound. Now swing the spoon so it hits a table or a chair one time. You will hear a sound like a bell. That's because you made the spoon vibrate. The vibrations travel along the string to your ears.

Try a fork, and see how the sound changes.

Try a bigger spoon.

Ask someone to touch the spoon.

As soon as someone touches the spoon, the sound stops. When the vibrations stop, there is no sound. Something must move, or vibrate, to make every sound that you hear.

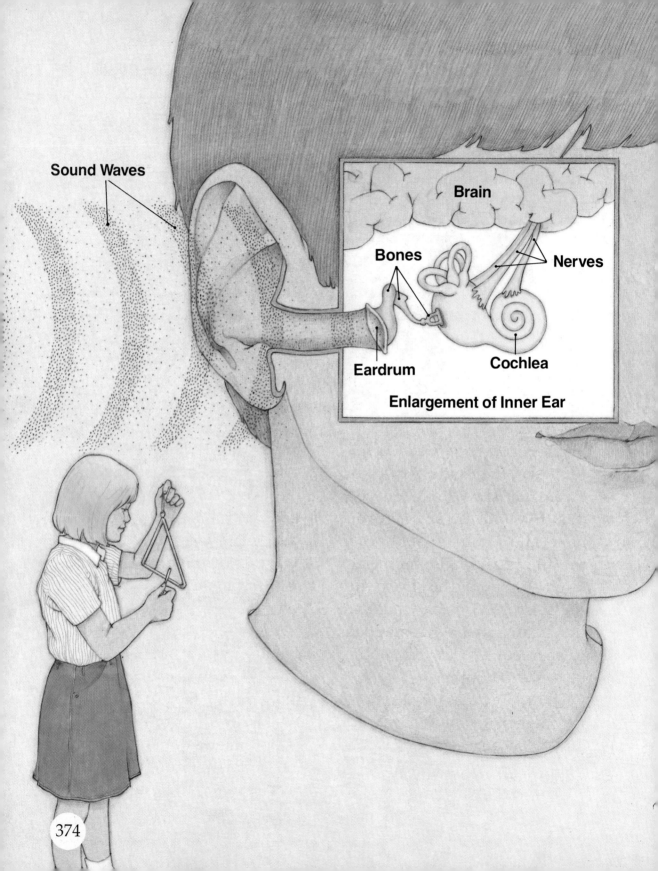

Sound Waves

Brain

Bones

Nerves

Eardrum

Cochlea

Enlargement of Inner Ear

Ears and Hearing

When something vibrates, it makes the air all around it vibrate. Air can move back and forth rapidly, just as the strings in a piano can.

You hear sounds because air vibrates. Air carries vibrations to your ear.

The outer part of your ear catches the vibrations and carries them into the opening of your ear. Inside your ear there is a tunnel. The vibrations go down the tunnel and strike against a thin wall. This is your eardrum.

When vibrations hit your eardrum, they make it vibrate. The eardrum vibrates like the top of a drum.

Behind your eardrum there is a chain of three small bones. When the eardrum vibrates, these bones vibrate also. They carry the vibrations deep inside your ear. They go to a part of the ear that is called the cochlea.

The cochlea is shaped like a small ball. It has liquid inside it. Nerves that connect the ear to the brain dip into this liquid.

When vibrations reach the cochlea, the liquid inside vibrates. The vibrations make signals in the nerves, and the nerves carry the signals to the brain.

Your brain changes the signals to what we call sounds.

A sound is made. Vibrations travel to your ear. They vibrate the eardrum and the cochlea. Signals are sent to your brain and you hear the sound. All this happens in less than a second.

When you hear a sound, find out what is vibrating.

Is something vibrating fast or slowly?

Is the sound high or low?

How does the sound get to your ears?

Listen. What do you hear?

1. What must happen for a sound to be made?
2. What makes a sound high or low?
3. The author suggested several ways a person could create sounds using common objects. Explain how three of these sounds are made.
4. Name a sound that you enjoy hearing. Why do you enjoy hearing that sound?
5. Why is the piano a good example to use in a discussion of fast and slow vibrations?
6. What does a person's brain do to help a person hear a sound?

You have learned that *SQ3R* stands for *survey, question, read, recite,* and *review.* Tell what you would do to complete the *survey* step for the selection "High Sounds, Low Sounds."

Prewrite

The sound a cow makes is "moo." The special name for words, like *moo*, that sound like what they mean is *onomatopoeia*. Copy the chart below and fill in the sound that belongs with each item. The sounds should be examples of onomatopoeia.

1. Clocks	_tick_	**2.** Snakes	
3. Bees		**4.** Cats	

Compose

Think of sounds you might hear at a circus. What sound would a popcorn maker make? What animals would you hear? If you entered a very old house that had been closed up for years, what sound would the door make as you opened it? Use one of these ideas or one of your own to write a paragraph about your experience. Include at least two examples of onomatopoeia.

Revise

Read your paragraph. Did you include at least two examples of onomatopoeia? Did the onomatopoeia make it easier to imagine the sounds?

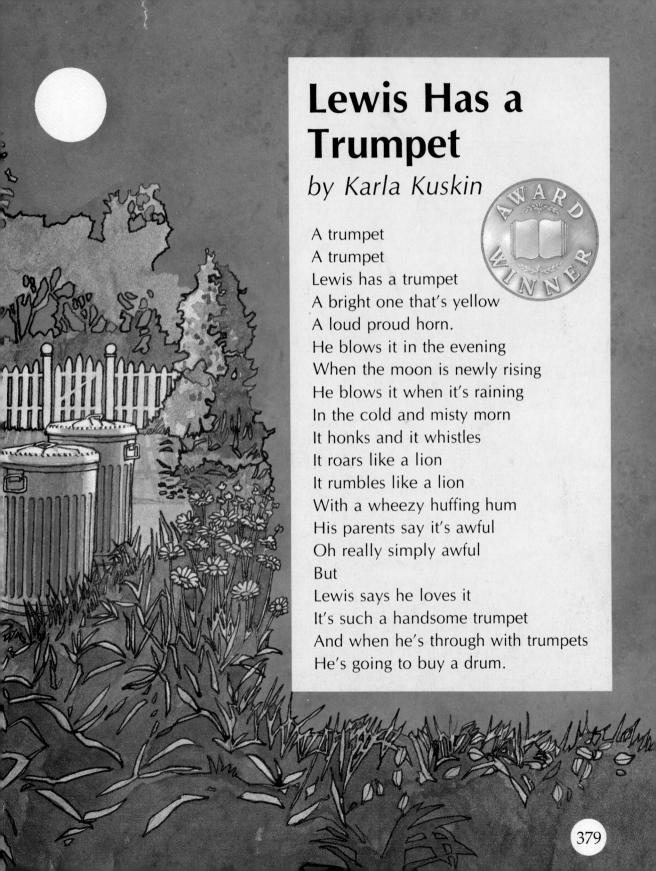

Lewis Has a Trumpet

by Karla Kuskin

A trumpet
A trumpet
Lewis has a trumpet
A bright one that's yellow
A loud proud horn.
He blows it in the evening
When the moon is newly rising
He blows it when it's raining
In the cold and misty morn
It honks and it whistles
It roars like a lion
It rumbles like a lion
With a wheezy huffing hum
His parents say it's awful
Oh really simply awful
But
Lewis says he loves it
It's such a handsome trumpet
And when he's through with trumpets
He's going to buy a drum.

Read to find out how a prince discovers the answer to the riddle of the drum.

As you read, refer to the list of Spanish words and their meanings given at the beginning of the story.

The Riddle of the Drum

based on a tale from Tizapán, Mexico, translated and retold by Verna Aardema

and adapted as a play by Anne Maley

Spanish Glossary

jacaranda (hä·kä·rän′dä) A tropical tree with blue flowers

olé (ō·lä′) A shout of approval; great

rebozo (rä·bō′sō) A long scarf

señor (sen·yôr′) Mister

sí (sē) Yes

tacos (tä′kōs) Fried tortillas

Tizapán (tē·sä·pän′) A place in central Mexico hundreds of years ago

tortillas (tôr·tē′yəs) Round, flat cakes of cornmeal usually eaten hot with a filling

uf (o͞of) An expression of disgust, like *ugh*

uno, dos, tres, cuatro, cinco (o͞o′nō, dōs, träs, kwä′trō, sēn′kō) One, two, three, four, five

CHARACTERS

Narrator
Wizard
King
Guard
Chorus
Prince Tuzán (tōo·sän')
Corrín Corrán (kôr·rēn' kôr·rän'), the runner
Voices 1–6
Tirín Tirán (tē·rēn' tē·rän'), the archer
Oyín Oyán (ō·yēn' ō·yän'), the hearer
Soplín Soplán (sō·plēn' sō·plän'), the blower
Comín Comán (kō·mēn' kō·män'), the eater
Princess Fruela (frōo·ā'lä)
Old Woman

Scene One

Setting: At the king's palace

Narrator: There was a king in Tizapán who had a beautiful daughter named Fruela. The king loved Fruela so much that he decided that whoever married her would have to prove himself worthy. So the king asked a wizard to make a strange drum.

Wizard: (*enters, carrying a drum*) Good day, Your Majesty. (*He bows to the King.*) Here is your drum, at last.

King: (*looking curious*) Ah, Wizard. Tell me its story.

Wizard: (*proudly*) The drum is just as you desired. The drumhead is made from a kind of leather that no one has ever used before. It is as black as jet. (*He strikes the drum.*) Its sound is like thunder on a distant mountain. (*He lowers his voice.*) And only you and I know that the drumhead is made of . . . (*He whispers the words in the king's ear.*)

King: (*smiling*) Well done! Now let us send this drum throughout the land to find a man who is worthy of my daughter Fruela.

Narrator: Everywhere the guard went, the children would fall in line behind him and join in with the song.

Guard, Chorus: (*singing together with the drum*)
Tum-te-dum!
The head of the drum-te-dum!
Guess what it's from-te-dum!
And marry the Princess Fruela.

Scene Two

Setting: On the road toward the palace

Narrator: Now, a handsome prince from a nearby land heard about the riddle of the drum. So he set out to try to win the princess. On the way, he met a man who was running as if a coyote were nipping at his heels.

Prince Tuzán: (*shouting*) Stop! Stop, señor! Why do you run so fast? Is something chasing you?

Corrín Corrán: (*proudly*) No, señor. I run for fun, for I am the runner, Corrín Corrán.

Prince Tuzán: I am Prince Tuzán. I'm on my way to the king, to try to win the princess. If you will help me, I shall reward you.

Corrín Corrán: (*bowing to the prince*) I'll do what I can. Lead the way, and I will follow.

Voice 1: Then on and on went Prince Tuzán,

Voice 2: Behind him the runner, Corrín Corrán.

Chorus: The two marched on toward the palace.

Narrator: Soon they met a man who carried a bow and a quiver of arrows.

Prince Tuzán: Good day, señor. I am Prince Tuzán. What is your name?

Tirín Tirán: (*pulling on his bow*) I am the archer, Tirín Tirán. Let me show you what I can do. (*He draws out an arrow and puts it into his bow.*)

Narrator: Then Tirín Tirán tossed his hat high in the air and shot an arrow through it.

Prince Tuzán: (*surprised*) Olé! Come along and help me win the princess, and I shall reward you.

Voice 1: Then on and on went Prince Tuzán,

Voice 2: Behind him the runner, Corrín Corrán,

Voice 3: Behind him the archer, Tirín Tirán.

Chorus: They all marched on toward the palace.

Narrator: Farther on, they came upon a man who had the largest ears Prince Tuzán had ever seen. He was lying under a tree with one huge ear pressed to the ground.

Prince Tuzán: Hello, señor. What are you doing?

Oyín Oyán: (*looking up*) I am the hearer, Oyín Oyán. I am listening to the talk at the palace. Another suitor for the princess has just guessed wrong.

Prince Tuzán: (*eagerly*) Do you know the right answer?

Oyín Oyán: (*getting up and laughing*) No, but I know all the wrong ones. I know that it isn't (*in a singsong voice*) duck skin or buck skin, goat skin or shoat skin, mule skin or mole skin, mare skin or bear skin—or even armadillo!

Prince Tuzán: Then come along. If you can keep me from guessing wrong, I shall reward you.

Voice 1: Then on and on went Prince Tuzán,

Voice 2: Behind him the runner, Corrín Corrán,

Voice 3: Behind him the archer, Tirín Tirán,

Voice 4: Behind him the hearer, Oyín Oyán.

Chorus: They all marched on toward the palace.

Narrator: They hadn't gone far when they came upon a man who was running a windmill. With his head held back and his cheeks puffed out, he blew—and the windmill turned faster and faster.

Prince Tuzán: How extraordinary!

Soplín Soplán: (*shrugging*) Quite ordinary for me, señor. I am the blower, Soplín Soplán.

Prince Tuzán: I am Prince Tuzán. Come along with us. Help me win the princess, and I shall reward you.

Voice 1: Then on and on went Prince Tuzán,

Voice 2: Behind him the runner, Corrín Corrán,

Voice 3: Behind him the archer, Tirín Tirán,

Voice 4: Behind him the hearer, Oyín Oyán,

Voice 5: Behind him the blower, Soplín Soplán.

Chorus: They all marched on toward the palace.

Narrator: They were all becoming tired and hungry when they came upon a man who was cooking a whole ox over a fire.

Prince Tuzán: Señor, are you cooking all this meat for yourself?

Comín Comán: (*nodding and smiling*) Sí. I am the eater, Comín Comán. For me, this is just one big piece of meat. But come and share my meal.

Prince Tuzán: Thank you, señor. (*They sit down and begin to eat.*) When we are finished, come and help me win the princess, and I shall reward you.

Voice 1: Then on and on went Prince Tuzán,

Voice 2: Behind him the runner, Corrín Corrán,

Voice 3: Behind him the archer, Tirín Tirán,

Voice 4: Behind him the hearer, Oyín Oyán,

Voice 5: Behind him the blower, Soplín Soplán,

Voice 6: Behind him the eater, Comín Comán.

Chorus: They all marched on toward the palace.

Scene Three

Setting: At the king's palace

Narrator: Soon they rounded the top of a hill and saw the palace on the far hillside. Far away, the princess was on her balcony. She and her father were talking. Oyín Oyán put his ear to the ground and overheard these words.

Princess Fruela: (*pointing*) Papa, look! A prince is coming!

King: (*looking into the distance*) Sí! And he has uno, dos, tres, cuatro, cinco attendants! Too bad he has to die—just because he doesn't know that the drumhead is made from the skin of a . . .

Narrator: That was when the king said the word! Oyín Oyán leaped up so fast, his ears flapped.

Oyín Oyán: (*shouting*) I heard the answer to the riddle! (*He whispers it in the prince's ear.*)

Narrator: Then Prince Tuzán and his men went on to the palace, where they were brought before the king.

Prince Tuzán: (*bowing low*) Your Majesty, I have come to solve the riddle of the drum.

King: (*sternly*) Do you know that if you fail, you will lose your life?

Prince Tuzán: (*calmly*) Sí, I know. Show me the drum.

Guard: (*enters, singing and beating the drum*)
Tum-te-dum!
The head of the drum-te-dum!
Guess what it's from-te-dum!
And marry the Princess Fruela!

Narrator: Prince Tuzán ran his fingers over the thin, black skin of the drum. He tapped out a little rhythm and began to speak.

Prince Tuzán: (*in a sing-song voice as he taps*) It isn't duck skin or buck skin, goat skin or shoat skin, mule skin or mole skin, mare skin or . . .

King: (*shouting*) Don't tell me what it isn't! Tell me what it is!

Prince Tuzán: (*thoughtfully*) It looks to me like this is the skin of a very large flea!

King: (*angrily*) Uf! I can't believe it! You're right! (*He speaks more quietly.*) But there are two more things you must do before you marry my daughter! First, one of your servants and one of my servants will race to the sea and fetch water. If mine returns first, you lose your life!

Narrator: Then Corrín Corrán stepped forward.

Corrín Corrán: Prince Tuzán, allow me to run for you.

Narrator: Then up stepped an old woman in a long, gray dress with a black rebozo around her shoulders.

Old Woman: (*smiling*) And I will run for the king!

Narrator: Corrín Corrán laughed at that. But after they began to run, he discovered that the old woman had magic powers. He had to run with all his might just to keep up with her. Side by side they raced down the valley, past a jacaranda tree, over a hill, and onto the beach. At the sea, they filled their small bottles with water and both turned back at the same moment.

Corrín Corrán: (*to himself*) What is wrong? I cannot seem to beat her! But I must win and save the prince's life!

Narrator: So Corrín Corrán went faster and reached the jacaranda tree just ahead of the old woman. But she was ready with her magic.

Old Woman: (*loudly*) Sleep! Go . . . to . . . sleep!

Corrín Corrán: (*falls under the tree, snoring*) Z-z-z-z!

Narrator: Oyín Oyán heard her words, and he heard the runner snoring. So he spoke to the archer.

Oyín Oyán: (*excitedly*) Tirín Tirán! Shoot the tree! Wake up the runner!

Narrator: The archer sent an arrow into the tree just above the sleeping runner. Zap! Corrín Corrán woke up and leaped into the race, but by now the woman was far ahead.

Old Woman: (*laughing*) I hear you behind me, but you will never catch me!

Narrator: Then Soplín Soplán puffed out his cheeks and aimed a strong wind at her. The wind lifted her up and carried her — kicking and screeching — all the way back to the jacaranda tree. Then Corrín Corrán won the race. The king, of course, was upset.

King: (*protesting*) You cheated, Prince Tuzán! But I will not punish you. You still have one last task to do. Before the sun sets, one of your servants must eat a cartload of food. If he fails, you die!

Narrator: So a cart filled with food was brought in, and Comín Comán set to his task.

Comín Comán: (*licking his lips*) Ah! Tacos, tortillas, meat, puddings! This will be a nice little lunch.

Narrator: Before evening, Comín Comán had eaten everything — even the cart! When the last task was

done, the king finally gave Prince Tuzán the Princess Fruela in marriage. The two lived together happily for many years. But what happened to the five faithful servants?

Voice 2: The faithful runner, Corrín Corrán, (*He bows.*)

Voice 3: The faithful archer, Tirín Tirán, (*He bows.*)

Voice 4: The faithful hearer, Oyín Oyán, (*He bows.*)

Voice 5: The faithful blower, Soplín Soplán, (*He bows.*)

Voice 6: The faithful eater, Comín Comán, (*He bows.*)

Chorus: They all lived well at the palace.

1. How did the prince discover the answer to the riddle of the drum?

2. What three things did Prince Tuzán have to do before he could marry Princess Fruela?

3. When did you first begin to think that each of the five faithful servants would somehow help Prince Tuzán?

4. Which of the servants do you think was the most helpful to the prince? Why?

5. How were the faithful servants rewarded for helping the prince?

In the story "The Riddle of the Drum," many Spanish words are used. Match the words below with their meanings.

1. olé   a. A tropical tree
2. jacaranda   b. Yes
3. rebozo   c. An expression of disgust; ugh
4. sí   d. A shout of approval
5. señor   e. Mister
6. tortillas   f. A long scarf
7. uf   g. Round, flat cakes of cornmeal

Prewrite

Prince Tuzán used the extraordinary talents of five servants to win the contest. Copy the chart and complete each sentence by writing what you would do if you had the talent of that servant. The first two are done for you.

> **1.** If I could shoot an arrow like Tirín Tirán, I would hit the bull's-eye every time.
>
> **2.** If I could blow like Soplín Soplán, I would blow a sailboat across the ocean.
>
> **3.** If I could run like Corrín Corrán, I would ▨▨▨▨
>
> **4.** If I could hear like Oyín Oyán, I would ▨▨▨▨
>
> **5.** If I could eat like Comín Comán, I would ▨▨▨▨

Compose

Write a paragraph describing one of the talents listed in the chart above. Tell why you would choose to have this talent and what you might do if you had it.

Revise

Check your work to be sure you have described the talent well. Make changes if they are needed.

Connotation and Denotation

A word may have two kinds of meanings. The first is its dictionary meaning, or its **denotation.** If someone asked you what a word meant, you would give the word's denotation. The second kind of meaning is the word's **connotation.** This is made up of the feelings, thoughts, or ideas that a word suggests. If someone asked you what a word made you think of, you would give the word's connotation.

For example, the denotation of the word *fireplace* is "a place or opening in which a fire is built." However, to some people the word *fireplace* may suggest a warm, cozy room on a winter day. To others, it may suggest hours of chopping wood.

People react to words in different ways, based on their past experiences. Think about the word *snow.* Everybody knows the denotation of *snow.* Snow is white flakes of frozen water that fall to the ground in winter. However, the connotation of the word *snow* is different for different people. To some, the word *snow* may suggest sledding or skiing. To others, the word *snow* may suggest shoveling the walk or dangerous driving conditions. If you have never seen snow, the word may have a much different connotation in your mind.

Writers know that words can have both a denotation and a connotation. They know that some words bring out strong feelings in people. Read the following story. As you read, think about the denotations and connotations of the words the writer has used. Which words have strong connotations?

When Danny came home from school, there was a letter from Aunt Doris on the kitchen table.

"Your aunt has sent you an early birthday present," Danny's mother said. "She told me it has something to do with athletic activity."

Danny thought, "Oh, boy, tickets to a football game in the city!" He knew that Aunt Doris worked near the football stadium.

Danny opened the letter, and a card dropped out. He picked it up and read it slowly. It said: "This card entitles you to three free dance lessons at the Midtown Dance Club."

The words *birthday, present, athletic, football,* and *dance* all have strong connotations. Notice how the writer has used these words in the story. First, the reader expects to learn about a birthday present. Most people like birthday presents. Next, the writer suggests that the present has to do with athletics, perhaps football. People react in different ways to these words. Some people enjoy football. Some do not like it at all. The final word with a strong connotation is *dance*. How did you feel when you read the last sentence of the story? What did you think of when you read the words *dance lessons*?

As you read and write, remember that words can make you feel and think in certain ways.

Being left-handed helped Mike to get on a baseball team. Read to find out how playing baseball leads Mike to join a dance class.

As you read, watch for words that have both a connotation and a denotation.

Just Because I'm Left-Handed

by Linda McCollum Brown

This whole mess started just because I'm left-handed.

Last month Tim and Jeff talked me into signing up for Little League. Now, baseball is okay and all, but it isn't my favorite thing to do. Just give me my clarinet or a chemistry set or a tennis racket or a book to read—especially a mystery—and I'm happy. But Tim and Jeff are my best friends. They said that a lefty can really do a right-handed pitcher in, and that I could help their team a whole lot.

So, I figured, why not? The Panthers' coach, Mr. Goodwin, said, "Hey, great—a southpaw!" I can't stand it when people call me a southpaw (I mean, does that make them northpaws?), but other than that he is okay. He is a real strong ballplayer, a super athlete.

Mom said I could ride the bus to practice so I wouldn't have to bother Mrs. Neumerski, our after-school babysitter, for a ride. I never miss supper

because we eat late anyhow, since Mom gets home from work late.

Everything was going fine until my sister Kathie (she's only in third grade) saw that article in the newspaper. I wish she didn't like to read so much! What's worse is that she has to tell everyone about what she reads.

I was all set to dive into my cherry pie after supper one night when she said, "Hey, Mom, I just read a really good article in the *Times*. It's about how some football and baseball players take ballet lessons."

"Ballet lessons?" Mom asked, looking up.

"Ballet lessons!" I almost choked on a mouthful of cherries.

"Yes, ballet lessons," Kathie answered, "during the off-season to help them keep in shape. Some of them even do it during the playing season because it helps them be more graceful."

"Oh, next I suppose you'll say that I should take ballet lessons," I said, laughing real hard. "What a joke!"

"Well," she said, looking at Mom and me, "our whole dancing school is going to do *The Nutcracker* for Christmas this year. The only trouble is there aren't enough boys, and I told Mrs. Goodwin that when baseball season ends, Mike would like to stay in shape and that he would come and . . ."

"You *what*?" This time I really did choke. "Me, dancing? No way!"

Mom glared at me. She turned to Kathie. "You know, dear, you mustn't promise something like that unless you ask Mike about it first."

Then she turned to me, and I could tell by the look in her eye that I was doomed. "However, Mike, it might be a good idea. You love music, and you

complain that you don't get enough exercise during the winter."

"It's not winter now," I sputtered.

"No, but they really do need some tall boys practicing now to be ready to dance *The Nutcracker* at Christmas. I was talking to Mrs. Goodwin the other day. Why don't you give it a try? If you still don't like it after a month or so, then you can drop it," Mom said. I could tell by her tone of voice there was no use trying to talk her out of it.

So now, there I was. The next day was my first—ugh—ballet lesson. If Jeff or Tim or any of the other guys had found out about it, I think I would have just died.

"Hey, Mom, can you call Jeff and tell him I'm sick or something? I was supposed to go over to his house tomorrow after practice, but now I've got that dumb dancing lesson."

"That won't be necessary, dear," Mom had said, giving me her you-know-we-don't-do-that-kind-of-thing look. "Jeff just called to say his uncle will be visiting him tomorrow, so it wouldn't work out anyway."

The next day Jeff was sure quiet at practice. He didn't even talk about his uncle coming, so I figured maybe he didn't like him or something. After practice Coach Goodwin said to me, "Can I give you a lift to the dancing school?"

"Sh-h-h!" I hissed, looking around quickly to make sure no one had heard him. "You mean *you're* going over there?"

"Sure," he said. "I teach the boys' class."

"You do?" I couldn't believe what I was hearing.

"Right," he answered. "I used to dance with a ballet company full-time until I injured my knee. You know, you've got to be in excellent physical shape to be a good dancer, just like any other athlete."

He might have told me more, but just then we reached his car. And what do you know—Jeff was sitting in the car, looking as miserable as I had felt earlier. Tim and some of the other guys were twirling around on their toes in the dust beside the car. "Jeff's going to dance like this," Tim hooted as he spun around. The rest of the guys were laughing.

Right then I wanted to run the other way, straight home—fast. But Jeff sure looked all alone. Besides, if I had to go to dancing class, it would be a lot more fun

to have one of my friends there, too. So I called out loud, "Hey, Jeff, did you know you have to be in great shape to be a good dancer? Some of the best ballplayers take ballet lessons to stay in shape for the season."

Tim and the other guys just stood there in the dust. I guess they didn't know what to say to that.

Jeff grinned and looked a little better. I never thought that anything Kathie said would make me or my friends feel better, but I'm glad that I remembered her *Times* article.

Then I remembered something else. "Hey, Jeff, what about your uncle?"

He rolled his eyes. "Aw, I just made that up. I couldn't tell you where I was really going."

This may not be so bad after all. I guess we can give it a try.

1. Why did Kathie suggest that Mike take ballet lessons?

2. On the day of Mike's first ballet lesson, what happened at baseball practice?

3. Do you think there was any connection between Mrs. Goodwin, the ballet teacher, and Mr. Goodwin, the coach? Why?

4. Find the sentence on page 399 that lets you know that Mike's mother would not make excuses for him.

5. Why did Mike feel better about taking ballet lessons after talking with Coach Goodwin?

All words have a denotation, or dictionary meaning. A word may also have a connotation, or the feelings, thoughts, or ideas that the word suggests. Think about the word *ballet*. Ballet is a dance in which formal steps and movements are performed. What was the connotation of the word *ballet* for Mike in "Just Because I'm Left-Handed"? What do you think of when you hear the word *ballet*?

Prewrite

Copy and complete the flow chart below. Show how being left-handed resulted in Mike's taking ballet lessons. Each boxed idea should lead to the next boxed idea.

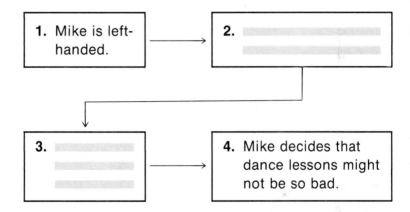

1. Mike is left-handed.

2.

3.

4. Mike decides that dance lessons might not be so bad.

Compose

The flow chart does not have to stop at the fourth step. Choose an activity for Mike that could be the result of the dance lessons. Write a paragraph to explain how he could become involved in this activity.

Revise

Read your paragraph carefully. Check to be sure that your paragraph has a main idea and enough supporting details.

Read to find out how one man made his dream of dancing come true not only for himself but also for others.

As you read, try to decide what characteristics make this selection biographical.

Ballet Is for Everyone

by Susanne Banta Harper

Arthur was tired. But he was happy and excited, too. He could hardly wait to tell his family and friends the good news.

"I did it," he told his best friend. "I passed the audition." Arthur Mitchell had been accepted to study dance at the New York City School of Performing Arts.

"Congratulations," his friend said, and he made a prediction. "You're going to be one of the best dancers at the school. I know it."

When classes began, it was clear that Arthur Mitchell did have exceptional talent. He was especially good at jazz dancing. He could move sleekly like a cat or rapidly like a fly. He could make angry, sharp movements or jaunty, bouncy ones. When Arthur danced in the jazz style, he was part of the music.

But Arthur studied more than just jazz dancing. He also studied ballet. He worked to train his legs to turn outward as classical ballet required. He practiced the exercises at the *barre* with special care so that he would develop the control of his body needed to perform the difficult steps perfectly. He loved the jumps and turns. When he leaped into the air, he seemed to fly. When he turned on one foot, he seemed to spin like a top. The harder Arthur worked at ballet, the more he came to love it.

Arthur kept in touch with his old friends as he studied. He told them that ballet was very hard work. "But," he said, "I think I would like to make it my career."

Some of his friends tried to discourage him. "Stick with jazz, Arthur," they said. "Ballet is for white people."

Arthur considered that advice. In the early 1950's there were no black dancers in any major ballet company. But Arthur Mitchell loved ballet.

I know it won't be easy, he thought. But I have worked hard and plan to work even harder. I know I can do it.

His mind made up, Arthur Mitchell entered the School of American Ballet. My friends are wrong, he thought. Ballet is for everyone.

Some of the students and some of the parents did not like having Arthur at the school. One father complained, "I do not want my daughter to dance with that black boy. He should not be here." Some other parents agreed.

The teachers at the school did not agree. They could see how talented Arthur Mitchell was. They encouraged him to continue. While Arthur was at the School of American Ballet, his abilities were noticed by the directors of the New York City Ballet. They invited him to join their company. Arthur was thrilled.

In 1955 Arthur Mitchell became the first black dancer to perform with a major ballet company. Audiences quickly came to love him and his wonderful dancing.

Arthur had succeeded in doing what he set out to do. He received praise from dance critics and warm applause from audiences, who loved him. He became a leading dancer. Yet at times he was troubled. He thought of the children in Harlem, where he had grown up. Those children had never seen ballet and did not have the opportunity to study it.

Ballet is for everyone—I am an example of that, he thought. But maybe that is not enough.

Finally, Arthur Mitchell decided to leave the New York City Ballet, and he announced what he was going to do. "I must try to bring ballet to other black people. I am going to start a new ballet company, a black ballet company."

Again some of his friends warned him. "Don't do it, Arthur," they said. "It's impossible. Where would you get the dancers?"

"I will recruit and train young people from Harlem. I will teach them to be first-rate dancers," Arthur replied.

The task before Mitchell was enormous. Also, the money to carry out his dream was scarce. At first all he could afford for his new dance school was a rented garage. Later the school moved to a church basement. The school attracted many students. Arthur made them work hard to master the classical technique. "I can do it, and you can, too," he told the students when they became discouraged.

After much hard work and training, Arthur Mitchell decided that he had a group good enough to perform for the public. The Dance Theater of Harlem was born. They performed many classical ballets. When they danced *Swan Lake,* the audiences saw swans gliding gracefully through the sad story. When they danced *Firebird,* audiences responded excitedly to the rapid leaps and turns of the magic bird. When they performed *Dougla,* which the Dance Theater of Harlem made famous, audiences responded to the jazz rhythms with enthusiasm. The Dance Theater of Harlem was a success wherever it went.

Eventually, the reputation of the company became so great that many dancers were eager to join it. One day when Arthur Mitchell was holding auditions, some of the dancers who competed were not black. He decided to hire some of them.

Later he was criticized by some people for hiring white dancers for the Dance Theater of Harlem. They said that they thought his company was for black dancers. Why hire white dancers?

"That's easy to explain" was Arthur Mitchell's answer. "The Dance Theater of Harlem needs dancers. And, as we have proved, ballet isn't just for white people or just for black people. Ballet is for everyone."

1. How did Arthur Mitchell help others make their dream of dancing come true?

2. How did Arthur's opinions differ from those of his friends over the years?

3. Do you think it was difficult for Arthur to switch from jazz dancing to ballet? Explain.

4. What words did the author use to help you picture the ballets *Swan Lake* and *Firebird*?

5. How did Arthur answer people who criticized him for hiring white dancers?

A biography is a true story about a real person. It gives information about the person's life and tells why the person is well-known or what he or she has done. Give at least two examples of what Arthur Mitchell did to become famous.

Prewrite

Arthur Mitchell's talent and determination helped him become successful. What other words could you use to describe him? Copy the list below. Add at least two more of Arthur Mitchell's qualities.

Arthur Mitchell
1. talented
2. determined
3. enjoys dancing
4. _____
5. _____

Compose

Write a paragraph about someone you know or have read about who has been a success in life. What qualities helped that person become successful? Does the person have any of the same qualities as Arthur Mitchell? What other qualities does the person have?

Revise

Look over your work. Have you explained how certain qualities helped the person to become successful? Make any necessary changes.

Point of View

Read the following paragraphs:

I sat down at the piano, feeling a bit nervous. As I placed my fingers on the keys, I was suddenly glad I had spent so much time practicing. I took a deep breath, then began to play.

The pianist sat down at the piano, placing her hands carefully upon the keys. She drew a deep breath before she began to play.

Both of these paragraphs tell about the same event. However, the paragraphs tell about the event from different points of view. The **point of view** in a story depends upon who is telling the story.

When an author uses a character in a story as the narrator, the story is said to be told from the **first-person point of view.** You know what the character says, does, and thinks because the character tells you. It is almost as if the character is speaking to you. Words that are often used with first-person point of view are *I, me, my, we, us,* and *our.* Look again at the first paragraph about the pianist. It is written from the first-person point of view.

Another point of view used in many stories is the **third-person point of view.** The third-person point of view does not use a character in the story to tell what is happening. Instead, the author uses an unseen narrator who is watching and reporting the action. Words that are often used with third-person point of view are *he, she, him, her, his, they, them,* and *their.* The second paragraph about the pianist is written in the third person.

Turn back to the selection "Just Because I'm Left-Handed," which begins on page 396. From what point of view is that selection written? What words give you a clue?

"Just Because I'm Left-Handed" is written from the first-person point of view. The main character, Mike, tells what is happening to him, using the words *I, me,* and *my.*

Now look at "The Queen Who Couldn't Bake Gingerbread," which begins on page 352. From what point of view is that selection written? What words give you a clue?

"The Queen Who Couldn't Bake Gingerbread" is written from the third-person point of view. An unseen narrator tells you about the Queen and King. The words *she, her, he, him, his,* and *they* are used.

Read and think about the characteristics of these two different points of view:

- In the first person, a character seems to be telling the story. The words *I, me, my, we, us,* and *our* are often used.
- In the third person, someone who is not part of the story seems to be watching the action and reporting what is happening. The words *he, she, him, her, his, they, them,* and *their* are often used.

As you read, notice from which point of view the author has chosen to write.

Beverly Cleary

When Beverly Cleary was a child, she wondered why there were no books written about children like her. Most books at that time were about wealthy English children or people on the frontier. When she grew up, she began to write stories about ordinary American children. Children today enjoy reading her stories. More than four million copies of her books have been sold.

Beverly Cleary was born in Oregon. She lived on a farm for the first few years of her life. Her mother had been a teacher, and she would recite stories and poems from memory for Beverly.

The small town near which they lived had no library, so Beverly's mother started one in an unused room over a bank. Beverly Cleary remembers that time well. She says, "My mother arranged for the state library to have crates of books shipped in. I don't remember how often, but I remember hanging over those crates looking for the children's books." It was during this time that Beverly Cleary learned to love books.

After Beverly graduated from college, she entered the School of Librarianship at the University of Washington in Seattle. There she specialized in library work with children. She was a children's librarian in Yakima, Washington, until she married Clarence Cleary and moved to California. The Clearys had twins, a boy and a girl, who are now grown up.

Beverly Cleary's first book, *Henry Huggins,* was published in 1950. She has written several more books about Henry, his friend Beezus, and her little sister Ramona, characters whose realistic adventures are filled with humor. These characters have become the favorites of many readers. In fact, the Clearys have a ten-gallon mailbox to hold all the letters Beverly Cleary receives from children who read her books.

Children often ask Beverly Cleary where she finds the ideas for the books she writes. She answers, "From my own experience and from the world around me." She tells children to read widely while they are growing up, and when the time comes for them to write, they will find their own way of writing. She tells them to read, look, listen, think, and write. She also advises children to keep a diary as a way to practice their writing.

Beverly Cleary has won many prizes for the books she has written, including a Newbery Medal for the book *Dear Mr. Henshaw.* You will be reading a selection from *Dear Mr. Henshaw* next. As you read, think about how Beverly Cleary feels about children and their writing.

Leigh Botts wants to be a writer. Read to find out how his favorite author helps Leigh to help himself.

As you read, notice the point of view from which the selection is written. Why do you think it is written from this point of view? Also, watch for the misspelled words in Leigh's early letters.

Dear Mr. Henshaw

by Beverly Cleary

May 12

Dear Mr. Henshaw,

My teacher read your book about the dog to our class. It was funny. We licked it.

Your freind,
Leigh Botts (boy)

December 3

Dear Mr. Henshaw,

I am the boy who wrote to you last year when I was in the second grade. Maybe you didn't get my letter. This year I read the book I wrote to you about called *Ways to Amuse a Dog.* It is the first thick book with chapters that I have read.

My teacher taught me a trick about the word *friend*. The *i* goes before *e* so that at the end it will spell *end*. Keep in tutch.

Your fri*end*,
Leigh (Lee) Botts

November 13

Dear Mr. Henshaw,

I am in the fourth grade now. I made a diorama of *Ways to Amuse a Dog*, the book I wrote to you about two times before. Now our teacher is making us write to authors for Book Week. I got your answer to my letter last year, but it was only printed. Please would you write to me in your own handwriting? I am a great enjoyer of your books.

Your best reader,
Leigh Botts

October 2

Dear Mr. Henshaw,

I am in the fifth grade now. You might like to know that I gave a book report on *Ways to Amuse a Dog*. The class liked it. I got an A−. The minus was because the teacher said I didn't stand on both feet.

Sincerely,
Leigh Botts

November 7

Dear Mr. Henshaw,

I got your letter and did what you said. I read a different book by you. I read *Moose on Toast*. I liked it almost as much as *Ways to Amuse a Dog*. It was really funny the way the boy's mother tried to think up ways to cook the moose meat they had in their freezer. One thousand pounds is a lot of moose.

Your number 1 fan,
Leigh Botts

September 20

Dear Mr. Henshaw,

This year I am in the sixth grade in a new school in a different town. Our teacher is making us do author reports to improve our writing skills, so of course I thought of you. Please answer the following questions.

1. How many books have you written?
2. Is Boyd Henshaw your real name or is it fake?
3. Why do you write books for children?
4. Where do you get your ideas?
5. What is your favorite book that you wrote?
6. Do you like to write books?
7. What is the title of your next book?
8. Please give me some tips on how to write a book.

I need your answer by next Friday. This is urgent!

Sincerely,
Leigh Botts

November 15

Dear Mr. Henshaw,

At first I was pretty upset when I didn't get an answer to my letter in time for my report, but I worked it out okay. I read what it said about you on the back of *Ways to Amuse a Dog* and wrote real big on every other line so I filled up the paper.

When your letter finally came I didn't want to read it to the class, because I didn't think Miss Martinez would like silly answers. But she said I had to read it. The class laughed when I came to the part about your favorite animal was a purple monster who ate children who sent authors long lists of questions for reports instead of learning to use the library. Anyway, thank you for answering my questions.

Your writing tips were okay. I could tell you meant what you said. Don't worry. When I write something, I won't send it to you. I understand how busy you are with your own books.

That list of questions you sent for me to answer really made me mad. Nobody else's author put in a list of questions to be answered, and I don't think it's fair to make me do more work when I already wrote a report. I'm not going to answer them, and you can't make me. You're not my teacher.

Yours truly,
Leigh Botts

P.S. Do you really write books because you have read every book in the library and because writing beats mowing the lawn or shoveling snow?

November 16

Dear Mr. Henshaw,

Mom found your letter and your list of questions which I was dumb enough to leave lying around. She says I have to answer your questions because authors are working people like anyone else, and if you took time to answer my questions, I should answer yours. She says I can't go through life expecting everyone to do everything for me.

Well, I got to go now. It's bedtime. Maybe I'll get around to answering your questions, and maybe I won't. There isn't any law that says I have to. Maybe I won't even read any more of your books.

Disgusted reader,
Leigh Botts

November 20

Dear Mr. Henshaw,

Mom is nagging me about your dumb old questions. She says if I really want to be an author, I should follow the tips in your letter. I should read, look, listen, think, and *write*. So here goes.

1. Who are you?

Like I've been telling you, I am Leigh Botts, Leigh Marcus Botts. I don't like Leigh for a name because some people don't know how to say it or think it's a girl's name.

I am just a plain boy. This school doesn't say I am gifted and talented, but I am not stupid either.

2. What do you look like?

I am sort of medium. I don't have red hair or anything like that. In first and second grades kids used to call me Leigh the Flea, but I have grown. Now when the class lines up according to height, I am in the middle. I guess you could call me the mediumest boy in the class.

This is hard work. To be continued, maybe.

Leigh Botts

November 22

Dear Mr. Henshaw,

I wasn't going to answer any more of your questions, but Mom won't get the TV repaired because she says it was rotting my brain.

3. *What is your family like?*

Since Dad went away, my family is just Mom and me. We used to live in a mobile home outside Bakersfield in California before Mom and Dad got divorced.

Dad drives a big truck, a cab-over job. That means the cab is over the engine. His big rig sure is a beauty, with a bunk in the cab and everything. His rig, which truckers call a tractor but everyone else calls a truck, has ten wheels, two in front and eight in back so he can hitch up to anything—flatbeds, refrigerated vans, a couple of gondolas.

In school they teach you that a gondola is some kind of boat in Italy, but in the U.S. it is a container for hauling loose stuff like carrots.

My hand is all worn out from all this writing, but I try to treat Mom and Dad the same so I'll get to Mom next time.

Your pooped reader,
Leigh Botts

November 23

Mr. Henshaw:

Why should I call you "dear," when you are the reason I'm stuck with all this work? It wouldn't be fair to leave Mom out so here is Question 3 continued.

Mom works part-time for Catering by Katy which is run by a real nice lady Mom knew when she was growing up. Mom and Katy and some other ladies make fancy food for weddings and parties. They also bake for restaurants. Mom is a good cook.

Your ex-friend,
Leigh Botts

November 24

Mr. Henshaw:
Here we go again.

4. Where do you live?

After the divorce Mom **and** I moved from Bakersfield to Pacific Grove, which is on California's Central Coast.

We live in a little house, a *really* little house, that used to be somebody's summer cottage. Now it is what they call a garden cottage.

Next door is a gas station that goes ping-ping, ping-ping every time a car drives in. They turn off the pinger at 10:00 P.M. Most of the time I am asleep by then.

Sometimes when the gas station isn't pinging, I can hear the ocean roaring and the sea lions barking. They sound like dogs.

Two more questions to go. Maybe I won't answer them. So there. Ha-ha.

Still disgusted,
Leigh Botts

November 27

Mr. Henshaw:

Okay, you win, because Mom is still nagging me, and I don't have anything else to do. I'll answer your last two questions.

5. Do you like school?

School is okay, I guess.

6. Who are your friends?

I don't have a whole lot of friends in my new school. A new boy in school has to be pretty cautious until he gets to know who's who. Maybe I'm just a boy nobody pays much attention to. The only time anybody paid much attention to me was in my last school when I gave the book report on *Ways to Amuse a Dog.* After my report some people went to the library to get the book.

I wish somebody would ask me over sometime.

There, Mr. Henshaw. That's the end of your crummy questions. I hope you are satisfied for making me do all this extra work.

> Fooey on you,
> Leigh Botts

December 4

Dear Mr. Henshaw,

I am sorry I was rude in my last letter when I finished answering your questions. Maybe I was mad about some other things.

When you answered my questions, you said the way

to get to be an author was to *write*. You underlined it twice. Well, I sure did a lot of writing, and you know what? Now that I think about it, it wasn't so bad when it wasn't for a book report or a report on some country or anything where I had to look things up in the library. I even sort of miss writing now that I've finished your questions.

Are you writing another book? Please answer my letter so we can be pen pals.

Still your No. 1 fan,
Leigh Botts

December 12

Dear Mr. Henshaw,

I was glad to get your postcard. Don't worry. I get the message. You don't have a lot of time for answering letters. That's okay with me, because I'm glad you are busy writing a book.

Something nice happened today. When I was hanging around at school waiting for the first bell to ring, I was watching Mr. Fridley, the custodian, raise the flags. Maybe I better explain that the state flag of California is white with a brown bear in the middle. When he pulled the flags to the top of the flagpole, the bear was upside down with his feet in the air. I said, "Hey, Mr. Fridley, the bear is upside down."

This is a new paragraph because Miss Martinez says there should be a new paragraph when a different person speaks. Mr. Fridley said, "Well, so it is. How would you like to turn him right side up?"

So I got to pull the flags down, turn the bear flag the right way, and raise both flags again. Mr. Fridley said maybe I should come to school a few minutes early every morning to help him with the flags. It was nice to have somebody notice me.

I've been thinking about what you said on your postcard about keeping a diary. Maybe I'll try it.

Sincerely,
Leigh Botts

December 13

Dear Mr. Henshaw,

I bought a composition book like you said. It is yellow with a spiral binding. On the front I printed

Diary of Leigh Marcus Botts

Private—Keep Out

This Means You!!!!!

When I started to write in it, I didn't know how to begin. I felt as if I should write "Dear Composition Book," but that sounds dumb. So does "Dear Piece of Paper." The first page still looks the way I feel—blank. I don't think I can keep a diary. I don't want to be a nuisance to you, but I wish you could tell me how. I am stuck.

Puzzled reader,
Leigh Botts

December 21

Dear Mr. Henshaw,

I got your postcard with the picture of the bears. Maybe I'll do what you said and pretend my diary is a letter to somebody. Maybe I'll pretend I am writing to you because when I answered all your questions, I got the habit of beginning, "Dear Mr. Henshaw." Don't worry. I won't send it to you.

Thanks for the tip. I know you're busy.

Your grateful friend,
Leigh Botts

FROM THE PRIVATE DIARY OF LEIGH BOTTS

Friday, December 22

Dear Mr. Pretend Henshaw,

This is a diary. I will keep it, not mail it.

I guess I don't have to sign my name to a diary letter the way I sign a real letter that I would mail.

Wednesday, January 3

Dear Mr. Pretend Henshaw,

I got behind in my diary during Christmas vacation because I had a lot of things to do such as go to the dentist for a checkup, get some new shoes, and do a lot of things that don't get done during school.

Wednesday, January 10

Dear Mr. Pretend Henshaw,

I read over the letter you wrote that time answering my questions and thought about your tips on how to write a book. One of the tips was *listen*. I guess you meant to listen and write down the way people talk, sort of like a play.

January 12

Dear Mr. Henshaw,

This is a real letter I am going to mail. Maybe I had better explain that I have written you some other letters that are really my diary which I keep because you said so and because Mom still won't have the TV repaired. She wants my brain to stay in good shape. She says I will need my brain all my life.

Guess what? Today the school librarian stopped me in the hall and said she had something for me. She told me to come to the library. There she handed me your new book and said I could be the first to read it. I must have looked surprised. She said she knew how much I love your books since I check them out so often. Now I know Mr. Fridley isn't the only one who notices me.

I am on page 14 of *Beggar Bears*. It is a good book. I just wanted you to know that I am the first person around here to get to read it.

Your No. 1 fan,
Leigh Botts

January 15

Dear Mr. Henshaw,

I finished *Beggar Bears* in two nights. It is a really good book. At first I was surprised because it wasn't funny like your other books, but then I got to thinking (you said authors should think) and decided a book doesn't have to be funny to be good, although it often helps. This book did not need to be funny.

I hope your book wins a million awards.

Sincerely,
Leigh Botts

January 19

Dear Mr. Henshaw,

Thank you for sending me the postcard with the picture of the lake and mountains and all that snow. Yes, I will continue to write in my diary even if I do have to pretend I am writing to you. You know something? I think I feel better when I write in my diary.

My teacher says my writing skills are improving. Maybe I will be a famous author someday. She said our school, along with some other schools, is going to print a book of work of young authors, and I should write a story for it. The writers of the best work will win a lunch with a Famous Author. I hope the Famous Author is you.

That's all for now. I am going to try to think up a story. Don't worry. I won't send it to you to read. I know you are busy and I don't want to be a nuisance.

Your good friend,
Leigh Botts the First

FROM THE DIARY OF LEIGH BOTTS

Saturday, January 20

Dear Mr. Pretend Henshaw,

Every time I try to think up a story, it turns out to be like something someone else had written, usually you. I want to do what you said in your tips and write like me, not like somebody else. I'll keep trying because I want to be a Young Author with my story printed.

Monday, February 5

~~Dear Mr. Henshaw~~,

I don't have to pretend to write to Mr. Henshaw anymore. I have learned to say what I think on a piece of paper.

Today after school I felt so rotten I decided to go for a walk. I wasn't going any special place, just walking. I had started down the street past some shops when I came to a sign that said "Butterfly Trees." I had heard a lot about those trees where monarch butterflies fly thousands of miles to spend the winter. I followed arrows until I came to a grove of mossy pine and eucalyptus trees with signs saying "Quiet."

The place was so quiet that I tiptoed. The grove was shady. At first I saw only three or four monarchs flitting around. Then I discovered some of the branches looked strange, as if they were covered with little brown sticks.

Then the sun came out from behind a cloud. The sticks began to move, and slowly they opened wings and turned into orange and black butterflies, thousands of them quivering on one tree. Then they began to float off through the trees in the sunshine. Those clouds of butterflies were so beautiful I felt good all over and just stood there watching them until the fog began to roll in, and the butterflies came back and turned into brown sticks again. They made me think of a story Mom used to read me about Cinderella returning from the ball.

I felt so good I ran all the way home.

Thursday, February 8

I started another story which I hope will get printed in the Young Writers' Yearbook. I think I will call it *The Ten-Foot Wax Man*. All the boys in my class are writing weird stories full of monsters, lasers, and creatures from outer space. Girls seem to be writing mostly poems or stories about horses.

February 15

Dear Mr. Henshaw,

I haven't written to you for a long time, because I know you are busy, but I need help with the story I am trying to write for the Young Writer's Yearbook. I got started, but I don't know how to finish it.

My story is about a man ten feet tall who drives a big truck. The man is made of wax, and every time he crosses the desert, he melts a little. He makes so many trips and melts so much he finally can't handle the gears or reach the brakes. That is as far as I can get. What should I do now?

The boys in my class who are writing about monsters just bring in a new monster on the last page to finish off the villains with a laser. That kind of ending doesn't seem right to me. I don't know why.

Please help. Just a postcard will do.

Hopefully,
Leigh Botts

February 28

Dear Mr. Henshaw,

Thank you for answering my letter. I was surprised that you had trouble writing stories when you were my age. I think you are right. Maybe I am not ready to write a story. I understand what you mean. A character in a story should solve a problem or change in some way. I can see that a wax man who melts until he's a puddle wouldn't be there to solve anything and melting isn't the sort of change you mean. I suppose somebody could turn up on the last page and make candles out of him. That would change him all right, but that is not the ending I want.

I asked Miss Martinez if I had to write a story for Young Writers, and she said I could write a poem or a description.

Your grateful friend,
Leigh

FROM THE DIARY OF LEIGH BOTTS
VOL. 2

Thursday, March 1

I am getting behind in this diary for several reasons, including working on my story and writing to Mr. Henshaw (really, not just pretend). I also had to buy a new notebook because I had filled up the first one.

I finally gave up on my story about the ten-foot wax man, which was really pretty dumb. I thought I would write a poem about butterflies for Young Writers because a poem can be short.

Saturday, March 17

Today is Saturday, so this morning I walked to the butterfly trees again. The grove was quiet and peaceful, and because the sun was shining, I stood there a long time, looking at the orange butterflies floating through the gray and green leaves and listening to the sound of the ocean on the rocks. I thought I might write about them in prose instead of poetry, but on the way home I got to thinking about Dad and one time when he took me along when he was hauling grapes and what a great day it had been.

Tuesday, March 20

Yesterday Miss Neely, the librarian, asked if I had written anything for the Young Writers' Yearbook, because all writing had to be turned in by tomorrow. When I told her I hadn't she said I still had twenty-four hours and why didn't I get busy? So I did, because I really would like to meet a Famous Author. My story about the ten-foot wax man went into the wastebasket.

Finally I dashed off a description of the time I rode with my father when he was trucking the load of grapes down Highway 152 through Pacheco Pass. I put in things like the signs that said "Steep Grade, Trucks Use Low Gear," and how Dad down-shifted and how skillful he was handling a long, heavy load on the curves. I put in about the hawks on the telephone wires and about that high peak where Black Bart's lookout used to watch for travelers coming through the pass so he could signal to Black Bart to rob them, and how the leaves on the trees along the stream at the bottom of the pass were turning yellow and how good the grapes smelled in the sun. Then I copied the whole thing over in case neatness counts and gave it to Miss Neely.

Monday, March 26

Today wasn't the greatest day of my life. When our class went to the library, I saw a stack of Yearbooks and could hardly wait for Miss Neely to hand them out. When I finally got mine and opened it to the first page, there was a monster story, and I saw I hadn't won first prize. I kept turning. I didn't win second prize which went to a poem, and I didn't win third or fourth prize, either. Then I turned another page and saw Honorable Mention and under it:

A Day on Dad's Rig
by
Leigh M. Botts

There was my title with my name under it in print. I can't say I wasn't disappointed because I hadn't won a prize, I was. I was really disappointed about not getting to meet the mysterious Famous Author, but I liked seeing my name in print.

Some kids were mad because they didn't win or even get something printed. They said they wouldn't ever try to write again which I think is pretty dumb. I have heard that real authors sometimes have their books turned down. I figure you win some, you lose some.

Friday, March 30

Today turned out to be exciting. In the middle of second period Miss Neely called me out of class and asked if I would like to go have lunch with the famous author, Angela Badger. I said, "Sure, how come?"

Miss Neely explained that the teachers discovered that the winning poem had been copied out of a book and wasn't original so the girl who submitted it would not be allowed to go and would I like to go in her place? Would I!

Miss Neely telephoned Mom at work for permission. Then she drove all the winners in her own car to the hotel, where some other librarians and their winners were waiting in the lobby. Then Angela Badger arrived, and we were all led into the dining room which was pretty crowded. One of the librarians told the winners to sit at a long table with a sign that said Reserved. Angela Badger sat in the middle and some of the girls pushed to sit beside her. I sat across from her.

There I was face to face with a real live author who seemed like a nice lady, plump with wild hair. I couldn't think of a thing to say because I hadn't read her books. Some girls told her how much they loved her books, but some of the boys and girls were too shy to say anything. Nothing seemed to happen until Mrs. Badger said, "Why don't we all go help ourselves to lunch at the salad bar?"

Getting lunch took longer than in a school cafeteria.

I was still trying to think of something interesting to say to Mrs. Badger while I chased garbanzo beans around my plate with a fork. A couple of girls did all the talking, telling Mrs. Badger how they wanted to write books exactly like hers.

Mrs. Badger tried to get some of the shy people to say something, without much luck, and I still couldn't think of anything to say. Finally Mrs. Badger looked straight at me and asked, "What did you write for the Yearbook?"

I felt myself turn red and answered, "Just something about a ride on a truck."

"Oh!" said Mrs. Badger. "So you're the author of *A Day on Dad's Rig*!"

Everyone was quiet. None of us had known the real live author would have read what we had written, but she had and she remembered my title.

"I just got honorable mention," I said, but I was thinking, she called me an author. *A real live author called me an author.*

"What difference does that make?" asked Mrs. Badger. "Judges never agree. I happened to like *A Day on Dad's Rig* because it was written by a boy who wrote honestly about something he knew and had strong feelings about. You made me feel what it was like to ride down a steep grade with tons of grapes behind me."

"But I couldn't make it into a story," I said, feeling a whole lot braver.

"Who cares?" said Mrs. Badger with a wave of her hand. "What do you expect? The ability to write stories comes later, when you have lived longer and have more understanding. *A Day on Dad's Rig* was splendid work for a boy your age. You wrote like you, and you did not try to imitate someone else. This is one mark of a good writer. Keep it up."

I noticed a couple of girls, who had been saying they wanted to write books exactly like Angela Badger, exchange embarrassed looks.

"Gee, thanks," was all I could say. Everyone got over being shy and began to ask Mrs. Badger if she wrote in pencil or on the typewriter and did she ever have books rejected and were her characters real people and what did it feel like to be a famous author?

I didn't think answers to those questions were very important, but I did have one question I wanted to ask which I finally managed to get in at the last minute

when Mrs. Badger was autographing some books people had brought.

"Mrs. Badger," I said, "did you ever meet Boyd Henshaw?"

"Why, yes," she said, scribbling away in someone's book. "I once met him at a meeting."

"What's he like?" I asked over the head of a girl crowding up with her book.

"He's a very nice young man with a wicked twinkle in his eye," she answered. I think I have known that since the time he answered my questions when Miss Martinez made us write to an author.

On the ride home everybody was chattering about Mrs. Badger this, and Mrs. Badger that. I didn't want to talk. I just wanted to think. A real live author had called *me* an author. A real live author had told me to keep it up. Mom was proud of me when I told her.

The gas station stopped pinging a long time ago, but I wanted to write all this down while I remembered.

March 31

Dear Mr. Henshaw,

I'll keep this short to save you time reading it. I had to tell you something. You were right. I wasn't ready to write an imaginary story. But guess what! I wrote a true story which won Honorable Mention in the Year-book. Maybe next year I'll write something that will win first or second place. Maybe by then I will be able to write an imaginary story.

I just thought you would like to know. Thank you for your help. If it hadn't been for you, I might have handed in that dumb story about the melting wax trucker.

Your friend, the author,
Leigh Botts

P.S. I still write in the diary you started me on.

You may want to read more of Leigh's diary and his letters to Mr. Henshaw in the book Dear Mr. Henshaw *by Beverly Cleary.*

1. How did Mr. Henshaw help Leigh to become a better writer?

2. Name three people, besides Mr. Henshaw, who encouraged Leigh to write. How did each one encourage him?

3. Why do you think that Mr. Henshaw sent Leigh the list of questions?

4. Look back at the closings of the letters Leigh wrote to Mr. Henshaw. Find three that reflect how Leigh felt about answering Mr. Henshaw's questions.

5. How did Angela Badger give Leigh more confidence in his ability to write?

The point of view in a story depends upon who is telling the story. In "Dear Mr. Henshaw," Leigh Botts is telling the story. He is a character in the story, and he is also the narrator. Therefore, this story is written from the first-person point of view. Why do you think Beverly Cleary used the first-person point of view for this story?

Thinking About "Symphonies"

You have just completed a unit called "Symphonies." You have learned that a symphony is a blending of music by an orchestra. However, you know that other forms of expression can be "symphonies," too. Music, art, and dance all shared the stage in this unit. In your reading, you met real musicians, artists, and dancers. You found out what is important to them. Itzhak Perlman loves to play the violin. Trina Schart Hyman wants only to draw. Leontyne Price cares deeply about singing. Arthur Mitchell is excited about dance. How are all these people alike? They all find joy in what they do.

You also met some fictional characters in this unit. You read about a boy who loved music in spite of some problems. You read about a queen who learned to play the slide trombone—partly because she couldn't bake gingerbread! You met a prince who needed friends to help him solve a riddle. These fictional characters, too, are alike. They all came from the imaginations of writers. Writers must be blenders, too. They must create a symphony with words. Leigh Botts discovered how difficult—and exciting—this can be.

Think about what you have read. Can you still hear the slide trombone? Can you see Trina Schart Hyman dressed as Little Red Riding Hood? Can you feel the rhythms of the Dance Theater of Harlem?

1. You read a biographical selection and an autobiographical selection in this unit. How was the writing in "Leontyne Price: Opera Superstar" different from the writing in "Self-Portrait: Trina Schart Hyman"?

2. Think about how Itzhak Perlman might have felt if he had played the violin in Haydn's orchestra in "The Boy Who Loved Music." Do you think he would have wanted to leave Esterhaza as much as Karl did? Why or why not?

3. Arthur Mitchell in "Ballet Is for Everyone" and Mike in "Just Because I'm Left-Handed" both had problems with friends. How were their problems alike? How were they different?

4. Lewis had a trumpet, and the queen had a slide trombone. Compare the sounds Lewis made on his trumpet with the sounds the queen made at first on her slide trombone. How were they alike?

5. Which selection in this unit do you think Leigh Botts would have liked the most? Why?

6. Which selection in this unit did you like the most? Why?

Read on Your Own

What's So Funny, Ketu? by Verna Aardema. Dial. In this African tale, a villager saves the life of a snake. As a reward, he is allowed to hear animals think.

The Piano Makers by David Anderson. Pantheon. This book tells and shows how a grand piano is made. It covers every step from cutting the wood to polishing the finished piano.

Let's Make a Movie by Giovanni Belgrano. Scroll. This book tells how you can make your own movie. It shows how to plan and write the script, how to film the story, and how to direct the movie.

Dear Mr. Henshaw by Beverly Cleary. Morrow. In his letters to his favorite author, ten-year-old Leigh talks about his problems at home and at school.

Pieter Brueghel's "The Fair" by Ruth Craft. Atheneum. This book takes a close look at a famous painting, "The Village Fair," and tells stories about the people in it.

Frogs and the Ballet by Donald Elliott. Gambit. This book introduces ballet steps and shows how they are used to create a ballet. You may be surprised to see frogs in ballet clothes demonstrating the steps.

You Can't Be Timid with a Trumpet: Notes from the Orchestra by Betty Lou English. Lothrop. A conductor and seventeen musicians from famous orchestras talk about their instruments and their music.

Music by Carol Greene. Childrens Press. This book tells about musical instruments and some of the great composers. It also shows why music is a language that the whole world can understand.

Saint George and the Dragon by Margaret Hodges. Illustrated by Trina Schart Hyman. Little, Brown. A knight slays a terrible dragon who has been frightening the countryside for years.

Emma by Wendy Ann Kesselman. Doubleday. When a 72-year-old woman receives a special gift of paints for her birthday, she is inspired. She captures many aspects of her life in her beautiful paintings.

Taking Pictures by Nina Leen. Holt. This book tells how to use a camera and how to take good pictures, both indoors and outdoors.

Making Musical Things by Ann Wiseman. Scribner's. This book shows how to make many musical instruments, using common objects. Instruments you can make include a milk-carton guitar and a tin-can harp.

Unit 4

Memories

People remember many different events in their lives. They recall good times and bad times. They remember special friends from long ago. They think of special occasions spent with family members. They remember favorite places they have been. They think fondly of objects that have special meaning. People like to talk about their memories and share them with others. Memories are an important link with the past.

In "Memories" you will read about some of the places, persons, and experiences that have been important parts of someone's life. You will read two tall tales—stories that are remembered for years because they are so much fun to listen to and to read. You will also read about ways to save memories.

As you read the selections, think about why certain memories and objects became important to the characters in the selections.

Personal Narrative

A story that begins *I will remember this day for as long as I live* is probably a personal narrative. The word *narrative* means "story." A **personal narrative** is the story of a personal experience, told from the point of view of the person who lived it. The person telling the story may be real, as in an autobiography, or fictional, such as the character Tom in "The Midnight Fox."

How do you know when you are reading a personal narrative? Several clues may help you. A personal narrative is told from the first-person point of view, using the words *I, me, my, mine, we, our,* and *us.* Another clue is that the writer speaks to the reader and expresses thoughts and feelings about an important experience or event in his or her own life.

Read the following paragraph. Look for clues that tell you that it is part of a personal narrative.

We didn't have running water. Every time we wanted water for bathing or drinking or washing clothes, we had to go get water from a neighbor's pump. We got so tired of carrying those buckets of water, and we were some kind of glad when Papa finally put a pump on our back porch.

The use of the word *we* is one clue that this paragraph is personal narrative. The writer is telling a personal experience from the first-person point of view. She is speaking directly to the reader and is sharing her feelings.

Read the following pairs of sentences. Which pair is an example of personal narrative? Why?

1. I always got scared when I walked across the bridge. Then one day I decided to be brave.
2. Yoshiko was afraid to walk across the bridge. Then one day she decided to be brave.

The first pair is an example of personal narrative. The sentences are written in the first person. The writer is speaking directly to the reader about feeling afraid.

Read the two paragraphs below. Decide which one is an example of personal narrative and why. Then change the other paragraph to make it an example of personal narrative.

Nothing had gone right that morning. First my alarm clock didn't work. Then I missed the school bus. I was sure it was the start of a bad day.

Kim could hardly wait for the airplane to land. She knew that her grandparents would be meeting her at the gate. This was the first time she had been allowed to travel alone to see them.

As you read the personal narratives in this unit, look for the following characteristics:

• It is written in the first person.
• It tells about the writer's personal experiences.
• It shows the writer's thoughts and feelings.

447

In this selection, you will read about one woman's memories of "how it used to be" when she was young.

As you read, think about what makes this selection a personal narrative.

Childtimes

by Eloise Greenfield
and Lessie Jones Little
with material by Pattie Ridley Jones

Pattie Frances Ridley was born in Bertie County, North Carolina, in 1884. She grew up in the town of Parmele. *Pomma-lee*, as everyone called it, was a town where two railroads crossed and a lumber company had built a mill. When the lumber company came to Parmele, many people followed, looking for jobs. Pattie Ridley's father was one of them. Here is Pattie's story, as she remembers it.

Papa's Jobs

We were living in a little place called Robersonville, about three miles from Parmele, when Papa heard about the mill going up. He had been down sick with a bad case of rheumatism around that time, and Mama and all of us had been real worried about him, but he was better by then and walking on crutches. So early one morning he took the train to go see about getting a job.

They hired Papa, and that's when we moved to Parmele. Papa got seventy-five cents a day for feeding the horses that pulled the wagonloads of machines — saws and things — from the train station to the mill. And when all the machinery was in, he got the job of cooking at the clubhouse where the company's officers lived, and cleaning up their bedrooms and the dining room. The clubhouse was different from most all the houses around Parmele. It had radiators, and pipes running from the mill, for steam heat in the wintertime. There was even a bathtub, it was in the dining room, and pipes for hot and cold running water, and hardly anybody had that in their houses.

Papa worked at the clubhouse until the mill closed down, and then he stayed on as the night watchman. After all the machines had been taken out and shipped away, Papa spent his nights there, watching those empty buildings.

Water

We didn't have running water. At first we had a well out in the backyard, until it started caving in and Papa had to get rid of it. He filled it in with dirt. Then every time we wanted water for bathing or drinking or washing clothes, we had to go get water from a neighbor's pump. We got so tired of carrying those buckets of water, and we were some kind of glad when Papa finally put a pump on our back porch.

Chores

We had right much work to do, in the house and out in the garden, too. We planted and weeded, and dug up sweet potatoes, and picked butter beans. Papa let us sell the beans and keep the money for ourselves.

We had to keep the yards clean, too, front and back. Most people didn't have grass in their yards. They had dirt yards, and we would sweep our yards every day, get up all the loose dirt, and leave them brushed clean, with the brush strokes the yard broom made looking almost like a design.

My sister Mary and I did the cooking. Some weeks she cooked and some weeks I cooked. We had one of those big iron stoves that you put coal in to make a fire, and that stove would get so hot, not just on the cooking eyes, but all over. When we did the ironing, we'd set the irons on the stove to heat them up. Our irons were heavy. They were made of real iron, even the handles, and we had to use a thick piece of cloth to hold them. We had four or five irons, and we'd iron with one until it got too cool and then we'd pick up another one, and keep on like that until we got the ironing done.

We had feather beds. The mattresses were stuffed with chicken feathers, and we had to turn them over nearly every day, and we couldn't miss a day shaking them up and smoothing out all the lumps. They had to be exactly right, just as smooth and neat, or Mama would make us do them all over again.

We didn't pull our bedspreads all the way up over the pillows the way a lot of people do nowadays. We had pillow shams that Mama had made, white cotton material that she cut in the shape of the pillow and embroidered. Sometimes she put lace around the edges, and she kept them starched so stiff and ironed so pretty. We would tack the top of the sham on to the head of the bedstead with thumbtacks, and after we finished making up the rest of the bed, we'd stand the pillows up and let the shams hang down in front of them. It was a pretty sight. Then at night when we went to bed we'd fold the shams back over the head of the bedstead so they wouldn't get wrinkled.

When you finished making up a bed, you knew better than to sit on it. Wherever you sat, those chicken feathers would mash flat and they'd stay mashed, and then you'd have to take everything off and start all over, shaking and patting to get it right again. We wouldn't ever sit on the bed. We already had enough chores to do, and we sure didn't want to do anything twice.

School

The school we went to was a one-room schoolhouse, a little square building with a big old potbellied stove inside. In the winter, the boys used to take turns going to school early in the morning to start the fire in the stove. That fire would be just blazing when the rest of us got there, and the room would be so warm.

Our seats were long benches, and we didn't have desks. We wrote on slates in our laps with a little piece of chalk. Mr. Highsmith—that was our teacher—he used to walk up and down between the benches, smiling, while we studied our books. Spelling books, reading books, arithmetic books. We had to study, study, study. We'd be some kind of glad when twelve o'clock came and we could go out for recess.

Most of the time we played in the schoolyard, but sometimes when the weather was nice and warm, we'd walk a ways from the school to a road where there were all these mulberry trees with ripe mulberries just waiting to be picked. We'd find some lightwood knots, those little pieces of pine wood you see lying in the woods sometimes, and we'd throw them up at the branches to knock the berries down. We had the best old time eating and getting our faces and hands all purple and sticky.

When recess was over, Mr. Highsmith would ring this little bell like the one Mama rang for us to come in to dinner. But if we were right in the schoolyard, he wouldn't ring the bell. He'd come to the schoolhouse door and call, "Books! Books!" He meant it was time for us to get back to those books and study some more.

The Jones Family

When I was about fourteen, a Mr. and Mrs. Jones moved to Parmele. Edmund and Eliza Knight Jones and their ten children. There were three sons and seven daughters. The Jones family bought two acres of land not far from our house, and they had a one-and-a-half-story house built on it. Two large rooms and a hall were on the first floor, and the second floor was an attic with a real low ceiling. It was so low, a grown person couldn't stand up in it, so it was used for the boys to sleep in.

Mrs. Jones loved to read. She used to teach school sometimes, and she loved books. She wanted all of her children to be able to read, so she taught the big ones and the big ones taught the little ones. Mrs. Jones used to sell chicken eggs for ten cents a dozen to buy books for her children. A book cost fifteen cents, and that was a lot of money back then.

One day there was a big windstorm in Parmele, and I mean that was some storm! It blew the Jones's house over. Nobody got hurt, but Mrs. Jones and two of her daughters had to go to work to save money for a new house. They went to Greenville and worked in the tobacco factory, pulling the stems off the tobacco leaves, until they had enough money. The family did most all the work on the new house themselves. They couldn't afford to buy nails, and their fingers bled from pulling the nails out of the old house to use again.

My favorite person in the Jones family was William, the oldest one of their children. When I got old enough to have a fella, William was my fella. We went to church together and sang in the choir together. And Sunday evenings, Mama would let us go for a walk down to the train station to watch the trains come in and see the people passing through town. I was old enough to wear long dresses by then, and I would get all prettied up on a Sunday, and William would come and get me.

My little sisters, Mary and Leah, always wanted to go with us on our walks. They kept begging and begging until one day I told them to come on and go. So William and I were walking along kind of slow, and I was holding the back of my dress with one hand the way I'd seen the ladies do, lifting it up just the tiniest little bit. Well, I happened to look back, and what were Mary and Leah doing but just switching along, holding the backs of their dresses, mocking me and giggling to beat the band!

Well, the Jones family were our neighbors for a good long while. My brother John married Roberta, one of the daughters, and on December 30, 1903, William Jones and I got married.

After we were married, we stayed with his family for a while until he could finish the house he had started building, and then we went to live in our own three-room house. William and I had six children. Four of them lived to grow up—four daughters. One of them was Lessie.

Pattie Ridley Jones is the first of three women in her family who have recorded their memories of growing up. In the book Childtimes, *Mrs. Jones, Lessie Little, and Eloise Greenfield tell the story of three generations of one American family.*

1. Name three ways that life is different today from when Pattie Ridley was a young girl.

2. What were three chores for which the Ridley children were responsible?

3. What did you think was the most interesting part of Pattie's story?

4. What clues in the selection helped you to know that Pattie thought the officers' clubhouse was not only *different* from, but *better* than, the other houses in Parmele?

5. Pattie Ridley said that her favorite person in the Jones family was William. How do you know that this was true?

Tell why each of the following details seems to come from a personal narrative:

1. We had right much work to do, in the house and out in the garden, too.

2. One day there was a big windstorm in Parmele, and I mean that was some storm!

456

Prewrite

"Childtimes" is a personal narrative because it was told by the person who lived through the experiences in the story. Copy the following sentences. Below each sentence, write another sentence that tells about the experience as if it were part of a personal narrative.

1. A small puppy scratched at the door.

2. The snow and ice made travel very dangerous.

Compose

Imagine that you were a child when Pattie Ridley was young. Write two or more paragraphs that describe an ordinary day in your life. Write the paragraphs as a personal narrative.

Revise

Is your writing in the form of a personal narrative? Does your story have a beginning, middle, and ending? Make any revisions that are needed.

In this personal narrative, memories of the past lead to an unexpected friendship. Read to find out how the friendship begins.

As you read, think about the mood and tone of the selection.

This Is What I Know

by Denise Gosliner Orenstein

I haven't always lived here.

My mother is a teacher. Last summer, we moved from New York City to live on Klawak, an island in Alaska. This island has only small buildings. My mother says we will learn a new way of life. I don't know about that.

My name is Shawn. My hair is red and curly. When we first moved to this island, everyone stared. I thought they stared because my hair is red. I hate my hair.

I learned a bunch of things when I moved here—like how to clean a fish without feeling funny and slimy, and how to find salmonberries in the spring. My friend Vesta taught me that.

I want to tell you about my friend Vesta. Her hair is short and dark. She knows how to tie three different kinds of rope knots with her eyes closed, and she can hop backward on ice without slipping.

Vesta is a Tlingit Indian. I'm not. My mother says I'm Caucasian, but I can't pronounce that. The kids at school say I'm white. I can pronounce that.

This is what I know: There are five kinds of Native people living in Alaska. "Native" means people who have always lived in a place. The five kinds of Native people are Eskimo, Athabascan, Haida, Aleut, and Tlingit. You pronounce the word "Tlingit" like this: Klinget. I don't know why.

My friend Vesta has a grandfather who loves me. It wasn't always like that. I used to be scared of Vesta's grandfather because he was so old and quiet, and sometimes his hands shook. When I visited Vesta's house, her grandfather would stare at me. I thought he didn't like me because my hair is red.

This is how I felt when I first moved to Klawak and met Vesta's grandfather: I was sad. I missed New York City and my friends from my New York school. There's a lot of sky and water around Klawak, and I didn't know what to do with it all. It rained a lot. My hair got curlier. I couldn't wear my sneakers because my feet got wet and muddy. My mother bought me a pair of ugly green boots. I felt lonely.

Vesta was the only one at school who was nice to me. Vesta sat next to me in class and lent me her red pen. One day she invited me to visit her house after school. That made me feel better.

At Vesta's house, her mother made us a special drink from oranges, cinnamon, and many other spices. We were drinking it when Vesta's grandfather came in. He was carrying a walking stick and wore a brown parka. It had a hood like my jacket. He was tall. He walked slowly, looked at me, but didn't speak. My hair started to feel very red. I decided to go home.

Now, this is the part that gets surprising. At least, I didn't expect what happened to happen. Vesta moved away to another town. Her father got a job in a cannery in a place called Ketchikan. Vesta and her mother had to go to Ketchikan, too.

This is what I know: There are a lot of fish in Alaska. Many people all over the state go fishing for a living. That's their regular job. All the fish that are caught are sent to places across the United States. A cannery is a place where fish are cleaned and put into cans to be sent away. Vesta's father went to work in one of those canneries.

After Vesta left, nothing was the same. No one in school whispered with me or passed me notes and funny drawings. No one in school invited me to their homes.

One day, when I came home from school, my mother called me into the kitchen. She was making deer stew. Sometimes people call it "venison." I don't know why.

"Shawn," my mother said, stirring the stew with a big wooden spoon, "I made some stew for Vesta's grandfather. With the family away, he needs a little looking after."

I didn't say anything. Vesta's grandfather seemed old enough to look after himself. My mother put the spoon down.

"I'd like to give some of this stew to Vesta's grandfather for dinner. I think he would appreciate a hot meal."

I looked away. I knew what was coming.

"Shawn," my mother continued, "would you please take a bowl of the stew over to Vesta's grandfather's house after school tomorrow?" I pulled at my hair. A bunch of curls were stuck in a big knot.

"Why do I have to?" I asked.

"I just finished telling you, Shawn," Mother said very slowly. "Vesta's grandfather is living all alone. He's an old man and can hardly cook a big meal for himself. It seems to me that you would want to do something for your friend's grandfather."

I bit my lip. "Well, I don't," I said. Then I ran out of the room.

My mother says that sometimes I can be stubborn. My mother followed me into my room. I was lying on my bed with my head under the pillow. My mother sat down next to me and put her hand on my back.

This is what I know: My mother has soft hands. They feel good against your back if you just might cry.

"Honey," my mother said softly, stroking my back. "I know living here has been a big adjustment for you. I know that you're trying hard."

I took the pillow off my head and looked up. Maybe there were tears on my face. My mother put her arms around me and held me for a while. Sometimes I love my mother so much, my heart hurts.

The next day, after school, I poured a bunch of deer stew into a bowl. I wondered whether the bowl was big enough. Vesta's grandfather might eat a lot. Next I covered the bowl with tinfoil so it wouldn't fall out while I was walking. I sat down and stared at the bowl of deer stew for a long while.

I might have felt a little scared.

When I knocked on Vesta's grandfather's door, no one answered. I knocked again, then pushed the door gently. It opened halfway.

"Hello," I said softly.

"Hello," I said again, louder. I looked inside. Vesta's grandfather was sitting at the kitchen table, cutting a piece of wood with a knife. He didn't look up. I walked into the house and put the bowl of stew on the table for Vesta's grandfather.

"My mother and I thought you might like some deer stew," I said. "My mother made it. Some people call deer 'venison.' I don't know why."

Vesta's grandfather reached out and touched the bowl with his fingertips. Then he looked up.

This is what I know: Vesta's grandfather's face is different from any other face I've seen. His skin is the color of wood, the lines on his face like the grain of wood. His eyes are very dark, very large, and very still. I held my breath.

Vesta's grandfather looked beautiful to me. I'm not sure why.

Vesta's grandfather put one hand on my arm and pointed to a chair.

"Sit down," he said. Vesta's grandfather had never spoken to me before. I sat down next to him. He picked up the piece of wood again and began cutting it with a knife. I had seen other men in Klawak cut wood like that. It's called carving. It's a kind of artwork. Vesta's grandfather began to talk as he carved. This is what he said:

"This wood is like the pulse of a wrist. It's full of motion and warm inside the hand. What I am carving is alive." I watched the piece of wood change shape as Vesta's grandfather carved. It looked like magic.

All at once, I could see the shape of a small, curved paddle. Suddenly, I wasn't scared of Vesta's grandfather anymore.

"Are you carving a paddle?" I asked Vesta's grandfather.

He nodded and said: "This is a paddle like those from long ago. All we had in those days were paddles to move our boats. We had no engines. Even then, we carved our paddles like pieces of art. When I was small, like you, my uncle taught me to carve as I am carving now. He handed down what he knew. My uncle was an artist from way back, and he taught me not to do anything halfway. The Tlingit people treat art as something alive, something to be respected."

"Have you ever carved a totem pole?" I asked Vesta's grandfather.

This is what I know: A totem pole is a tree without any branches. The bark is carved with all kinds of animals and painted all different colors. There are a lot of totem poles in Klawak.

Vesta's grandfather nodded. "The totem pole here in Klawak," he said, "the one with the fox on top? I carved that."

I couldn't believe it. The fox totem pole was my favorite. Vesta's grandfather continued talking: "A person making totem poles has learned to study the animals. First, I had to study the fox. The fox is a lively creature, and runs around like a small child. The fox is the symbol of a child." He smiled and touched my hair. "Your hair is red, the same color as the fox. You are lively and fast, like the small animal the Tlingit people admire."

I was beginning to think that Vesta's grandfather didn't dislike me anymore. "What do the other totem pole animals mean?" I asked Vesta's grandfather.

He was quiet for a moment, and then he said: "The crab is the symbol of the thief because he has so many hands. The mosquito represents teaching. When a mosquito bites, you start itching. Sometimes learning hurts."

"Did you paint the totem poles you carved?" I asked. "Totem poles are so big, so tall. How did you reach way up to paint them?"

Vesta's grandfather laughed. "You paint the totems when they are lying down across the ground," he said, "before they are placed upright to stand in the sky. Long ago, we used paintbrushes made from wild bushes, and made all different kinds of paints from nature around us. Some paints were made from tree bark, some from blueberries and blackberries. These old Indian paints last for hundreds of years. They never fade in the sun. Now, these paints from long ago are gone. Very few people remember them."

Vesta's grandfather put the paddle on the table next to the bowl of deer stew. It was finished. He looked at me.

"This paddle is for you," he said. "Take it home."

I felt funny. The paddle was so beautiful. I didn't feel right taking Vesta's grandfather's paddle home. He picked up the paddle and handed it to me. It felt warm, warm from the heat of his hands.

Vesta's grandfather looked at me. "The Tlingit does not turn down any gift," he said, "but accepts it with open arms."

That is when Grandfather and I became friends.

This is what I know: In the late afternoon, the Klawak sky turns pink. If you walk up the hill behind the schoolyard, you can see totem poles shine in the moving light. Stand under the one with the red fox on top. Hold your breath. Hear the sounds from long ago.

1. How did Shawn become friends with Vesta's grandfather?

2. Why did Shawn feel different from the other kids at school?

3. What did Vesta's grandfather tell Shawn about carving a totem pole?

4. Why do you think that moving to Klawak was a big adjustment for Shawn?

5. What did Vesta's grandfather say to Shawn that made her feel better about her appearance?

6. What gift did Vesta's grandfather give to Shawn? Why do you think he gave her that?

Apply

the

Skills

Look back at the selection to answer the following questions about mood and tone.

1. Find the words on page 460 that tell how Shawn felt when she first moved to Klawak.

2. Looking at the picture on page 463, describe Shawn's mood.

468

Prewrite

Look at the story titles and questions below. In each list, the questions could be used to create details for the story. Copy the lists and add at least two more *how, when, where,* or *why* questions that could be used to create details.

Moving to a New Place	A New Friendship
1. Where did you move? 2. When did you move? 3. 4.	1. Where did you meet? 2. When did you meet? 3. 4.

Compose

Write a short paragraph that describes either moving to a new place or making a new friend. Use one of the lists above to help you decide what details need to be included.

Revise

Check your paragraph carefully. Have you answered *how, when, where,* and *why* questions in your paragraph? If not, revise your work by adding sentences to your paragraph.

Every family has memories to share. Families also share other things, such as family traits. Read to find out where family traits come from and how they are passed from one generation to another.

As you read, use the chart given to help you understand what a family tree is.

Me and My Family Tree

by Paul Showers

There are many ways to picture your family. One way to show your family is to start with one of your ancestors. You show him and his wife (or her and her husband) and all their children. Then you show the children's children, and so on until it comes to you. This is called your *family tree*.

Here is just a part of my family tree. It starts with my great-great-grandfather, Dan Kelly, who had red hair. He and his wife, Martha, had four sons and three daughters.

One of his daughters was my great-grandmother. She and her husband had three sons and three daughters. One of their sons was my grandfather. He and his wife had two sons and two daughters.

One of their sons had red hair. He is my father. My father's brother is my uncle and my father's sisters are my aunts.

470

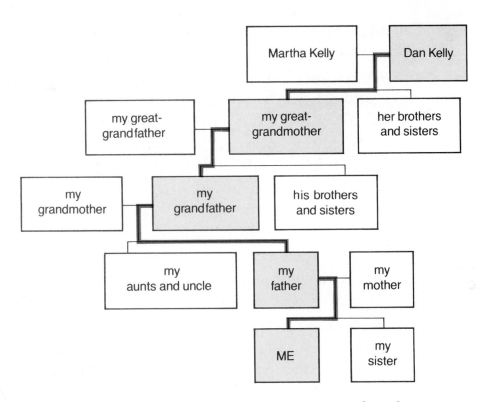

I don't know many of the people on my family tree. Most of them were dead before I was born, but I have pictures of some of them.

This is my great-great-grandfather, Dan Kelly— one of my ancestors. He had a red beard and red hair. My father says Dan Kelly passed his hair down to us.

The things your ancestors pass down to you are called *traits*. Red hair is a trait. Brown hair, straight hair, and curly hair are traits. The shape of your ears and hands, the color of your eyes, the color of your skin—these are all traits people get from their ancestors.

All the traits from all your ancestors are called your *heredity*. Every living thing has heredity. A dog, an elephant, a goldfish—each one gets traits from its ancestors. Even plants have heredity.

For a long time people didn't understand heredity. They didn't know where traits came from. Some people thought they came only from the mother, and others thought traits came only from the father. Over a hundred years ago Gregor Mendel began to study heredity. He started with plants.

Gregor Mendel was a monk. He grew peas in the monastery garden. Some of his pea plants had red flowers. When pollen from a red flower fell on another red flower, seeds were formed. Plants with red flowers grew from these seeds. Mendel also had pea plants with white flowers. Their seeds always grew into plants with white flowers.

Mendel decided to try an experiment. He took a little brush and scraped pollen from the red flowers. He brushed this pollen onto the white flowers. This is called *cross-pollination*.

Mendel cross-pollinated many pea plants in his garden. He carefully saved all the seeds from the cross-pollinated flowers. The next year he planted these seeds and watched them grow into new plants. When flowers came out on the new plants, they were all red. None of these "children" of the red and white plants had white flowers.

When these "children" made seeds, Mendel

planted the seeds the next year. The plants that grew from these seeds were the "grandchildren" of his red and white pea plants. Most of the "grandchildren" plants had red flowers, but some of them had white flowers. The white trait had been passed down from the ancestors to some of the "grandchildren" plants.

Mendel repeated this experiment many times. He also studied other traits of his pea plants. He cross-pollinated short plants and tall plants. He kept track of the seeds of hundreds of them. Mendel grew peas for nearly ten years, and he found out some important things about heredity.

He learned that traits come from the ancestors of both the mother and the father. Sometimes these traits—like red hair or long legs—are not seen in the children, but they may show up again in the grandchildren or great-grandchildren.

What Mendel learned about pea plants is true of other living things. It is true of some traits in birds and fish, dogs and cats, and other animals. It is true of some traits in people.

People are much harder to study than pea plants, of course. They have many more traits, and their traits are all mixed-up. However, we can still see some traits from the ancestors in the children and grandchildren.

I get my red hair from my father and my great-great-grandfather. My mother is short, like *her* mother. Perhaps I will be short like them, or I may be tall like my father and his ancestors. I can't tell yet. I don't know all the traits that will come to me from my ancestors. I am still growing.

1. How did the narrator get her red hair and other traits?

2. What kind of experiments did Mendel perform to study heredity?

3. What happened to the red and white pea plants in Mendel's experiments?

4. Name a trait that you might have inherited from one of your ancestors.

5. In the selection, why are the words *traits*, *heredity*, and *cross-pollination* written in italics?

6. What makes us different from each other?

Use the chart on page 471 to help you draw a family tree for one set of Mendel's pea plants. Start with two red "parent" plants. Each red "parent" has its own pair of "parents" — one red and one white (the "grandparents"). Draw the "grandparents" above the "parents." The two red "parents" also have four "children" plants. Three of the "children" are red and one is white. Draw the "children" below the "parent" plants.

Prewrite

Your appearance is based on traits that you inherited from your ancestors. Copy the chart below. It lists different traits that can be inherited. Complete the chart by filling in information about yourself and a person you know.

	Eye Color	Hair Color	Curly/Straight Hair	Tall or Short
1.				
2.				

Compose

Use the information from the chart to write a paragraph that tells what you or the other person looks like. You may add information that is not listed on the chart.

Revise

Read your paragraph. Is it a good description of the person you were writing about? Add more details if your description is not complete.

Multiple Meanings

Point is a word that has many, or multiple, meanings. *Point* can mean "to show direction." *Point* can mean "main idea." *Point* can also mean "an exact moment in time." Perhaps you know other meanings of the word *point*.

The context in which a word is used determines the meaning of that word. Read the following sentence:

Did the ship's compass point north or south?

By reading the sentence and using context clues, you know that *point* in this sentence means "to show direction." The words *compass, north*, and *south* give you clues to the right meaning.

Many words have multiple meanings. When you come to a multiple-meaning word in your reading, choose the meaning that makes sense in the sentence. Use context clues to help you decide which meaning is correct.

Read the following paragraph and decide on the meaning of *free* as it is used in the sentence. Explain the meaning. Then tell which context clues helped you know the meaning.

On my first plane trip, my ticket did not cost a cent. Mom got the free ticket because she had taken so many business trips on that one airline.

You probably figured out that *free* means "not costing anything." The context clues in the first sentence ("did not cost a cent") help make that meaning clear. What are some other meanings of the word *free*?

Sometimes you cannot figure out a word's meaning from the context in which it appears. Then you may have to find the word's meaning in a dictionary. If several meanings are listed, select the definition that makes the best sense in the sentence.

Read the following sentence:

"I hope I can *land* this fish," said Jennifer when she felt a tug on her fishing line.

If you look up the word *land* in a dictionary, you will find multiple meanings of this word. Four of the meanings are given below. Which one is the right meaning for the word *land* as it is used in the sentence?

land: 1. Ground or soil. **2.** To bring to a landing, as a plane. **3.** To catch and bring in. **4.** To come to rest on a surface, as after a fall.

Make up your own sentences for the other three meanings of *land*.

In your reading, when you find a word with multiple meanings, remember how you can decide which meaning is the correct one. Try to use context clues to help you. If you cannot find a word's meaning from context clues, use a dictionary. Always choose the meaning that makes sense in the sentence.

In this tall tale, read to find out about little Stormy's childhood and why he was meant to be "the greatest sailor ever to sail the sea."

As you read, look for words that have multiple meanings.

Little Stormy

by Harold W. Felton

Tall tales about Alfred Bulltop Storm-along, the greatest sailor who ever lived, have been told for many years. Some people say that Stormy was born one night in a hurricane that hit the New England coast.

When his mother saw her baby, she smiled and said, "His eyes are blue and green, blue-green, like the sea."

His father seemed to grow two inches with pride as he gazed into the eyes of his son. "You come from a long line of men who went down to the sea in ships," he said. "They were iron men who sailed wooden ships. You will be a man of iron, too."

The neighbors said, "My, what a big baby!"

His parents named him Alfred Bulltop: Alfred Bulltop Stormalong.

His mother was right. His father was right. The neighbors were right. Everything they had said about him was true.

He was a big baby, and the neighbors were bug-eyed when they saw that the baby had a full set of teeth. He was such a big baby, his parents had to blow a foghorn to wake him up.

No cradle was big enough for little Stormy, so they used a whaleboat. No room in the house was big enough for a whaleboat, so his father anchored it out in the bay. That is where little Stormy spent the first days of his youth.

There it was that he laughed and played with the sharks when they came close enough for him to reach out and pat their fins. For a time sharks were his only playmates, and he swam and wrestled with them. He was always careful not to hurt them.

Stormy was a curly-headed boy with a freckled face. He was a happy baby and almost never caused any trouble. But one day he turned over suddenly in his whaleboat cradle, starting a tidal wave that washed away six lobster shacks and almost wrecked the town pier.

After that he was always careful not to make any sudden movements. But it was very hard for such a big baby to stay still all the time.

Stormy's parents fed him whale milk and clam chowder and plenty of fish, lobster, baked beans, and brown bread. His appetite was good, and he put away great quantities of food. He liked clam chowder especially and ate a lot of it. He spooned it out of a washtub with a spoon as big as a half-bushel scoop. He grew quickly, as might be expected.

Stormy had salt water in his blood. One day a tall, thin pine tree floated near his cradle. It had been uprooted by a storm. Stormy pulled it out of the water and stripped the branches off. He held it out at arm's length and yelled at it. He yelled so loud the bark peeled off.

Using the tree trunk for a mast and his blanket for a sail, he rigged up his whaleboat cradle as a sailboat. As soon as he got the boat under way, he turned its prow and put out from the bay, into the ocean.

"Avast and ahoy!" he shouted with glee.

With a voice that sounded like a foghorn, he broke into song. As his boat dipped and rose in the waves, he sang: "Oh, a sailor's life is the life for me!"

Stormy soon outgrew his baby cradle-boat. As he grew bigger, he built and traded for larger and still larger boats. He was out sailing every minute he was not in school or doing his chores.

One morning he took his friend Jonathan out in his boat before school to set some lobster traps. By the time they were through, the rising wind had changed. The boys faced a long journey home, going against the wind for the first leg of their trip. A peninsula two miles long and half a mile wide lay between them and the schoolhouse.

"What are we going to do?" asked Jonathan. "It will take us an hour or more to tack down to the tip of the peninsula before we can come around and sail with the wind at the stern." He gazed sadly over the stretch of land that separated them from the schoolhouse.

"I know what to do," said Stormy. He turned the rudder and the boat came around. The sail filled and bent low as the boat moved right toward the shore of the peninsula.

"Hey! What are you doing?" Jonathan shouted. "You'll run the boat aground!"

"Maybe not," said Stormy. "The peninsula is smooth, and it's wet with dew."

"Dew? What has dew got to do with it?"

Stormy smiled. Then his lips firmed. He held the rudder steady and kept an eye on the sail. There could be no slack in it. He must keep it full and tight.

The wind stayed with him, and under his expert hand
the boat sailed over the wet sand of the beach and onto
the dew-damp grass. As lightly as a butterfly flitting from
flower to flower, the boat sped across the half-mile of
peninsula and down into the water on the other side, just
in time for school.

The schoolmaster and the other children, who were
standing in the schoolyard, were amazed.

"That boy is a real sailor," the schoolmaster said. "A
real sailor! He can sail in shallower water than anyone I
ever saw or heard of!"

When Stormy was eleven years old, he had to start
shaving. His beard was as tough as the bristles on a brush,
and his hair was as thick and strong as rope yarn. At
twelve he finished school.

He studied so hard the last year he was in school that he finished the last three grades in one year. He had to do it, because he had grown so much that the seats in the schoolhouse wouldn't have held him if he had stayed another year.

"I'm ready to go," he said.

"Go where?" his father asked.

"Into the world, to find my place in it," Stormy said.

His father and his mother nodded. So did the neighbors and the schoolmaster.

"But where in the world will you go?" his father asked.

"I will go down to the sea in ships. Salt water is in my blood," he said.

"Just as the Stormalongs have always done," his father said. "The ships are wooden ships, but you will be a man of iron."

1. Why did the schoolmaster say that Stormy was a "real sailor"?

2. List three ways in which Stormy was unusual when he was born.

3. What do you think Stormy meant when he said that he had salt water in his blood?

4. What sentence in the beginning of the story shows that Mr. Stormalong was proud of his new son?

5. Where will Stormy go to find his place in the world?

Use the context of the following sentences to select the correct meaning for the underlined word.

1. "They were <u>iron</u> men who sailed wooden ships."
   strong   useful metal

2. "It will take us an hour or more to <u>tack</u> down to the tip of the peninsula."
   short nail   sail against the wind

Prewrite

This chart lists believable and unbelievable things about Stormy. Copy the chart and fill in details about a new character. Decide what will be believable about your character and what will be exaggerated.

STORMY	OTHER CHARACTER
Believable	
Went to school Had parents Had a friend	
Exaggerated	
Had a whaleboat for a cradle Played with sharks Could sail across land	

Compose

Use details from the chart to write a paragraph describing your character. Include real and exaggerated details.

Revise

Read your work. Does it include real and exaggerated details? Add more details if needed.

In this tall tale, Josh McBroom sets matters straight by recalling how his "wonderful one-acre farm" got started. Read to find out how Josh turned his one-acre disaster into a success.

As you read, decide for yourself what could be true and what is exaggerated.

McBroom Tells the Truth

by Sid Fleischman

One summer day, Josh McBroom, his dear wife Melissa, and their eleven children left their Connecticut farm. They piled everything into their old car and headed West, where the land is good and the sun shines all winter. On the way through Iowa, they met up with farmer Hector (Heck) Jones, who had some neighboring farm- land to sell. Quick as a wink, Heck Jones had sold them eighty acres—for only ten dollars. The McBrooms thought they had made a good deal. Then Heck Jones took them out to see their new land.

We gazed with delight at our new farm. It was broad and sunny, with an oak tree on a gentle hill. There was one defect, to be sure. A boggy-looking pond spread across an acre beside the road. You could lose a cow in a place like that, but we had got a bargain — no doubt about it.

"Mama," I said to my dear Melissa. "See that fine old oak on the hill? That's where we'll build our farm-house."

"No you won't," said Mr. Heck Jones. "That oak is not on your property."

"But, sir—"

"All that's yours is what you see under water. Not a rock or a tree stump in it."

I thought he must be having his little joke, except that there wasn't a smile to be found on his face. "But, *sir*!" I said. "You clearly stated that the farm was eighty acres."

"That's right."

"That marshy pond hardly covers an acre."

"That's wrong," he said. "There are a full eighty acres—one piled on the other, like griddle cakes. I didn't say your farm was all on the surface. It's eighty acres deep, McBroom. Read the deed."

I read the deed. It was true.

"*Hee-haw! Hee-haw!*" he snorted. "I got the best of you, McBroom! Good day, neighbor."

He scurried away, laughing up his sleeve all the way home. I soon learned that Mr. Heck was always laughing up his sleeve. Folks told me that when he'd hang up his coat and go to bed, all the stored-up laughter would pour out his sleeve and keep him awake nights. But there's no truth to that.

I'll tell you about the watermelons in a minute.

Well, there we stood gazing at our one-acre farm that wasn't good for anything but jumping into on a hot day. And that day was the hottest I could remember. The hottest on record, as it turned out. That was the day, three minutes before noon, when the cornfields all over Iowa exploded into popcorn. That's history. You must have read about that. There are pictures to prove it.

I turned to our children. "Will*jill*hester*chester*peter-*polly*timtommarylarryandlittleclarinda," I said. "There's always a bright side to things. That pond we bought is a mite muddy, but it's wet. Let's jump in and cool off."

That idea met with favor, and we were soon in our

swimming togs. I gave the signal, and we took a running jump. At that moment such a dry spell struck that we landed in an acre of dry earth. The pond had evaporated. It was very surprising.

My boys had jumped in headfirst, and there was nothing to be seen of them but their legs kicking in the air. I had to pluck them out of the earth like carrots. Some of my girls were still holding their noses. Of course, they were sorely disappointed to have that swimming hole pulled out from under them.

But the moment I ran the topsoil through my fingers, my farmer's heart skipped a beat. That pond bottom felt as soft and rich as black silk. "My dear Melissa!" I called. "Come look! This topsoil is so rich it ought to be kept in a bank."

I was in a sudden fever of excitement. That glorious topsoil seemed to cry out for seed. My dear Melissa had a sack of dried beans along, and I sent Will and Chester to fetch it. I saw no need to bother plowing the field. I directed Polly to draw a straight furrow with a stick and Tim to follow her, poking holes in the ground. Then I came along. I dropped a bean in each hole and stamped on it with my heel.

Well, I had hardly gone a couple of yards when something green and leafy tangled my foot. I looked behind me. There was a beanstalk traveling along in a hurry and looking for a pole to climb on.

"Glory be!" I exclaimed. That soil was *rich*! The stalks were spreading out all over. I had to rush along to keep ahead of them.

By the time I got to the end of the furrow, the first stalks had blossomed, and the pods had formed, and they were ready for picking.

You can imagine our excitement. Will's ears wiggled. Jill's eyes blinked. Chester's nose twitched. Hester's arms flapped. Peter's missing front teeth whistled. Tom stood on his head.

"Will*jill*hester*chester*peter*polly*tim*tom*mary*larry*and-little*clarinda*," I shouted. "Harvest those beans!"

Within an hour we had planted and harvested that entire crop of beans. Was it hot working in the sun! I sent Larry to find a good acorn along the road. We planted it, but it didn't grow near as fast as I had expected. We had to wait an entire three hours for a shade tree.

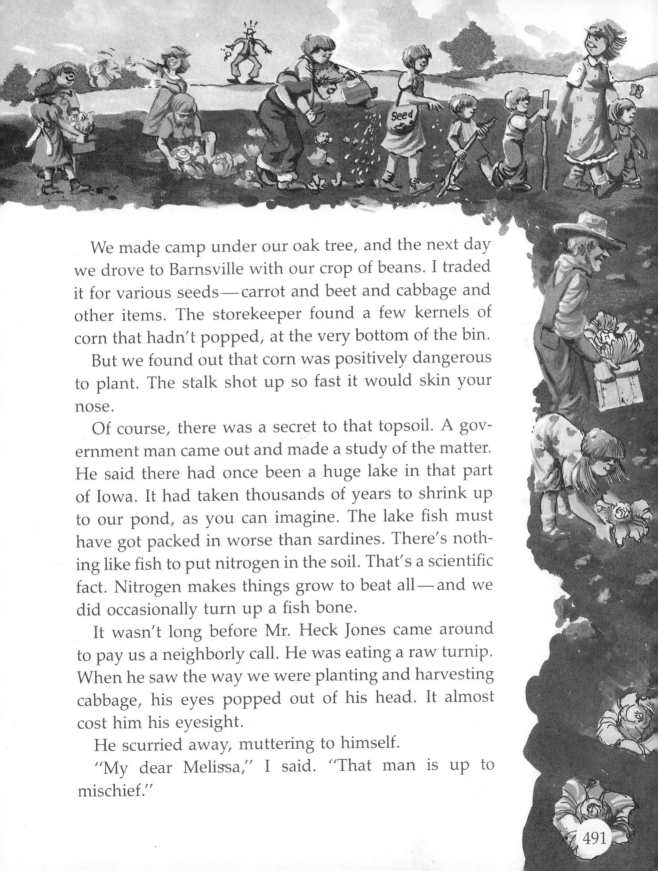

We made camp under our oak tree, and the next day we drove to Barnsville with our crop of beans. I traded it for various seeds—carrot and beet and cabbage and other items. The storekeeper found a few kernels of corn that hadn't popped, at the very bottom of the bin.

But we found out that corn was positively dangerous to plant. The stalk shot up so fast it would skin your nose.

Of course, there was a secret to that topsoil. A government man came out and made a study of the matter. He said there had once been a huge lake in that part of Iowa. It had taken thousands of years to shrink up to our pond, as you can imagine. The lake fish must have got packed in worse than sardines. There's nothing like fish to put nitrogen in the soil. That's a scientific fact. Nitrogen makes things grow to beat all—and we did occasionally turn up a fish bone.

It wasn't long before Mr. Heck Jones came around to pay us a neighborly call. He was eating a raw turnip. When he saw the way we were planting and harvesting cabbage, his eyes popped out of his head. It almost cost him his eyesight.

He scurried away, muttering to himself.

"My dear Melissa," I said. "That man is up to mischief."

491

Meanwhile, we went about our business on the farm. I don't mind saying that before long we were showing a handsome profit. Back in Connecticut we had been lucky to harvest one crop a year. Now we were planting and harvesting three, four crops a *day*.

There were things we had to be careful about—weeds, for one thing. My youngsters took turns standing weed guard. The instant a weed popped out of the ground, they'd race to it and hoe it to death. You can imagine what would happen if weeds ever got going in rich soil like ours.

We also had to be careful about planting time. Once we planted lettuce just before my dear Melissa rang the noon bell for dinner. While we ate, the lettuce headed up and went to seed. We lost the whole crop.

One day, back came Mr. Heck Jones with a grin on his face. He had figured out a loophole in the deed that had made the farm ours.

"Hee-haw!" he laughed. He was munching a radish. "I got the best of you now, Neighbor McBroom. The deed says you were to pay me *everything* in your purse, and you *didn't*."

"On the contrary, sir," I answered. "Ten dollars. There wasn't another cent in my purse."

"There were *moths* in the purse. I seen 'em flutter out. Three milky white moths, McBroom. I want three moths by three o'clock this afternoon, or I aim to take back the farm. *Hee-haw!*"

Off he went, laughing up his sleeve.

Mama was just ringing the noon bell, so we didn't

have much time. Confound that man! He did have his legal point.

"Will*jill*hester*chester*peter*polly*tim*tom*mary*larry*and-little*clarinda*!" I said. "We've got to catch three milky white moths! Hurry!"

We hurried in all directions. But moths are next to impossible to locate in the daytime. Try it yourself. Each of us came back empty-handed.

My dear Melissa began to cry, for we were sure to lose our farm. I don't mind telling you that things looked dark. Dark! That was it! I sent the youngsters running down the road to a lonely old pine tree and told them to rush back with a bushel of pine cones.

Didn't we get busy though! We planted a pine cone every three feet. They began to grow. We stood around anxiously, and I kept looking at my pocket watch. I'll tell you about the watermelons in a moment.

Sure enough, by ten minutes to three, those cones had grown into a thick pine forest.

It was dark inside, too! Not a ray of sunlight slipped through the green pine boughs. Deep in the forest I lit a lantern. Hardly a minute passed before I was surrounded by milky white moths—they thought it was night. I caught three on the wing and rushed out of the forest.

There stood Mr. Heck Jones waiting with the sheriff to foreclose.

"*Hee-haw! Hee-haw!*" old Heck laughed. He was eating a quince apple. "It's almost three o'clock, and you can't catch moths in the daytime. The farm is mine!"

"Not so fast, Neighbor Jones," said I, with my hands cupped together. "Here are the three moths. Now, skedaddle, sir, before your feet take root and poison ivy grows out of your ears!"

He scurried away, muttering to himself.

"My dear Melissa," I said. "That man is up to mischief. He'll be back."

It took a good bit of work to clear the timber, I'll tell you. We had some of the pine milled and built ourselves a house on the corner of the farm. What was left we gave away to our neighbors. We were weeks blasting the roots out of the ground.

We'd see Mr. Heck Jones standing on the hill in the distance, watching. He wasn't going to rest until he had pried us off our land.

Then, late one night, I was awakened by a hee-hawing outside the house. I went to the window and saw old Heck in the moonlight. He was cackling and chuckling and heeing and hawing and sprinkling seed every which way.

I pulled off my sleeping cap and rushed outside.

"What mischief are you up to, Neighbor Jones!" I shouted.

"*Hee-haw!*" he answered, and scurried away, laughing up his sleeve.

I had a sleepless night, as you can imagine. The next morning, as soon as the sun came up, that farm of ours broke out in weeds. You never saw such weeds! They heaved out of the ground and tumbled madly over each other—chickweed and milkweed, thistles and wild morning glory. In no time at all the weeds were in a tangle several feet thick and still rising.

We had a fight on our hands, I tell you! "Will*jill*-hester*chester*peter*polly*tim*tom*mary*larry*andlittle*clarinda*!" I shouted. "There's work to do!"

We started hoeing and hacking away. For every weed we uprooted, another reseeded itself. We were a solid month battling those weeds. If our neighbors hadn't pitched in to help, we'd still be there burning weeds.

The day finally came when the farm was cleared, and up popped old Heck Jones. He was eating a big slice of watermelon. That's what I was going to tell you about.

"Howdy, Neighbor McBroom," he said. "I came to say good-bye."

"Are you leaving, sir?" I asked.

"No, but *you* are."

I looked him squarely in the eye. "And if I don't, sir?"

"Why, *hee-haw*, McBroom! There's heaps more of weed seed where that came from!"

As my youngsters gathered around, Mr. Heck Jones made the mistake of spitting out a mouthful of watermelon seeds.

Things did happen fast!

Before I had quite realized what he had done, a watermelon vine whipped up around old Heck's scrawny legs and jerked him off his feet. He went whizzing every which way over the farm. Watermelon seeds were flying. Soon he came zipping back and collided with a melon. In no time watermelons went galloping all over the place, and they were knocking him about something wild. He streaked here and there. Melons crashed and exploded. Old Heck was so covered with melon pulp he looked as if he had been shot out of a ketchup bottle.

It was something to see. Will stood there wiggling his ears. Jill blinked her eyes. Chester twitched his nose. Hester flapped her arms like a bird. Peter whistled through his front teeth, which had grown in. Tom

stood on his head. Little Clarinda took her first step.

By then the watermelons began to play themselves out. I figured Mr. Heck Jones would like to get home as fast as possible. So I asked Larry to fetch me the seed of a large banana squash.

"*Hee-haw!* Neighbor Jones," I said, and pitched the seed at his feet. I hardly had time to say good-bye before the vine had him. A long banana squash gave him a fast ride all the way home. I wish you could have been there to see it. He never came back.

That's the entire truth of the matter. Anything else you hear about McBroom's wonderful one-acre farm is an outright fib.

1. What was the one-acre disaster, and how did the McBrooms turn it into a success?

2. Describe two different ways that Heck Jones tried to cheat or trick the McBrooms.

3. How do you know that the McBrooms' neighbors must have liked them?

4. What did Josh McBroom say that made you think that watermelons would play an important part in the story?

5. How do you know that Heck Jones did not cause the McBrooms any more trouble after he rode a banana squash home?

Many exaggerations are used in tall tales. The sentences below are from the story. Decide whether they could be true or whether they are examples of exaggerations. Explain.

1. "I sent Larry to find a good acorn along the road."

2. "That was the day, three minutes before noon, when the cornfields all over Iowa exploded into popcorn."

Prewrite

Read the numbered sentences below. Each is about a different event. Listed under each event is an exaggerated detail about the event. Copy and complete each list by adding at least three more exaggerations about each event.

1. Today is a very cold day.
   a. All the oceans are frozen solid.
   b. _____
   c. _____
   d. _____

2. Denise's dog barks loudly.
   a. People two states away can hear it bark.
   b. _____
   c. _____
   d. _____

Compose

Choose one of the numbered sentences above. Use it and the details from the list to write an exaggerated story of the event. Include three examples of exaggeration in your story.

Revise

Read your story carefully. Does it contain at least three examples of exaggeration? If not, revise your work.

Supporting Details

Many paragraphs have a topic, a main idea, and supporting details. The **topic** of a paragraph tells you what the paragraph is about. The **main idea** is the most important statement the paragraph makes about the topic. **Supporting details** are the facts that help explain and support the main idea.

The topic of a paragraph, or of several paragraphs, may be stated directly in a title or a heading. The topic can usually be stated in a single word or phrase. The main idea may be stated directly in a sentence within the paragraph, or the main idea may be unstated. If the main idea is unstated, you should use the details given in the text to help you decide what the main idea is.

Read the following heading and paragraph:

Bicycle Safety

All bicycles should be equipped with safety devices. Bicycles should have headlights and taillights so that the riders can be seen clearly at night. Bells are helpful when bicycle riders must warn someone of the riders' approach.

The topic and the main idea of this paragraph are both directly stated. The topic is *bicycle safety*. The first sentence of the paragraph states the main idea. The last two sentences are details that support the main idea. Notice how the supporting details give you more information about the main idea.

Now read the next heading and paragraph. The paragraph tells about some stories by Aesop [ē′säp], a famous storyteller. Look for the topic and the main idea. Remember that the main idea may not actually be stated. Then look for details that support or explain the main idea.

Aesop's Fables

Aesop wrote a fable about a greedy fox who wanted some grapes. He wrote another fable about a group of mice who discussed tying a bell on a cat. In other stories, Aesop told about an ant who rescued a dove, a hare who challenged a tortoise to a race, and a mouse who became friends with a lion.

The topic of this paragraph is *Aesop's fables*. The unstated main idea is *Many of Aesop's fables are about animals that talk and act like people*. In the paragraph there are several examples of animals that talk and act like people. Each of these examples is a detail that supports the unstated main idea. These supporting details also give readers a better understanding of the main idea.

Read the paragraph at the top of the following page. Look for the topic and main idea as you read. What supporting details are given? How do these details explain the main idea?

Desert camels have padded feet that help them walk through burning desert sands. Because they lose very little water through sweating, camels can go a long time without becoming thirsty. Their eyes and noses can close up tight to keep out blowing sand. On long trips, camels can get energy by burning up the fat they have stored in their humps.

The topic of this paragraph is *desert camels*. The main idea, however, is unstated. You might phrase the unstated main idea this way: *Camels are well suited to desert life.* Four supporting details explain this main idea: Camels have padded feet; they can store water; they can tightly close their eyes and noses; and they can store fat in their humps. Each detail is a fact about the camel's body, and these facts explain why the camel is well suited to desert life.

As you read informational articles, ask yourself what the topic is. Then look for the main idea. If the main idea is not stated, use the details to help you decide what the unstated main idea is. Then put the main idea into your own words.

Textbook Application: Supporting Details in Science

Read the following article from a science textbook. Find the topic and the main idea of the article. Is the main idea stated or unstated? Then look for details that support the main idea. The sidenotes will help you.

One way we use the oceans is for their resources (ri sôr′siz). A **resource** is a useful material taken from the earth. Minerals are resources found in the oceans. Some minerals are found in small black rocks on the ocean floor. These rocks are called **nodules** (noj′ülz). Nodules contain minerals such as copper and nickel.

Food from the sea is also an important resource. People eat fish and also feed fish to livestock. Seaweed has many uses. Did you know that seaweed is used to make some types of ice cream, candy, and medicines?

Natural gas and oil are resources that can be found beneath the ocean floor. As our oil and natural gas supplies on land are used up, we will need the oil and gas under the oceans.

> The topic of this article is *ocean resources.* The main idea is stated in the first sentence.

> This is a detail that supports the main idea. It is one example of how we use the ocean for its resources. What other supporting details can you find in the last two paragraphs?

The tides can be used to produce energy. This is called tidal power. The rise and fall of the water supplies the energy to make electricity. Someday tidal power may be a common energy source along the shores.

—*Silver Burdett Science*, Silver Burdett

Textbook Application: Supporting Details in Health

Read the following article from a health textbook. Look for the topic of the article and the main idea. The main idea of this article is unstated. Then look for details that support the main idea. The sidenotes will help you.

The topic of this article is *the tooth.* The unstated main idea is *The tooth is made up of many parts.*

Here is one detail that supports this main idea. What are four other details that support this main idea?

Smile into a mirror and look at one of your teeth. You are looking at only part of the tooth. The part you can see is called the **crown.** Almost half of the tooth is hidden by your gums. Your gums are the pink tissue around your teeth. The hidden part of the tooth is called the **root.** The roots of your teeth go through your gums and into your jawbone.

A tooth has many layers. Each layer is different. The picture shows the different parts of the tooth.

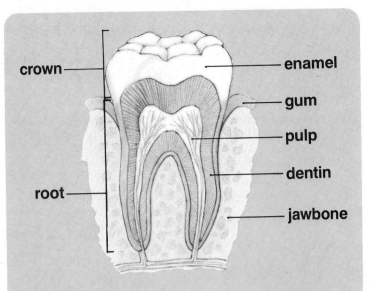

crown — enamel — gum — pulp — dentin — root — jawbone

The **enamel** is the outer layer. It makes a thin, hard shell around the tooth. Enamel is even harder than bone. It protects your tooth. **Dentin** is a thick layer under the enamel. Dentin is hard, too. But it is not as hard as enamel.

Dentin and enamel are made by the living part of the tooth. This part is the **pulp.** It is in a hollow space in the very middle of the tooth. The pulp is soft tissue with nerves and blood vessels. The pulp works to keep the rest of the tooth healthy.

—*HBJ Health*, Harcourt Brace Jovanovich

As you read, look for the topic, main idea, and supporting details of articles. Remember that the main idea may be stated or unstated. If you are not sure what the main idea is, the supporting details can help you find it. The supporting details explain or provide more information about the main idea.

In this historical biography, read to find out about the things that went well and the things that did not go so well on Paul Revere's midnight ride.

As you read, pay attention to the details that give you more information about the events of that famous night.

And Then What Happened, Paul Revere?

by Jean Fritz

Paul Revere lived in Boston, Massachusetts, over two hundred years ago. He was a man of many talents, who crafted things from silver and even made false teeth. Beginning in 1765, however, Paul devoted his talents to helping America win its independence from England. Paul became a leader of the Sons of Liberty, a secret club that wanted freedom from British rule. He was also an express rider who rode his horse between towns carrying secret messages and news. Paul carried many messages on many rides, but only one ride is remembered in history. This is the story of Paul's Big Ride to Lexington.

In the winter of 1774, Paul Revere became Massachusetts's Number One express rider. He also became a secret agent. It looked more and more as if the English soldiers in Boston meant to make war on America, and Paul's job was to try to find out the English plans. So he patrolled the streets of Boston at night, delivered messages, and kept himself ready at all times to warn the countryside.

He was far too busy now to write in his Day Book. He was too busy to make many silver teapots or whittle many teeth.

Sometimes on his missions things went just right. He got past the sentries, got through the snow, kept his horse on the road, and kept himself on his horse.

Sometimes things went poorly. Once the English found him in a rowboat snooping around Castle Island in Boston Harbor. So they stopped him, questioned him, and locked him up. He stayed locked up for two days and three nights.

Paul knew that all his rides were small compared with the Big Ride that lay ahead. Nothing should go wrong with this one. In the spring, everyone agreed, the English would march into the countryside and really start fighting. When they did, Paul Revere would have to be ahead of them.

On Saturday, April 15, it seemed that spring had arrived. Boats for moving troops had been seen on the Charles River. English scouts had been observed on the road to Lexington and Concord. A stableboy had overheard two officers making plans.

Dr. Joseph Warren was directing Patriot activities in Boston. At 10:45 on Tuesday night, April 18, he sent for Paul Revere. Other messengers had been dispatched for Lexington and Concord by longer routes. Paul was to go, as planned, the same way the English were going—across the Charles River. He was to alarm the citizens so that they could arm themselves, and he was to inform John Hancock and Samuel Adams, Boston's two Patriot leaders who were staying in Lexington. Paul was to leave now.

He had already arranged a quick way of warning the people of Charlestown across the river. Two lanterns were to be hung in the steeple of the North Church if the English were coming by water; one lantern if they were coming by land.

So Paul rushed to the North Church and gave directions. "Two lanterns," he said. "Now."

Then he ran home, flung open the door, pulled on his boots, grabbed his coat, kissed his wife, told the children to be good, and off he went—his hat clapped to his head, his coat-tails flying. He was in such a hurry that he left the door open, and his dog got out.

On the way to the river Paul picked up two friends, who had promised to row him to the other side. Then all three ran to a dock near the Charlestown ferry where Paul had kept a boat hidden during the winter. Paul's dog ran with them.

The night was pleasant, and the moon was bright. Too bright. In the path of moonlight across the river lay an armed English transport. Paul and his friends would have to row past it.

Then Paul realized his first mistake. He had meant to bring cloth to wrap around the oars so the sound would be muffled. He had left the cloth at home.

That wasn't all he had left behind. Paul Revere had started out for his Big Ride without his spurs.

What could be done?

Luckily, one of Paul's friends knew a lady who lived nearby. He ran to her house, called at her window, and asked for some cloth. This lady was not a time waster. She stepped out of the flannel petticoat she was wearing and threw it out the window.

Then all he needed were his spurs. Luckily, Paul's dog was there, and luckily, he was well trained. Paul wrote a note to his wife, tied it around the dog's neck, and told the dog to go home. By the time Paul and his friends had ripped the petticoat in two, wrapped each half around an oar, and launched the boat, the dog was back with Paul's spurs around his neck.

Paul and his two friends rowed softly across the Charles River, slipped carefully past the English transport with its sixty-four guns, and landed in the shadows on the other side — safely. There a group of men from Charlestown who had seen the signal in the church steeple had a horse waiting for Paul.

Off Paul Revere rode on his Big Ride.

He kept his horse on the road and himself on his horse, and all went well until suddenly he saw two men on horseback under a tree. They were English officers. One officer sprang out and tried to get ahead of Paul. The other tried to overtake him from behind, but Paul turned his horse quickly and galloped across country, past a muddy pond, toward another road to Lexington.

And what happened to the officers?

One of them galloped into the mud and got stuck; the other gave up the chase. Paul continued to Lexington, beating on doors as he went, arousing the citizens. At Lexington he woke up John Hancock and Samuel Adams and advised them to leave town. Paul had a quick bite to eat, and then, in the company of two other riders, he continued to Concord, warning farmers along the way.

For a while all went well. Then suddenly from out of the shadows appeared six English officers. They rode up with their pistols in their hands and ordered Paul to stop. But Paul did not stop immediately.

"Stop!" one of the officers shouted. "If you go an inch farther, you are a dead man."

Paul and his companions tried to ride through the group, but they were surrounded and ordered into a pasture at one side of the road. In the pasture six other officers appeared with pistols in their hands.

One of them spoke like a gentleman. He took Paul's horse by the reins and asked Paul where he came from.

Paul told him, "Boston."

The officer asked what time he had left Boston.

Paul told him.

The officer said, "Sir, may I ask your name?"

Paul answered that his name was Revere.

"What! *Paul* Revere?"

Paul said, "Yes."

Now the English officers certainly did not want to let Paul Revere loose, so they put him, along with other prisoners, at the center of their group, and they rode off toward Lexington. As they approached town, they heard a volley of gunfire.

"What was that?" the officer asked.

Paul said it was a signal to alarm the countryside.

With this piece of news, the English decided they'd like to get back to their own troops in a hurry. Indeed, they were in such a hurry that they no longer wanted to be bothered with prisoners. So after taking away the prisoners' horses, they set the prisoners free.

And then what happened?

Paul Revere felt bad, of course, to be on his Big Ride without a horse. He felt uneasy to be on a moonlit road on foot. So he struck out through the country, across stone walls, through pastures, over graveyards, back into Lexington to see if John Hancock and Samuel Adams were still there.

They were. They were just preparing to leave town in John Hancock's carriage. Paul and Hancock's clerk, John Lowell, went with them.

All went well. They rode about two miles into the countryside, and then suddenly John Hancock remembered that he had left a trunk full of important papers back in a Lexington inn. This was a mistake. He didn't want the English to find those papers.

So what happened?

Paul Revere and John Lowell got out of the carriage and walked back to Lexington.

It was morning now. From all over the area, farmers were gathering on Lexington Green. As Paul crossed the green to the inn, there were between fifty and sixty armed men preparing to take a stand against the English. The English troops were said to be near.

Paul went into the inn, had a bite to eat, found the trunk, and carried it out, holding one end while John Lowell held the other. As they stepped on the green, the troops appeared.

And then what happened?

Paul and John held on to the trunk. They walked right through the American lines, holding on to the trunk. They were still holding on when a gun was fired. Then there were two guns, then a succession of guns firing back and forth. Paul did not pay any attention to who was firing or who fired first. He did not stop to think that this might be the first battle of a war. His job was to move a trunk to safety, and that's what he did.

The battles of Lexington and Concord did, of course, begin the Revolutionary War. They were victories for the Americans, who have talked about Paul Revere's ride ever since. Some things went well on Paul's ride. Some things went poorly, but people have always agreed that Paul's ride was a success.

1. On the night of Paul Revere's ride, what happened that he hadn't planned?

2. What was Paul Revere supposed to do on his Big Ride to Lexington?

3. What three things happened on April 15 to suggest the English planned to march?

4. What do you think was the most dangerous thing to happen during the Big Ride?

5. Why did the author use questions such as "And then what happened?" throughout the story?

6. How did the battles at Concord and Lexington prove that the ride was successful?

The following main ideas from the selection are in paragraphs on the pages listed. Name two details that help support or explain each main idea.

1. Sometimes Paul Revere's rides went smoothly. (page 507)

2. Paul Revere's life was in danger the night of the Big Ride. (pages 509–11)

Prewrite

The chart below lists some of the problems
Paul Revere had on his Big Ride. Copy the
chart and list how he solved each problem.
Look back at the selection if you need help.

Problems	Solutions
1. forgot cloth to muffle oars	
2. forgot spurs	
3. chased by English officers	
4. left without a horse	

Compose

Imagine that Paul Revere could not solve his
problems in the ways listed on your chart.
Choose one of the problems that Paul Revere
ran into, and write a paragraph that tells a different way he could have solved that problem.

Revise

Read your paragraph. Have you given a new
solution? Could your solution have happened
in Paul Revere's time? Does it allow him to continue his mission? Add any information that is
needed.

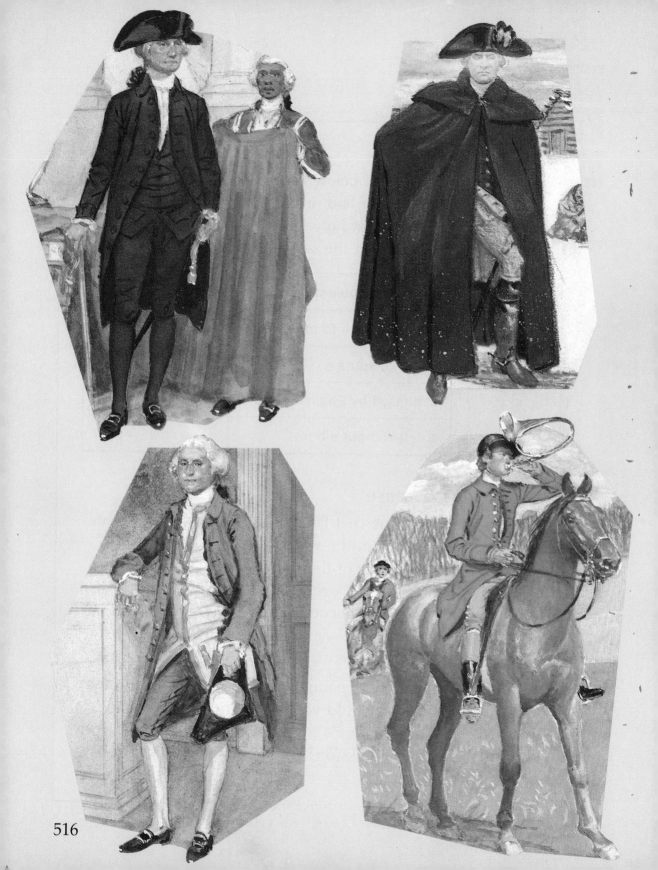

Which Washington?

by *Eve Merriam*

There are many Washingtons:
Which one do you like best?
The rich man with his powdered wig
And silk brocaded vest?

The sportsman from Virginia
Riding with his hounds,
Sounding a silver trumpet
On the green resplendent grounds?

The President with his tricorne hat
And polished leather boots,
With scarlet capes and ruffled shirts
And fine brass-buttoned suits?

Or the patchwork man with ragged feet,
Freezing at Valley Forge,
Richer in courage than all of them—
Though all of them were George.

Sequence

When you read a story, you know that the events are happening in a certain order. To help you see this order, or sequence, writers use time-order clues, such as times, days, and sometimes months. They also use word clues, such as *before, after, first,* and *then.* These clues help you to put the story events in the right order and to understand how the parts of the story are related.

Sequence is also important when you are solving problems in other subjects. If you are working a word problem in math, knowing how to sort the parts into the right order makes the problem much easier to solve. If you are doing a science experiment, knowing how to put the tasks in order makes your experiment more likely to work. When you have several jobs to do, knowing the right order in which to do them helps you make the best use of your time.

Problems can be solved more easily if you use a sequence of steps such as the one below. Read and think about each step in this sequence.

1. Identify or state the problem.
2. Gather the information you need.
3. Make a plan to solve the problem.
4. Carry out the plan.

Read about Josh's problem. As you read, think about how Josh might go about solving it.

One Saturday morning, Josh had some errands to run. It was already 11:00 A.M., and he was worried about getting his errands done before his baseball game at 1:00 P.M. Josh's father had given him money to buy paintbrushes, a hammer, and nails from the hardware store. Josh knew that the hardware store closed at noon on Saturday.

With his own money, Josh planned to buy his sister a birthday card and present. He would find those at the gift shop. If he had any money left over, he wanted to buy a book at the bookstore.

Josh solved his problem this way. First, Josh identified his problem. He needed to do all his errands and get to the baseball game in two hours.

Second, Josh gathered information. He made a list of all the things he needed to do and all the places he had to go.

Third, Josh made a plan. He knew that he needed to do some errands before he did others. Because the hardware store closed earlier than the other stores, Josh decided to go there first. At the hardware store he would buy the paintbrushes, hammer, and nails. After that, Josh would go to the gift shop. There he would buy his sister's present and card. If he had enough time and money left, he would make his last stop at the bookstore.

Fourth, Josh carried out his plan. Because Josh had sorted out everything, he could do his errands as quickly as possible and get to his baseball game on time.

Josh used the four steps and what he knew about sequence to solve his problem. Look again at the last four paragraphs. The words *first, second, third,* and *fourth* show you the sequence of steps that Josh followed.

These four steps can be applied to most problems. Knowing and using these steps will help you solve problems. Also, using what you know about sequence will help you develop your plan.

Remember these steps. Make them work for you.

1. Identify the problem.
2. Gather information.
3. Make a plan.
4. Carry out the plan.

Textbook Application: Using Sequence to Solve Problems in Science

Problem solving is an important skill in science. The following article is from a science textbook. Most of the work needed to solve this science problem has been done for you. Three of the four steps have been completed. Which step is necessary to solve this problem? Use the sidenotes to help you.

Is Air Matter?

One cup is full of pencils. Another is full of water. The third cup is empty. Is it really empty? Air is all around us, of course. What we call an "empty" cup is already filled with air.

Suppose you try to put marbles in the cup full of pencils or water. You have to move some of the pencils or water out of the way to do this. Pencils and water are **matter.** So are marbles. Matter takes up space. The pencils and water cannot take up the same space as the marbles.

Yet you *can* put the marbles in the cup full of air. Is air matter, then? Does it take up space?

These questions state the problem (step 1).

A Cup Full of Air

What happens when you push the mouth of a cup straight down into water? There is air in the cup. Both air and water are matter. They cannot take up the same space. Since the air has no way of leaving the cup, the water cannot enter. Paper inside the cup stays dry.

If you make a hole near the top of the cup, air can leave. Now the water can enter the mouth of the cup. The paper inside the cup gets wet.

When you put marbles into an "empty" cup, air leaves, too. The marbles push

These paragraphs provide the information you need to solve the problem (step 2).

aside the air in the cup. Air is a gas. The molecules that make up a gas move freely. The invisible molecules of air move out of the cup into the air around you.

ACTIVITY

Does Air Take Up Space?

You can use: paper towel, deep bowl filled with water, sharp pencil, paper cup

1. Stuff the paper towel into the bottom of the cup. Turn the cup upside down, and check that the paper towel cannot fall out.

2. Lower the cup *straight down* into the water in the bowl. Don't tilt the cup. Does the cup go down easily, or does something seem to be pushing it back? Then lift the cup straight up. Feel the paper inside the cup. Is it wet?

This activity is the plan to follow to solve the problem (step 3).

3. Now punch a hole in the side of the cup, near the top, with the pencil point. Lower the cup straight down into the water again. Does the cup go down more easily now? Lift the cup and touch the paper inside. Is it wet now?

How do you explain what happens to the paper each time?

—*HBJ Science,* Harcourt Brace Jovanovich

Step 4, carrying out the plan, is the missing step necessary to solve this problem. To carry out the plan, you would actually have to do the experiment.

Whenever you have a problem to solve, stop to think it through step by step:

1. Identify or state the problem.
2. Gather the information you need.
3. Make a plan to solve the problem.
4. Carry out the plan.

It was just an old desk—or was it? Read to discover why there was so much interest in the mysterious rolltop desk.

As you read, notice how Jenny uses her problem-solving skills to solve the mystery.

The Mystery of the Rolltop Desk

by Evelyn Witter

Jenny watched her mother pull the red pickup truck into the driveway. A large canvas-covered object was tied up in the back.

"What do you suppose Mom's bringing home this time?" her brother, Roger, asked.

At that moment Mrs. Marsh breezed through the door and turned to face them. Her face was pale. Her hands trembled.

"What did you buy?" Jenny asked.

"I was helping Mr. Sloan get ready for the auction, as I do every Friday. I saw a rolltop desk. I asked Mr. Sloan if I could buy it before the Saturday auction, and he said 'yes,' and so I did. Then a man came in and insisted on buying it. I said 'no,' but he kept insisting. Finally, I just left with the desk."

"That shouldn't make you nervous, Mom."

"Well, he followed me home!"

Now Jenny began to feel nervous. She parted the kitchen curtains and looked out the window. Clouds floated over the blue sky, and the sun shone brightly. Everything seemed peaceful. Then Jenny saw a man getting out of a small green car. He was neatly dressed in navy blue and had a bushy moustache. He was looking at their house.

"I see him!" Jenny exclaimed.

Mrs. Marsh looked out the window as the man turned to leave. "He's odd," she said. "He even grabbed me by the arm when I refused to sell the desk. He kept saying he just had to have that desk."

"What is so special about the desk?" Roger asked.

"Let's unload it. You can see for yourself," Mrs. Marsh suggested.

"I'll get Al to help," Jenny said as she hurried out. She was back in a few minutes with Alfred Miller, the boy who lived next door and who was her best friend.

Roger soon had the ropes untied and the canvas peeled away from the desk. Al had his father's moving helper—a platform on a roller that his father called a dolly. The boys carried the desk up the stairs and wheeled it into the living room.

When the desk was in place, Jenny told Al about the odd man who said he just had to have it.

"Why does he have to have this particular one?" Al asked.

"It's a good desk," Mrs. Marsh said. "It dates back to 1860."

Jenny studied the desk. It had eight big drawers, twenty pigeon holes, and sixteen little drawers.

"It would hold a lot of stuff," Jenny said.

"Why this desk?" Al asked again.

Jenny was about to give her opinion when she noticed the green car again. She grabbed a pencil and began writing.

"What are you writing?" her mother asked.

"His license number," Jenny replied.

"It really scares me to have that man hanging around like that," Mrs. Marsh said with a shudder.

That night Jenny helped her mother check all the windows and doors to see that they were locked. But Jenny had a strange feeling. Even though the house was locked up, if anyone really wanted to get in, she felt he would somehow be able to do it. She woke several times during the night.

Finally, since she couldn't sleep, she crept downstairs. She walked over to the desk and turned on the light near it. She kept asking herself what there was about the desk that made the man want it so much.

With nimble fingers Jenny touched every drawer and every pigeon hole. As far as she could see, there was nothing unusual about them.

Then Jenny gradually pulled the big desk away from the wall. She looked at the back of the desk and ran her fingers all around the back. The oak boards were smooth, but she found one spot where the varnish felt thicker than the rest. Jenny ran her fingers over that spot again. Then she thumped the spot with her fist. It sounded hollow!

She kept tapping the same spot. She could see a square crack beginning to form as she tapped.

Quickly she ran next door. She threw pebbles at Al's window to wake him. She wanted to share her discovery with Al.

After three throws, Al came to his window. "What's the matter?" he asked with a yawn.

"Hurry!" Jenny told him.

A few minutes later Al was in the Marsh's living room. As soon as he saw the square crack and thumped the back of the desk himself, he ran to the carriage house and got a chisel and hammer.

He worked quickly and quietly, and he and Jenny soon had the square pried loose.

There, lying in the circle of light from the lamp, was a piece of yellowed paper. It had some old-fashioned writing on it. In places the writing was almost all faded away. There were three ink blots between two of the lines.

The writing was hard to read, but Jenny and Al finally figured it out. It read:

Howe's fleet in Chesapeake Bay. Plans to attack Philadelphia. G. Washington.

"George Washington!" exclaimed Al.

"Written by George Washington!" echoed Jenny. "That's what the man really wants!"

"Keep it locked in your dresser," whispered Al as they moved the desk back into place. "I'll be back in the morning, and we'll tell your mom."

The next morning Jenny was awakened by her mother's call. "Jenny! Roger! Come down!"

Jenny threw on her robe and hurried downstairs. She saw desk drawers piled on the sofa and stacked on the floor. The desk was lying on its side, and the hole in the back was plain to see.

Jenny tried to draw her mother aside and tell her about the paper she and Al had found, but the police had already arrived.

"May we check this place out?" one officer asked.

While the police checked for fingerprints, Jenny told Roger about the paper. Then they met with Al in the carriage house at the back of the Marsh property.

"Should we tell them about the paper we found?" Al asked.

"We should," Jenny said.

"I don't believe the man in the green car was the one who broke in last night," Roger said thoughtfully. "He would know that Mom could identify him."

"Maybe," said Al, "but he sure looked suspicious yesterday when he parked his car around here."

"Let's go back to the house," Jenny said.

Back in the house they listened carefully to the questions the police asked and watched the shorter officer check for fingerprints. The tall police officer explained:

"We're checking these fingerprints against those of two men we apprehended last night. We're certain that these are the men who ransacked the rolltop desk. We know that these men have been convicted of break-ins in which valuable documents have been stolen. If these fingerprints match theirs, then we're certain that a valuable document is involved."

Just then the doorbell rang. When Jenny opened the door, she gasped and took three steps backward.

There stood the neatly dressed man who had been watching their house.

"I beg your pardon," he said in a low voice. "My name is Darrell Young. May I please speak with Mrs. Marsh?"

"My mother doesn't want to sell her desk," Jenny told him. She tried to be calm, but she knew the quiver in her voice told how frightened she was.

"I know," said the young man. "I must speak to her and explain about the desk."

Jenny hurried into the living room. "Mom! That man is here—that man in the green car—he's at the front door asking for you!"

"Show him in," ordered the tall police officer.

The man followed Jenny into the living room. He stopped short when he saw the police. He seemed to lose his dignified manner for a moment. A blush covered his neck, went up into his face, and reached the roots of his hair.

"I'm Darrell Young," he stammered. "I seem to have bungled this whole mission."

"What mission?" asked the police officer.

"I represent the Farley Museum," said Mr. Young. He drew out papers and gave them to the officer.

"These papers appear to be in order, Mr. Young," said the officer. "What is your business here?"

"This is my first assignment," explained Mr. Young. "I was to buy the rolltop desk. The museum traced this desk back to a man who was a Virginian. He bought the desk in 1860. The Virginian was the owner of a document signed by George Washington that dated back to the Revolutionary War. The museum had reason to believe that when the Virginian bought the desk, he transferred all the papers to it."

"The Revolutionary War document, too?" asked Jenny.

"Yes," nodded Mr. Young. "Well, I tried several times to get Mrs. Marsh to sell the desk, but she just wouldn't."

"Do you have any knowledge of two men who make a specialty of stealing documents?" one police officer asked.

"I do know of several rare documents that have been stolen in burglaries. It's possible that these thieves could have known about the Washington document and broken in here and stolen it," said Mr. Young.

"No they didn't!" cried Jenny. "I have it."

All eyes were on Jenny and Al as they told how they had found the secret hiding place before the thieves had broken into the house.

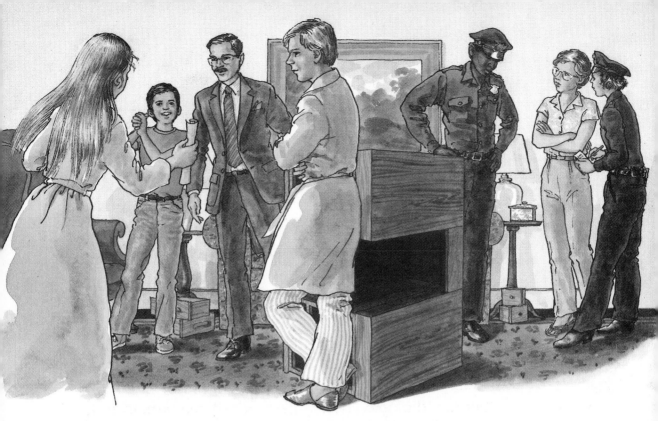

Jenny ran upstairs and brought the yellowed paper to Mr. Young.

"That's it!" cried Mr. Young, trembling with excitement. "And George Washington's signature is clear. This is indeed a great find!"

Everyone gathered around Mr. Young.

"We'll have to hold those men," said the tall police officer. "They didn't get what they were looking for, but these prints will probably prove that they did the breaking and entering."

"The museum will pay you handsomely for this document, Mrs. Marsh," Mr. Young cut in. "And of course, Jenny and Al will receive a citation for protecting a valuable historic document."

"They solved the mystery of the rolltop desk before any of us," Mrs. Marsh added proudly.

Jenny and Al smiled happily at each other.

1. What was so special about the rolltop desk?
2. What did Jenny find when she examined the desk?
3. Was Al's suggestion about locking the document in Jenny's dresser a good one? Why?
4. How did the author try to fool the reader?
5. Who solved the mystery of the rolltop desk?

Apply
the
Skills

Jenny and Al followed certain steps to solve the mystery. Put the sentences below in order to tell four of the steps they followed.

a. Then, Jenny gradually pulled the big desk away from the wall. She looked at the back of the desk . . .

b. She kept asking herself what there was about the desk . . .

c. All eyes were on Jenny and Al as they told how they had found the secret hiding place . . .

d. "Keep it locked in your dresser," whispered Al . . . "I'll be back in the morning, and we'll tell your mom."

Prewrite

Authors use words and pictures to describe characters, objects, and events in their stories. Copy the chart and complete it by adding at least one other word or phrase that describes each item. Use the words and the pictures in the selection to help you.

Darrell Young	Document	Rolltop desk
neatly dressed	old	made of oak

Compose

Imagine that you are Darrell Young and that the museum wants a report on your mission. Write a paragraph that tells about the events, starting with the auction. Include at least three descriptive sentences. Look at the chart for help.

Revise

Read your work carefully. Your paragraph should include several descriptive sentences. Add more details if they are needed.

Follow Directions

Almost every day, you follow some kind of directions. You may follow signs or other directions to get from one place to another. You may follow a series of steps to play a game, operate a computer, or make part of a meal.

When you are following written directions, the first thing you should do is read them from beginning to end. If necessary, read them more than once. All the steps are important and should be followed in the order in which they are given.

A recipe is one kind of written direction. A recipe usually lists the ingredients first. Then it gives the steps to be followed.

Important information may be found anywhere in a recipe. This is why it is necessary to read a recipe all the way through. You must be sure you understand what the directions call for before you begin.

Read the recipe for a vegetable salad at the top of the next page. There is an asterisk (*) beside the green beans in the ingredients list. At the end of the recipe there is another asterisk. What information about the green beans is given there? Why is this information important?

Spring Vegetable Salad

3 large carrots
1 cup fresh green beans*
1 can chick peas
1 cup cherry tomatoes

Wash the carrots and the tomatoes. Then peel the carrots. Cut one carrot into round slices, and put a layer of the slices in the bottom of a clear glass bowl. Add a cup of cooked green beans. Then cut a second carrot and arrange the slices on top of the beans. Add the chick peas. Next, cut the third carrot and put the slices in the bowl. Cut the cherry tomatoes in half, and place them in a layer on top of the carrots. Serve with your favorite dressing.

*Cook green beans and cool them before adding them to the salad.

The information given at the end of the recipe tells you that the green beans have to be cooked and cooled before they are put into the salad. If you started to make the salad without reading all the directions, you would have missed the information about the green beans. When you came to that part of the recipe, you would have had to stop to prepare the beans for the salad.

Look again at the recipe for the salad. You know what ingredients you need. However, you will also need other things that are not listed. You will need a pot for cooking the beans. You will also need tools to prepare the carrots and tomatoes, and to open the can of chick peas.

If you gather everything you need before you begin, then you will not have to stop to look for things. Reading through the directions before you begin helps you to be prepared and to avoid making mistakes.

Doing your schoolwork well also depends on knowing how to read and follow directions. When you take a test or work on an activity sheet, you must understand what to do. Otherwise, your answers may be wrong.

Sometimes misreading only a word or two can lead you to give a wrong answer. Read the following directions for an activity. Watch for the word *except*.

> Draw a line through all the boxes except the one with three dots.

If you read the directions carefully, then your answer would look like this. Your answer would be correct.

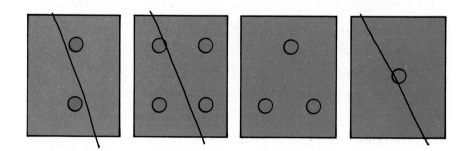

If you did *not* read the directions carefully, then you might think the directions said this:

> Draw a line through the box with three dots.

Your misunderstanding of the directions might then lead you to mark your paper like this. Your answer would be incorrect.

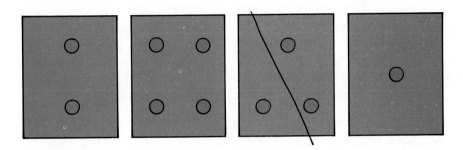

Directions can be helpful only if you know how to follow them.

- Remember to read the directions carefully, all the way through, before you use them.
- Read the directions as many times as you need to in order to understand them.
- When the directions come with a list of materials, be sure that you study both the list and the directions so that you can gather everything that you need before you begin.
- If the directions are given in steps, then be sure to follow the steps in order.

One way to "save time" is to save memories. Read to discover one way you can save memories now and enjoy them later.

As you read, pay attention to the directions that tell you how to "save time."

Saving Time

by Linda Beech

There is an old saying that goes something like this: *If you want to find out how far you have come, then look at where you have been.* Maybe this saying helps explain why people remember and study the past. By looking at the past and trying to understand it, people can learn more about themselves in the present.

Because the past is so important, scientists and historians study it in many ways. For example, scientists often dig deep into the earth, hoping to uncover some evidence of life from long ago. Sometimes they discover whole cities that have been buried for centuries. At other times, they find only a few tools, bits of clothing, and other objects. Yet scientists can sometimes fit these objects together, like pieces of a puzzle. These pieces may then tell the story of a whole civilization.

Archaeological dig

Not too long ago, people invented another way to save pieces of time for future generations to study. This invention is called a *time capsule*. A time capsule is a sealed container that holds many objects. These objects will tell people of the future what life was like in the past. A time capsule may hold such objects as pictures of cities and buildings, movies of people and events, and things that people use every day. When a capsule is sealed, it is sometimes placed in a special room or in the cornerstone of a building. A time capsule may also be buried deep in the earth, like objects from long ago.

The first time capsule was made in 1938. It was buried over fifteen meters underground at Flushing Meadows, on the spot at which the New York World's Fair of 1939 was to be held. The capsule is 2.3 meters long. It is to be opened in the year 6939, almost five thousand years from now.

In 1940 a huge time capsule was placed in an underground room at Oglethorpe University in Atlanta, Georgia. In it there are films, small models of cars and buildings, and other objects that tell what life was like in 1940. This time capsule is to be opened in the year 8113! Its location has been recorded in libraries and universities in different countries. This should improve its chances of being found. Other time capsules are buried in California, Canada, and Japan.

Not all time capsules must be opened so far in the future. Nor do time capsules have to be made with people of future generations in mind. A time capsule can be of use to anyone, even if it is put away for only a short time.

Oglethorpe University time capsule

Suppose, for example, that you want to remember some details of your life now, this year. You could make a simple time capsule that would help you record what you want to remember.

You might decide to make one time capsule for a whole year or one time capsule for each month of the year. You might make a time capsule for one of your interests, such as sports or music. You might make a time capsule on your birthday, to be opened on your birthday the following year. When you opened the capsule, you could see how much you had changed in that year's time.

When you are ready to make a time capsule, follow these steps:

1. Collect things that tell about you and what you are like now. You might want to include: photographs of you, your family, and your friends; samples of schoolwork; a TV or movie guide with your favorite shows underlined; and even letters and postcards from friends and family. You could select greeting cards you have received, cards or papers that show your activities and the clubs to which you belong, and samples of your hobbies. You might like to include party invitations and ticket stubs or programs from plays and sports events you have attended. Don't forget labels from containers of your favorite foods or from anything else you can think of.

2. Find a container for your time capsule items. A shoebox or a large envelope could make a good time capsule. A metal coffee can could be used, too. Be sure that your capsule has a lid or can be sealed.

3. Look through the items you have collected. Then decide how many will fit in your capsule. You might want to label some things to help you remember dates or names when you open your capsule. You might also want to make a list of the items in your capsule. This list can serve as a table of contents.

4. Place the items in your capsule and seal it.

5. Label and date the outside of the capsule. On the outside, also write: *To be opened on* ________. Add the date when the capsule should be opened.

6. Store your time capsule somewhere in your home, in a safe place—and don't forget to open it when the time comes!

Now use your imagination. Suppose you never did open your time capsule. It is the year 3000. Someone your age has found the time capsule you sealed and left behind. The person opens the capsule and begins to study the objects inside. Very slowly, this person learns what your life was like, a thousand years before. Can you imagine that? Could it really happen? Only time will tell.

1. According to this selection, what is one way that you can "save time"?

2. How does the saying *"If you want to find out how far you have come, then look at where you have been"* help explain why people remember and study the past?

3. What types of things can be put in a time capsule?

4. Why do you think a time capsule that was sealed in the year 2000 would be important in the year 3000?

5. Why is it important to label and date items in a time capsule?

Two directions for making a time capsule are missing. What are they? Are they needed?

1. Store your time capsule.

2. Look through the items you have collected.

3. Collect things that tell what you are like.

4. Label and date the time capsule.

Prewrite

The selection you have just read describes time capsules and explains how to make one. Think about what you might like to put in your own time capsule. List the items that you would include. Why would you save these things? How would they help someone know what you were like?

Compose

Choose one of the following activities.

1. Write a paragraph that describes three things you would put in a time capsule. Describe each one and tell why you would include it.

2. Pretend that you have just discovered a time capsule. Write a paragraph that describes what you find when you open it. Tell who might have buried the capsule, where you found it, and when it was buried.

Revise

Read your paragraph. Have you included all the information asked for in the activity you chose? Make any changes that are needed.

Telling Time

by *Lilian Moore*

Time ticks,
whispers,
rings,
sounds a chime,
a ping,
a tock,
or the long slow
bong
of a grandfather clock.

Time
on the sundial
is a
shadow,
making its rounds,
moving
till day is done
in secret
understanding
with the sun.

Read to find out about one family's special way of remembering.

As you read, look for the plot of the story — the problem and how it is solved.

The Patchwork Quilt

by Valerie Flournoy

Tanya sat restlessly on her chair by the kitchen window, watching Mama bake biscuits. She gazed through the window and saw her two brothers, Ted and Jim, and Papa building the new backyard fence.

"I'm gonna talk to Grandma," she said.

Grandma was sitting in her favorite spot—the big soft chair in front of the picture window. In her lap were scraps of materials of all textures and colors. Tanya recognized some of them. The plaid was from Papa's old work shirt, and the red scraps were from the shirt Ted had torn that winter.

"Whatcha gonna do with all that stuff?" Tanya asked.

"Stuff? These aren't stuff. These little pieces are gonna make me a quilt, a patchwork quilt."

Tanya tilted her head. "I know what a quilt is, Grandma. There's one on your bed, but it's old and dirty and Mama can never get it clean."

Grandma sighed. "It isn't dirty, honey. It's worn, the way it's supposed to be."

Grandma flexed her fingers to keep them from stiffening. She sucked in some air and said, "My mother made me a quilt when I wasn't any older than you. But sometimes the old ways are forgotten."

Tanya leaned against the chair and rested her head on her grandmother's shoulder.

Just then Mama walked in with two glasses of milk and some biscuits. Mama looked at the scraps of material that were scattered all over. "Grandma," she said, "I just cleaned this room, and now it's a mess."

"It's not a mess, Mama," Tanya said through a mouthful of biscuit. "It's a quilt."

"A quilt! You don't need these scraps. I can get you a quilt," Mama said.

Grandma looked at her daughter and then turned to her grandchild. "Yes, your mama can get you a quilt from any department store. But it won't be like my patchwork quilt, and it won't last as long either."

Grandma's eyes grew dark and distant. She turned away from Tanya and gazed out the window, absentmindedly rubbing the pieces of material through her fingers.

"Grandma, I'll help you make your quilt," Tanya said.

"Thank you, honey."

"Let's start right now. We'll be finished in no time."

Grandma held Tanya close and patted her head. "It's gonna take quite a while to make this quilt, not a couple of days or a week—not even a month. A good quilt, a masterpiece . . ." Grandma's eyes shone at the thought. "Why, I need more material. More gold and blue, some red and green. And I'll need the time to do it right. It'll take me a year at least."

"A year!" shouted Tanya. "That's too long. I can't wait that long, Grandma."

Grandma laughed. "A year isn't that long, honey. Makin' this quilt is gonna be a joy. Now run along and let Grandma rest." Grandma turned her head toward the sunlight and closed her eyes.

"I'm gonna make a masterpiece," she murmured, clutching a scrap of cloth in her hand, just before she fell asleep.

One August afternoon, Mama told Jim that his favorite blue corduroy pants were worn out. "We'll have to get you a new pair and use these old ones for rags," Mama said.

Jim was miserable. His favorite pants had been held together with patches; now they were beyond repair.

"Bring them here," Grandma said.

Grandma took part of the pant leg and cut a few blue squares. Jim gave her a hug and watched her add his patches to the others. "A quilt won't forget. It can tell your life story," she said.

The arrival of autumn meant school and Halloween. This year Tanya would be an African princess. She danced around in the long, flowing robes Mama had made from several yards of colorful material. The old bracelets and earrings Tanya had found in a trunk in the attic jingled noisily as she moved. Grandma cut some squares out of the leftover scraps and added Tanya to the quilt, too!

The days grew colder, but Tanya and her brothers didn't mind. They knew snow wasn't far away, but it was the end of November when Ted, Jim, and Tanya got their wish. They awoke one morning to find everything in sight covered with snow.

Tanya got dressed and flew down the stairs. Ted and Jim, and even Mama and Papa, were already outside.

"I don't like leaving Grandma in that house by herself," Mama said. "I know she's lonely."

Tanya pulled herself out of the snow, being careful not to ruin her snow angel. "Grandma isn't lonely," Tanya said happily. "She and the quilt are telling each other stories."

Mama glanced questioningly at Tanya. "Telling each other stories?"

"Yes, Grandma says a quilt never forgets!"

The family spent the morning and most of the afternoon sledding down the hill. Finally, when they were all numb from the cold, they went inside for milk and sandwiches.

"I think I'll go sit and talk to Grandma," Mama said.

"Then she can explain to you about our quilt—our very own family quilt," Tanya said.

Mama saw the mischievous glint in her youngest child's eyes.

"Why, I may just have her do that, young lady," Mama said as she walked out of the kitchen.

Tanya leaned over the table to see into the living room. Grandma was hunched over, her eyes close to the fabric as she made tiny stitches. Mama sat at the old woman's feet. Tanya couldn't hear what was said, but she knew Grandma was telling Mama all about quilts and how *this* quilt would be very special. Tanya sipped her milk slowly; then she saw Mama pick up a

piece of fabric, rub it with her fingers, and smile.

From that moment on both women spent their winter evenings working on the quilt. Mama did the sewing while Grandma cut the fabrics and placed the scraps in a pattern of colors. Even while they were cooking and baking all their holiday specialties during the day, at night they still worked on the quilt. Only once did Mama put it aside. She wanted to wear something special for the holidays, so she bought some gold material and made a beautiful dress. Tanya knew without asking that the gold scraps would be in the quilt, too.

When Tanya got downstairs one December morning, she found Papa fixing pancakes.

"Where's Mama?" asked Tanya.

"Grandma doesn't feel well this morning," Papa said. "Your mother is with her now till the doctor gets here."

"Will Grandma be all right?" Ted asked.

Papa rubbed his son's head and smiled. "There's nothing for you to worry about. We'll take care of Grandma."

Tanya looked into the living room. There on the back of the big chair rested the patchwork quilt. It was folded neatly, just as Grandma had left it.

"Grandma didn't want us to know she wasn't feeling well. She thought it would spoil our holidays," Mama told them later, her face drawn and tired, her eyes a puffy red. "Now it's up to all of us to be quiet and make her as comfortable as possible." Papa put an arm around Mama's shoulder.

"Can we see Grandma?" Tanya asked.

"No, not tonight," Papa said. "Grandma needs plenty of rest."

It was nearly a week later, the day before New Year's, when the children were permitted to see their grandmother. She looked tired and spoke in whispers.

"We miss you, Grandma," Ted said.

"And your muffins and biscuits," added Jim. Grandma smiled.

"Your quilt misses you, too, Grandma," Tanya said. Grandma's smile faded from her lips. Her eyes grew cloudy.

"My masterpiece," Grandma sighed. "It would have been beautiful. Almost half finished." The old woman closed her eyes and turned away from her grandchildren. Papa whispered it was time to leave. Ted, Jim, and Tanya crept from the room.

Tanya walked slowly to where the quilt lay. She had seen Grandma and Mama work on it. Tanya thought very hard. She knew how to cut the scraps, but she wasn't certain of the rest. Just then Tanya felt a hand resting on her shoulder. She looked up and saw Mama.

"Tomorrow," Mama said.

New Year's Day was the beginning. After the dishes were washed and put away, Tanya and Mama examined the quilt.

"You cut more squares, Tanya, while I stitch some patches together," Mama said.

Tanya snipped and trimmed the scraps of material till her hands hurt from the scissors. Mama watched her carefully, making sure the squares were all the same size. The next day was the same as the last—more snipping and cutting. But Mama couldn't always be around to watch Tanya work. Grandma had to be looked after. So Tanya worked by herself.

Then one night, as Papa read them stories, Jim walked over and looked at the quilt. In it he saw patches of blue—his blue. Without saying a word, Jim picked up the scissors and some scraps and started to make squares. Ted helped Jim put the squares in piles while Mama showed Tanya how to join them.

Every day, as soon as she got home from school, Tanya worked on the quilt. Ted and Jim were too busy with sports, and Mama was looking after Grandma, so Tanya worked alone. But after a few weeks she stopped. Something was wrong—something was missing, Tanya thought. For days the quilt lay on the back of the chair. No one knew why Tanya had stopped working. Tanya would sit and look at the quilt. Finally she knew. Some*thing* wasn't missing. Some*one* was missing from the quilt.

That evening before she went to bed Tanya tiptoed into Grandma's room, a pair of scissors in her hand.

She quietly lifted the end of Grandma's old quilt and carefully removed a few squares.

February and March came and went as Mama proudly watched her daughter work on the last few rows of patches. Tanya always found time for the quilt. Grandma had been watching, too. The old woman had been getting stronger and stronger as the months passed. Once she was able, Papa would carry Grandma to her chair by the window. Then she would sit and hum softly to herself and watch Tanya work.

"Yes, honey, this quilt is nothin' but a joy," Grandma said.

Summer vacation was almost here. One June day Tanya came home to find Grandma working on the quilt again! She had finished sewing the last few squares together; the stuffing was in place, and she was already pinning on the backing.

"Grandma!" Tanya shouted.

Grandma looked up. "Hush, child. It's almost time to do the quilting on these patches. But first I have some special finishing touches . . ."

The next night Grandma cut the final thread with her teeth. "There. It's done," she said. Mama helped Grandma spread the quilt full length.

Nobody had realized how big it had gotten or how beautiful. Reds, greens, blues, and golds, light shades and dark, blended in and out throughout the quilt. "It's beautiful," Papa said. He touched the gold patch, looked at Mama, and remembered.

Jim remembered, too. There was his blue and the red from Ted's shirt. There was Tanya's Halloween costume. And there was Grandma. Even though her patch was old, it fit right in.

They all remembered the past year. They especially remembered Tanya and all her work. So it had been decided. In the right-hand corner of the last row of patches was delicately stitched, "For Tanya from Your Mama and Grandma."